Studies in Childhood and Youth

Series Editors
Afua Twum-Danso Imoh
University of Sheffield
Sheffield, UK

Nigel Thomas
University of Central Lancashire
Preston, UK

Spyros Spyrou
European University Cyprus
Nicosia, Cyprus

Penny Curtis
University of Sheffield
Sheffield, UK

This well-established series embraces global and multi-disciplinary scholarship on childhood and youth as social, historical, cultural and material phenomena. With the rapid expansion of childhood and youth studies in recent decades, the series encourages diverse and emerging theoretical and methodological approaches. We welcome proposals which explore the diversities and complexities of children's and young people's lives and which address gaps in the current literature relating to childhoods and youth in space, place and time.

Studies in Childhood and Youth will be of interest to students and scholars in a range of areas, including Childhood Studies, Youth Studies, Sociology, Anthropology, Geography, Politics, Psychology, Education, Health, Social Work and Social Policy.

More information about this series at
http://www.palgrave.com/gp/series/14474

Giovanna Mascheroni · Donell Holloway
Editors

The Internet of Toys

Practices, Affordances
and the Political Economy
of Children's Smart Play

Editors
Giovanna Mascheroni
Department of Communication
Catholic University of the Sacred Heart
Milan, Italy

Donell Holloway
School of Arts and Humanities
Edith Cowan University
Mount Lawley, WA, Australia

Studies in Childhood and Youth
ISBN 978-3-030-10897-7   ISBN 978-3-030-10898-4   (eBook)
https://doi.org/10.1007/978-3-030-10898-4

Library of Congress Control Number: 2018965777

This Palgrave Macmillan imprint is published by the registered company Springer Nature Switzerland AG
The registered company address is: Gewerbestrasse 11, 6330 Cham, Switzerland

Preface and Acknowledgements

This book brings together diverse contributions on Internet connected toys from leading scholars in the field of children and media studies. The Internet of Toys is only the latest technological innovation aimed at children and an emerging application of the Internet of Things. It embodies a number of technological and sociocultural developments—the robotification of childhood, datafication and dataveillance, and the emergence of connected and hybrid play practices—that render it an excellent point of departure for those interested in understanding, more broadly, how children's lives, and their futures, are transforming. We are deeply grateful to the authors of the following chapters for providing innovative and thought-provoking research that helps the readers situate the Internet of Toys against the background of such broader sociocultural and media changes. Without their enthusiasm and commitment, this book would have not been possible.

Our interest in how digital media are embedded in children's everyday lives originated as members of the EU Kids Online network. In over ten years of EU Kids Online research, we became fully committed to going beyond media panics and researching media from the viewpoint of children and their families. While the Internet and digital media are undoubtedly an integral and pervasive component of children's everyday lives, we believe in the need for research that accounts for the varied ways in which children and their families face the challenges that digital media pose, and adapt and reinvent technologies so as to fit their everyday lives. A meaningful experience for the both of us was the comparative qualitative research into young (0–8) children's use of technology at home coordinated by the Joint Research Centre. More recently, the inspiration to direct our attention towards the Internet of Toys and Things for young children came from our participation in the COST Action IS1410, the digital literacy and multimodal practices of young children (DigiLitEY)—which also supported this publication. Therefore, we are deeply grateful to our EU Kids Online and DigiLitEY colleagues for helpful discussions and inspiration along the way, and especially to Stéphane Chaudron, Ola Erstad, Rosie Flewitt, Lelia Green, Leslie Haddon, Uwe Hasebrink, Claudia Lampert, Sonia Livingstone, Jackie Marsh, Tijana Milosevic, Kjartan Olafsson, Ingrid Paus-Hasebrink, Julian Sefton-Green, David Smahel, Elisabeth Staksrud, Anca Velicu, Dylan Yamada-Rice and Bieke Zaman. A special thank goes also to Nick Couldry and Andreas Hepp who inspired the theoretical backbone of our understanding of IoToys as media.

We are also grateful to the various opportunities we had to present and discuss our ideas, namely the Internet of Toys panel organised at the DigiLitEY meeting in Prague in November 2016; the two sessions we organised with DigiLitEY colleagues at the Cyberspace Conference in Brno in November 2017; and finally, the panel at the ICA 2018 Conference in Prague.

We are deeply grateful to our partners, Massimiliano Giacomello and David Holloway, for their love, patience and support.

Finally, a particular inspiration for both of us comes from children, first and foremost those in our families: we want to dedicate this book to Aiden, Angus, Clara and Patrick. We would also like to thank Archie, Laika and Scout, our non-human companions.

Milan, Italy   Giovanna Mascheroni
Fremantle, Australia   Donell Holloway
August 2018

Contents

Notes on Contributors

Thomas Apperley (Ph.D.) is a researcher and educator that specialises in digital games and other playful technologies. Tom is a University Researcher at the Centre of Excellence in Game Culture Studies at Tampere University.

Lorna Arnott is a Lecturer in the University of Strathclyde, UK. Lorna's main area of interest is in children's early experiences with technologies, particularly in relation to social and creative play. She also has a keen interest in research methodologies, with a specialist focus on consulting with children. Lorna is the convener for the Digital Childhoods Special Interest Group as part of the European Early Childhood Educational Research Association and is the Editorial Assistant for the *International Journal of Early Years Education*.

Alex Barco (Ph.D., 2017, La Salle—Ramon Llull University) is a postdoctoral researcher in the Amsterdam School of Communication Research (ASCoR) at the University of Amsterdam. His interests are on how social robots can have an impact in education for children with and without disabilities.

Lizzy Bleumers is a senior researcher at imec-SMIT, Vrije Universiteit Brussel. She has mainly conducted user research related to gaming, play, learning and participatory practice. To do so, she combines human-centred design research methods with living lab testing. Lizzy loves organising events that bring academia closer to the public, like the Ludic City Lectures on gameplay in an urban setting together with DiGRA Flanders and, currently, master classes for city representatives on research and developments in the smart cities domain.

Rita Brito is an Invited Assistant Professor in Lisbon College of Education, Polytechnic Institute of Lisbon, in Early Childhood Education Masters. She holds a degree in Early Childhood Education, a Ph.D. in Educational Technology and a postdoctoral research on the use of technologies by families and children up to 6 years old. Rita is a researcher at UIDEF—Institute of Education, University of Lisbon. Rita's research focuses on digital educational technology, children under 6 years old, Early Childhood Educators and Primary teachers training. She has published several journal and book articles in international journals and books. Rita is the author of http://www.Familia.com (2017).

Stéphane Chaudron works on research projects dedicated to Empowering Children Rights and Safety in emerging ICT at the Joint Research Centre of the European Commission. Her background is in Social Geography and Science Pedagogy. She has been for years in charge of the coordination of large European Research Networks dedicated to e-safety, New media education, Standardization and Science Teaching Education (UCLouvain, Imperial College London, European Schoolnet). She has been in charge of the coordination of EC's research project "Young Children (0–8) and Digital Technology" since 2014. Recently she has undertaken research on security and safety considerations of the Internet of Toys and explores the effect of the digital transformation on the concept of Identity, on the way users manage (or not) their personal data.

Chiara de Jong (M.A., 2017, Tilburg University) is a Ph.D. candidate at the Amsterdam School of Communication Research (ASCoR) at the University of Amsterdam. She investigates children's interaction with social robots and in particular children's acceptance of robots.

Rosanna Di Gioia is a researcher in the JRC Cyber and Digital Citizens' Security Unit. Her background is in Social Psychology and she has earned a master degree in Cognitive Processes and Technology from International Telematics University Uninettuno with a focus on Media Education, Social Cognition and Cyber-Risk Propensity and Assessment. In the past five years, she has been involved in projects on cyber-security, cyber-bullying and Empowering Citizens' Rights in emerging ICT. Her research interests include Privacy and Data Protection practices together with Digital Play. She is currently coordinating the development and dissemination of an edutainment in the format of a storytelling game introducing Data Protection Rights to (young) citizens. Previously, she contributed to development of the Happy Onlife toolkit raising awareness on Internet risks and opportunities. Currently, she is involved in projects exploring the digital transformation impact of the Internet of Toys and the Blockchain technologies in Energy Communities.

Patrícia Dias is Assistant Professor of the Faculty of Human Sciences and researcher at the Research Centre for Communication and Culture Studies at the Catholic University of Portugal. Holding a Ph.D. in Communication Sciences, her research interests are digital media, young children, mobile communication, marketing and public relations. She is author of *Living in the Digital Society* (2014) and *The Mobile Phone and Daily Life* (2008).

Dimitrios Geneiatakis holds a Ph.D. in the field of Information and Communication Systems Security from the Department of Information and Communications Systems Engineering of the University of Aegean, Greece. He has participated in various research projects in the area of information systems security. His current research interests are in the areas of security mechanisms in Internet telephony, Internet of Things, intrusion detection systems, network security and lately in software security. He is an author for more than fifty refereed papers in international scientific journals and conference proceedings. Currently, he is a scientific project officer within Joint Research Centre of European Commission. Previously, he was a lecturer at the Department of Electrical and Computer Engineering of the Aristotle University of Thessaloniki, Greece.

Seth Giddings (Ph.D.) is Associate Professor Digital Culture and Design within Winchester School of Art at the University of Southampton. Seth is a media and cultural theorist, and occasional media artist. Seth has published widely on new media, video games and play culture, and media theory. Recent research has centred on ethologies of the design of playful technologies, from mobile games to robots to playground swings.

Colette Gray is a Principal Lecturer in Early Childhood Studies at Stranmillis University College, Queen's University Belfast. Editor of the *International Journal of Early Years Education*, she continues to develop her research interests in the field of participatory research which children and marginalised groups, the impact of special needs on children's learning, and the ethical implications of research involving vulnerable groups.

Katriina Heljakka (Doctor of Arts, visual culture, M.A. Art History, M.Sc. Economics) is a toy researcher who holds a postdoctoral position at University of Turku (digital culture studies) and continues her research on toys, toy fandom and the visual, material, digital and social cultures of play in the Academy of Finland project Centre of Excellence in Game Culture Studies. Her current research interests include the emerging toyification of contemporary culture, toy design and the hybrid and transgenerational dimensions of ludic practices.

Donell Holloway is a Senior Research Fellow at Edith Cowan University, in Perth, Western Australia. She has authored or co-authored over 50 refereed journal articles, book chapters and conference papers and is in the process of writing a sole-authored book titled *Children's Digital Lives: The Parent Factor*. She is currently a chief investigator on two Australian Research Council grants, The Internet of Toys: Benefits and risks of connected toys for children, and Toddlers and tablets: exploring the risks and benefits 0–5s face online. As an ethnographic researcher, her work centres on the domestic contexts of children's media use.

Pirita Ihamäki received her M.A. in digital culture 2006, M.Sc. in marketing 2011 and her Ph.D. in digital culture 2015 from the University of Turku at Pori Unit. She is currently working as a consultant in the Sustainable Development Industrial Zone Project at Prizztech Ltd. She has also worked as a researcher at different universities. Her current research interests are game design, gamification, service design, toyification, the Internet of Toys and toy tourism.

Stine Liv Johansen (Ph.D.) is Associate Professor at Centre for Children's Literature and Media, Department of Communication and Culture, Aarhus University. Stine Liv Johansen studies children's use of and play with media, toys and technology in their everyday life in- and outside of institutional settings. She has written and published studies on for instance football as a mediatised play practice and YouTube as a site for children's playful practices. She is a member of the Danish Media Council for Children and Young People.

Ana Jorge (Communication Sciences Ph.D., University NOVA of Lisbon) is Assistant Professor at the Catholic University of Portugal and researcher at CECC. She has researched on children and youth as media audiences, as objects of representation in the media and as content producers. Her postdoctoral research focused on children and media education, particularly consumer literacy. She is member of COST DigiLitEY and European Literacy Network; previously, she was member of EU Kids Online and CEDAR networks, and of RadioActive101 project.

Ioannis Kounelis is a scientific project officer at the Joint Research Centre of the European Commission. His research activities focus on blockchain technologies, software security, especially on mobile devices, as well as Internet of Things security. He holds a M.Sc. and a Ph.D. degree in ICT security from the Royal Institute of Technology (KTH) in 2010 and 2015, respectively, while he received his B.Sc. degree in computer science from the Aristotle University of Thessaloniki in 2007.

Rinaldo Kühne (Ph.D., 2015, University of Zürich) is an Assistant Professor in the Amsterdam School of Communication Research (ASCoR) at the University of Amsterdam. His research focuses on media effects on young people, the communication between humans and artificial agents, cognitive and emotional mechanisms of media uses and effects, and methods in communication research.

Eva Lievens is an Assistant Professor of Law & Technology at Ghent University and a member of the Human Rights Centre and the Crime, Criminology & Criminal Policy Consortium. A recurrent focus in her research relates to human and children's rights in the digital environment. She is a member of the Flemish Media Regulator's Chamber for impartiality and the protection of minors, the associate editor of the *International Encyclopaedia of Laws—Media Law* and a contributor to the *European Audiovisual Observatory IRIS newsletter for Belgium.*

Vilmantė Liubinienė (Social Sciences, Sociology Ph.D., Kaunas University of Technology) is Professor at Kaunas University of Technology, Faculty of Social Sciences, Arts and Humanities, Lithuania. Her research fields are media linguistics, media literacy, localisation and translation, digital culture and intercultural communication, system of universal values, identity building, etc. She is a member of COST IS1410 Action "The digital literacy and multimodal practices of young children" and the European Commission's JRC project "Young Children (0–8) and Digital Technologies". ECREA Member since 2017.

Thomas Enemark Lundtofte is a Ph.D. fellow in Media Studies at the Department for the Study of Culture, University of Southern Denmark. Thomas researches how young children, ages 4 to 6 years, play with tablet computers. He has conducted fieldwork in the homes of seven Danish children using the POV methodology. His research on young children's play practices with tablet computers centres on their use of DR Ramasjang—an app provided by the National Danish Broadcasting Company (DR)—which is a common frame of reference within this particular age group in Denmark.

Ilse Mariën is working as a post-doc researcher at imec-SMIT, a research centre attached to the Vrije Universiteit Brussel (VUB) where she is leading several projects related to digital inequalities, e-skills and participation. In 2016, she successfully defended her Ph.D. that entails (1) a more contextualised and comprehensive theoretical framework for digital inequalities; and (2) a concise strategic framework for developing sustainable e-inclusion policies. Over the past 10 years, Ilse has built a great deal of expertise on (1) e-inclusion theories and policies, (2) doing research with vulnerable groups and groups at risk of digital and social exclusion and (3) innovative, interactive, participatory and action-oriented research methods.

Jackie Marsh is Professor of Education at the University of Sheffield, UK. Jackie has led numerous research projects engaging children, teachers, parents and children's media industry partners in research on young children's play and digital literacy practices in homes and schools. Jackie is Chair of COST Action IS1410, DigiLitEY, a European network of 35 countries focusing on research in this area (2015–2019). She is currently leading a 7-country project on makerspaces in the early years, MakEY http://makeyproject.eu (2017–2019) funded by the EU Horizon 2020 programme. Jackie has published widely in the field and is a co-editor of the *Journal of Early Childhood Literacy*.

Giovanna Mascheroni (Ph.D.) is a Senior Lecturer of Sociology of Media and Communications in the Department of Communication, Università Cattolica of Milan. She is part of the management team of EU Kids Online and co-chair of WG4 of the COST Action IS1410 DigiLitEY. Her work focuses on the social shaping and the social consequences of the Internet, mobile media and Internet of Toys and Things among children and young people, including online risks and opportunities, civic/political participation, datafication and digital citizenship.

Ingrida Milkaite is a doctoral student in the research group Law & Technology at Ghent University in Belgium. She is working on the research project "A children's rights perspective on privacy and data protection in the digital age: a critical and forward-looking analysis of the General Data Protection Regulation and its implementation with respect to children and youth". Ingrida takes part in the activities of the Human Rights Centre, is a member of the European Communication Research and Education Association (ECREA) and a contributor to the *Strasbourg Observers blog*.

Bjorn Nansen is a Senior Lecturer in Media and Communications at the University of Melbourne. His research focuses on emerging and evolving forms of digital media use in everyday and family life, using a mix of ethnographic, participatory and digital methods. His current research projects explore changing home media infrastructures and environments, children's mobile media and digital play practices, the digitisation of death and the body, and the datafication of sleep.

Benjamin Nicoll is a lecturer and researcher based in the School of Culture and Communication at the University of Melbourne, Australia. His research focuses on the history and critical theory of video games and video game platforms, with a particular focus on notions of technological failure and marginality in game history. He is currently developing a research project that examines the use and implementation of "game engines" in Australian game design contexts.

Patricia Núñez (Ph.D.) is Professor of Advertising and Public Relations at the Faculty of Information Sciences, Complutense University, Madrid. She is member of the research group SOCMEDIA: Study of the learning and leisure socio-communicative behaviour and competences developed by children and young people (digital natives) through the use of new media and ICT. Patricia chaired the TWG Advertisement Research of ECREA. She held visiting fellowships in several international universities, including the University of Sao Paulo (Brazil) and Helsinki (Finland).

Gabriela Oliveira holds a Master in Communication Sciences by the Catholic University of Portugal. Her research focuses on consumer behaviour, particularly on children, toys and technologies. Currently, she is research assistant at the Research Centre for Communication and Culture, at the same university.

Ioanna Palaiologou is an Academic Associate of the University College London, Institute of Education, UK and an educational psychologist. She completed her Ph.D. in 2003 and has worked both as a researcher in education and lecturer on Education and Early Childhood Studies in UK universities. She is a member of the executive committee of British Education Studies Association (BESA). She is also the Coordinator of the Special Interest Group (SIG) SIG on Transforming Assessment, Evaluation and Documentation Early Childhood Pedagogy in the European Early Childhood Education Research Association (EECERA).

Esther Martínez Pastor is Assistant Professor in the Faculty of Communication Sciences at the University Rey Juan Carlos de Madrid. She holds a Ph.D. in Communication Sciences and a degree in Advertising and Public Relations (University Complutense de Madrid) and Law (UNED). Her research is focused on advertising, emotions in advertising, kids and regulation. She elaborates an annual Report to evaluate "Self-Regulatory Code for Television spots of toys and Children" for the Spanish Association of Toy. She was involved in the project "the Analysis of the use and consumption of media and social networks on the Internet among Spanish adolescents. Characteristics and high-risk practices (CSO2009-09577)" funded by the Spanish Ministry of Science and Innovation.

Jochen Peter (Ph.D., 2003, University of Amsterdam) is a Full Professor in the Amsterdam School of Communication Research (ASCoR) at the University of Amsterdam. His research deals with young people's use of new communication technologies and its consequences for their psychosocial development.

Maarten Van Mechelen is a postdoctoral researcher at TU Delft specialised in the domain of Child–Computer Interaction. His current research focuses on early mastering of twenty-first-century skills through design-based learning. His teaching responsibilities include supervising M.A. and Ph.D. students and teaching a course on designing for and with children. Maarten holds master degrees in Graphic Design and Cultural Studies and a doctoral degree in Design Research (KU Leuven—UHasselt). In addition, he is a member of different organising committees including the ACM IDC 2018 conference.

Caroline L. van Straten (M.Sc., 2016, Utrecht University) works as a Ph.D. candidate in the Amsterdam School of Communication Research (ASCoR) at the University of Amsterdam. Her research investigates the psychological mechanisms underlying relationship formation between children and social robots.

Dylan Yamada-Rice is a Senior Tutor in Information Experience Design at the Royal College of Art. She is also a Senior Research Manager for Dubit, a company that specialises in strategy, research and digital for children's entertainment brands. Her research focuses on the design of digital storytelling, games and play on a range of platforms such as apps, augmented and virtual reality, as well as new content for television. She specialises in experimental visual and multimodal research methods.

Bieke Zaman is Assistant Professor at Mintlab, part of the Institute of Media Studies at KU Leuven. Her research focuses on digital media, children and interaction design from a communication sciences and Human–Computer Interaction perspective. Bieke is Associate Editor of the *International Journal of Child-Computer Interaction* and *Personal and Ubiquitous Computing*. She is Vice-Chair of the ECREA TWG on Children, Youth and Media; member of the EU COST Action IS1410 DigiLitEY, and member of the organising committee of the Interaction Design and Children conference.

List of Figures

List of Tables

1

Introducing the Internet of Toys

Giovanna Mascheroni and Donell Holloway

Introduction

The Internet of Things (IoT), where physical objects are embedded with electronics, sensors, software and connectivity that support the exchange of data, is a growing part of the Internet experience—including that of young children. A new generation of toys connected to the

In accordance with the Italian academic convention, we specify that while the general structure and the conceptual framework of the chapter were designed by the two authors jointly, Giovanna Mascheroni specifically wrote the following sections: *The Internet of Toys as Media* and *The Internet of Toys and the Datafication of Everyday Life*; Donell Holloway wrote the sections *The Internet of Toys as Toys* and *The Internet of Toys as Social Robots*.

G. Mascheroni (✉)
Department of Communication, Catholic University of the Sacred Heart,
Milan, Italy
e-mail: giovanna.mascheroni@unicatt.it

D. Holloway
School of Arts and Humanities, Edith Cowan University,
Mt Lawley, WA, Australia
e-mail: donell.holloway@ecu.edu.au

© The Author(s) 2019
G. Mascheroni and D. Holloway (eds.), *The Internet of Toys*,
Studies in Childhood and Youth, https://doi.org/10.1007/978-3-030-10898-4_1

Internet have been launched on the market in the past decade and are becoming increasingly commonplace (McReynolds et al., 2017). The Internet of Toys (IoToys) are very similar to other IoT devices, in that they consist of physical toys that are connected to the Internet—and, potentially, to other toys—through Bluetooth and Wi-Fi. They are equipped with sensors and voice/image recognition software and/or can be controlled and programmed via apps on smartphones or tablets (Holloway & Green, 2016). The first popular example of IoToys was toys-to-life, action figures such as Skylanders or Disney Infinity, that are connected to a video game by means of radio frequency identification (RFID), near-field communication (NFC) or image recognition software. The market for connected toys has expanded quickly and now includes dolls and teddy bears equipped with voice and image recognition, such as Hello Barbie, My Friend Kayla, CloudPets; robots, drones or other mechanical toys that are remotely controlled and/or programmable through apps, such as Anki Cozmo, Sphero SPRK and Dash & Dot; puzzle and building blocks such as Osmo; arts-to-life such as Play-Doh Touch; outdoor physical toys such as the Springfree Trampoline; and teddy bears that monitor the child's health parameters, such as Teddy *the Guardian.*

As a consequence of their being fitted with sensors and connected to networks, these toys gain "new skills [affordances] that are expressed in new forms of communication" (Bunz & Meikle, 2018, p. 1): they can react to various physical inputs (sounds, images, touch and movements); track children's behaviour and biometrical data, and/or measure the surrounding environment; interact with children on a personalised basis (e.g. by replying to their queries); and produce information (data) that is circulated through networks for analysis and interpretation. In this sense, physical toys have become *media* that "mediate what has not been mediated before" (Bunz & Meikle, 2018, p. 18).

This introduction aims to contextualise IoToys within the tradition of media and communications, set out the theoretical foundations for this volume and explore the notions of mediatization, datafication and robotification.

The Internet of Toys as Media

Our critical analysis of IoToys builds on and adapts Bunz and Meikle's (2018) media and communications perspective on the Internet of Things. We make the argument here that we have much to gain from an approach to Internet-connected and sensors-based playthings as *media*, for this will help us to understand and situate the social consequences of the entanglements of objects, data and communication practices that constitute the IoToys on both the micro-level of everyday life and the macro-level of broader social, political and economic implications. Therefore, before we delve deeper into the world of IoToys and new play practices, we need to theorise how and why we can understand Internet-connected playthings as media.

The Internet of Toys enables practices of "connected play" (Marsh, 2017), which criss-cross, connect and challenge the boundaries between dichotomised spaces and concepts: online and offline, digital and non-digital, material and immaterial, but also public and private, global and local. Media scholars, especially within the domestication of technology approach and its notion of double articulation, have long acknowledged the media's role in the reconfiguration of the boundaries between separate social spheres, such as private and public. Media are doubly articulated into private and public social contexts and cultures, for "information and communication technologies, uniquely, are the means (the media) whereby public and private meanings are mutually negotiated; as well as being the products themselves (through consumption) of such negotiations of meaning" (Silverstone, Hirsch, & Morley, 1992, p. 28). In focusing on the process through which media are absorbed into the places and contexts of family life, up to the point that they are taken for granted and normalised, domestication scholars emphasise the double articulation of information communication technologies (ICTs) into everyday life as both "*objects and media*: ICTs are doubly articulated into everyday life as machines and media of information, pleasure, communication" (Haddon & Silverstone, 2000, p. 251). We propose to extend the concept of double articulation to the study of IoToys, for it acknowledges both the material and communication dimensions of Internet-connected toys and the interrelation between the two. IoToys in their capacity as material objects are not dissimilar to other physical toys children are used to playing with. Their materiality is an important aspect of how children make sense of, normalise and incorporate the new generation of toys into their everyday play practices. However, IoToys are also, fundamentally, media, i.e. a means of communication "mediating between the private world of the household and the public sphere" (Livingstone, 2007, p. 16) or, as is becoming more common under surveillance capitalism, between the household and the commercial sphere (see below). They are sensory interfaces that allow children to access media content (be it bedtime stories, educational content or popular culture characters) and to communicate (e.g. they can send messages to their parents' smartphones through CloudPets or communicate with another VaiKai doll). Their symbolic value lies in both its content—the software, the media, the conversations—and "its meaning as an object – embedded as it is in the public discourses of modern capitalism" (Silverstone, 1994, p. 123).

However, there have been significant changes since the notion of the double articulation of media into everyday life was formulated within the domestication of technology approach. An increasing diversity of media has become integrated into our everyday lives. Digital media have become implicated in all sorts of social practices and processes and have sustained the emergence of a new business logic named "surveillance capitalism" (Zuboff, 2015)—we shall return to this later. The growing complexity of today's media system, and its increased interdependence, is what media scholars refer to as mediatization. The notion of mediatization emphasises the interrelation between social and cultural change, on the one hand, and a changing media environment, on the other. While mediatization can be traced back over the past five to six centuries, we have now entered an age of deep mediatization, in which "the social world is not just mediated but mediatized: that is, *changed* in its dynamics and structure by the role the media continuously (and recursively) play in its construction" (Couldry & Hepp, 2017, p. 15). By this, we do not argue that each and every social practice is mediated, but that the horizons for practices are represented and processed by a complex social world where digital media are both the resources and reference point for human agency (Couldry & Hepp, 2017).

The Internet of Things is part of this growing complexity, in which everyday life is reconfigured through "networks of connected things that create and distribute information" (Bunz & Meikle, 2018, p. 34). IoToys are just another component of the ecology of tracking and measuring that is generated by "sensing networks of connected things" (Bunz & Meikle, 2018, p. 2). While being networked and fitted with sensors, IoToys also combine the play affordances of physical toys (their tactile, functional, narrative and emotional features) with the affordances of the Internet of Things. This recombination adds a further layer of complexity to their double articulation in children's everyday lives. Not only does the child see, touch, feel, speak to and listen to an Internet-connected toy, the toy as a connected object can also track, see, speak and address them. The interaction between the child and the toy is, therefore, reconfigured as a bidirectional, multidimensional, multi-sensory experience that involves auditory, visual, haptic and kinetic communication, and in which the toy is repositioned not only as an interface, but as an actor in the communication process. The toy itself has gained agency, as it collects, generates, communicates and distributes data.

The notion of double articulation, then, is complicated by the newly acquired agentic capacities of network things. The materiality of media as objects, and the materiality of the communication infrastructures to which they are connected, is not a precondition for our communication *through* and *to* the connected things, but also for connected things to autonomously engage in communicative practices, configuring what, borrowing from Hartmann's work (2006), we could describe as triple articulation. We argue, therefore, for an extension to triple articulation, whereby the third dimension refers to the agency of things as producers of (big) data and, ultimately, knowledge (boyd & Crawford, 2012; Couldry & Hepp, 2017). That is, triple articulation accounts for the entanglement of media objects with broader processes of social, economic and political change that extend the surveillance business model of social media to playthings.

For these reasons, we believe that the definition of new media provided by Leah Lievrouw and Sonia Livingstone (2006) can complement and compensate for the challenges that a media- and data-saturated world poses to the concept of double articulation, as originally developed. They understand ICTs and their social contexts as comprising three dimensions:

- the artefacts and devices that enable and extend our ability to communicate;
- the communication activities or practices we engage into develop and use these devices; and,
- the social arrangements or organizations that form around the devices and practices (Lievrouw & Livingstone, 2006, p. 23).

The contributions collected in this volume variously address IoToys as (a) material artefacts that enable physical as well as connected play practices; (b) a combination of play and communicative practices, as well as the data practices in which the users and IoToys engage; and (c) new organisational forms, namely surveillance culture, datafication and surveillance capitalism, which reconfigure the meanings and value of play and communication practices, and, ultimately, of such toys as media. We, therefore, begin by exploring IoToys as material artefacts; we then delve into their transformation into robots; and finally, we look at the organisational practices that have developed around toys as networked, sensing media.

The Internet of Toys as Toys

A toy is a physical object that is used for play. A variety of objects can serve as toys (wooden spoons, cardboard boxes and rulers, to name a few). It is manufactured toys, nonetheless, that now form a substantial part of children's play culture in developed and developing countries, including connected toys. As a new category of toys, it is the digital connectedness and associated communicative affordances—whether they be beneficial or detrimental—of IoToys that are frequently promoted, critiqued and researched. Early childhood practitioners and early development experts also speculate whether IoToys (as opposed to physical toys) will deprive children of real-life authentic play, restrict children's socialisation with others and lead to a dominion model relationship with these toys. Also of concern is that these toys may limit children's curiosity and imagination as a consequence of their algorithmically generated scripts (Connected Toys, n.d.).

Offline Play with Connected Toys

In spite of these worries, there is now research that demonstrates that IoToys can, and do, serve as non-mediated, non-connected playthings, often when they are unplugged or disconnected (Coulton, 2015; Ihamäki, Pori, & Heljakka, 2018). Children do not necessarily need their IoToys to malfunction or lose connectivity to discover their offline affordances. Skylander figurines are a well-known example of this online/offline play (Coulton, 2015). These figurines, with their RFID tags, unlock access to a video game when placed on a "portal of power" (Payne & Steirer, 2014). Interestingly, however, much of the play that occurs with Skylanders happens when the video console is not in use. Children are collecting, trading and playing with these toy figurines—as well as using them to move forward within their video game play (Coulton, 2015).

Hybrid and Embedded Play

Children themselves make little differentiation between online and offline play and readily alternate and cross these boundaries when playing with connected toys. Connected toys, therefore, are conduits for both physical and digital play, as well as play that occurs between and through these spaces. This hybrid play can be further delineated into play with screenless IoToys—play that is labelled embedded play (Ruis, 2016). Embedded play refers to play with screenless, yet connected, toys or objects—where the child does not need to use a screen-based app to unlock a toy's digital play potential. This embedded play shifts the child's attention away from the screen and further towards the toy. Then, the toy itself becomes the only play interface (adapted from Ruis, 2016).

Designing Connected Toys

Conventional play objects have been categorised and theorised in a number of ways. They can be evaluated in terms of their affective (emotional), physical (tactile), functional (mechanical) and fictional (narrative) affordances (Ihamäki et al., 2018). They are also thought of as cultural artefacts that reflect or shape everyday life, as gendered playthings that reinforce gendered stereotypes, as agents of imagination and narrative making, and as artefacts that are implicit in children's identity making. Hinske, Langheinrich, and Lampe (2008) propose that good IoToy design needs to incorporate the same design principles that are applied to conventional toy design. This includes the toy being appealing to children in a sensory manner, being adaptable to a range of users and promoting child development. "Toys should encourage imagination and social play, stimulate physical or mental activity, and promote the discovery of new ways to play" (p. 2). They go on to suggest that designers of IoToys must aim for robustness in their toys in case of technological failures or connectivity issues, and that the digital technology embedded in a toy should not be essential to the children's play experience with it—so that when and if there is a malfunction or the toy is turned off for some reason, play may continue.

Education researchers, like Hinske et al. (2008), have also found that the offline, physical qualities of connected toys are as significant as their digital affordances. Ihamäki et al. (2018) found that children's play with Fisher-Price's Smart Bear, CogniToys' Dino and Wonder Workshop's Dash includes both online/offline and digital/physical play affordances. They investigated children's play with these toys in an early childhood setting and found that children's play behaviour with these toys was not always dependent on their digital affordances. The physical affordances of these toys also stimulated offline "imaginative play patterns such as treating the toy character as a companion that may be nurtured and played with" (p. 13). These toys provided for both instrumentally motivated play (coding, language skill development) when turned on and intrinsically motivated play (open-ended imaginative play) when turned off. Accordingly, children's understandings of the online/offline spaces in which they play require further exploration (Marsh et al., 2018) in order to extricate and understand these complexities and their relationship to children's learning and play.

To conclude, children make use of the multiple affordances of these toys, those associated with physical, real-world play and those associated with connected, digital play. The toys are treated simultaneously as material artefacts for tangible play and technical artefacts for virtual play. In this sense, the binaries made between offline/online play and physical/virtual play collapse and converge when children play with their connected toys in everyday, real-life situations. Thus, they are simultaneously situated in the digital, physical (and in-between) worlds of children. Well-designed IoToys, therefore, should allow children to participate in open-ended play with a physical toy, digital play with a connected toy and merged (in-between) play involving both the physical and the virtual.

The Internet of Toys as Social Robots

In the past century, robots were typically used in manufacturing—for manual labour and repetitive tasks (Ford, 2015). Nowadays, the continuing development of artificial intelligence (AI) or machine learning has significantly extended the scope and opportunity to develop more sophisticated and social robots. This includes leading-edge toys that are automated in such a way that they elicit social responses from or interaction with children. In addition, the miniaturisation and easy availability of sensors such as cameras, audio recorders and movement sensors—as well as cloud computing—has made these toys more affordable for manufacturers and consumers alike (Chaudron et al., 2017).

Social robots can be defined as embodied and sociable machines. Generally speaking, embodiment refers to the physical presence of an object or being (e.g. a robot) in a real-world environment. This physical presence can be either dynamic or static (Duffy, 2004). For instance, with no moving parts, CogniToy's Dino is a static embodied robot that uses speech recognition techniques and cloud computing to engage in conversations with children. Robot embodiments can also vary in appearance. Young children, in particular, can soon become fond of anthropomorphic robots (Breazeal et al., 2016; Paradeda, Ferreira, Martinho, Dias, & Paiva, 2016). Thus, most robots available for children are zoomorphic (animal like) or humanoid (human like) in appearance.

The sociability afforded to these social robots for children is to some degree in the eye of the child user (Kahn et al., 2012; Marsh, 2017). However, Breazeal (2003) suggests that different degrees of complexity in the design of robots increase or decrease a robot's level of sociability, as well as people's perceptions of them as social entities. These levels, or degrees, of robot sociability include *socially evocative, social interface, socially receptive* and *sociable. Socially evocative* robots are robots that "encourage people to anthropomorphize the technology in order to interact with it, but goes no further" (Breazeal, 2003, p. 169). An example of a socially evocative robot for children is Hasbro's Furby (Daily et al., 2017), which evokes (simulates) interactivity through its apparent ability to develop language skills. Each Furby begins by speaking only Furbish but is programmed to speak more English and less Furbish over time (Soltano, 2008) thus projecting learning and sociability without digitally interacting with its child owner.

Social interface describes a robot designed to communicate using human processes such as normal speech and social norms (Breazeal, 2003). These robots effectively mimic social norms but are not driven by them, as their social behaviour is only exhibited on an interface level. The Fisher-Price Think & Learn Teach 'n Tag Movi, for instance, can exhibit up to 60 different facial expressions as it directs children's play activities. However, it does not respond in any socially interactive manner to the child user. A *socially receptive* robot moves beyond the social interface and is essentially influenced by what the child does. These robots, like the WowWee CHiP Dog, learn through their interactions with children. Over time the CHiP Dog develops a distinctive personality that is determined, to some level, by how the child interacts with the toy. Finally, a *sociable* robot has the ability to do all of the aforementioned things, as well as having intentions or goals of its own (Serholt, 2017). "Such robots not only perceive human social cues, but at a deep level also model people in social and cognitive terms in order to interact with them" (Breazeal, 2003, p. 169). Anki's Cozmo Robot is considered a sociable robot in that it learns, adapts and responds to users. It is able to "recognise its user, read the emotions of its user and interpret the environment. In addition, it can show emotions based on the interactions with its user" (Demir, Caymaz, & Elci, 2017, p. 2).

Interactions between robots and children are different from those between adults and robots (Belpaeme et al., 2013). In addition, there are differing levels of built-in socialness of social robots available for children to use in domestic and educational settings. This adds complexity and variability to the manner in which children and robots interact with each other. It is, therefore, important that we understand children's interactions with social robots in terms of the embedded sociability of the robot and projected sociability from the child across different ages, genders and cultures and the other opportunities or risks that are afforded by automated social toys and the networked system they rely on.

The Internet of Toys and the Datafication of Everyday Life

As we have seen, once connected to sensing networks, these things (IoTs) gain new skills, including the ability to access, generate and communicate data about their users and the surrounding environment. Understanding "the politics of this agency is important, because [the] internet of things system might reduce or increase but surely will change the agency of the individual user" (Bunz & Meikle, 2018, p. 118). Through these Internet-connected and sensor-based things, users' behaviours are tracked, datafied, measured and, ultimately, predicted. Datafication can be defined as "the ability to render into data many aspects of the world that have not been quantified before" (Cukier & Mayer-Schoenberger, 2013), including social relations and emotions.

Dataveillance (Van Dijck, 2014)—that is the real-time monitoring and surveillance of citizens'/consumers' practices through digital technologies—has become so pervasive that data and information generated by automated processes now represent "a precondition for everyday life"

(Couldry & Hepp, 2017, p. 123). However, the algorithmic processes through which human behaviour is measured, evaluated and predicted are proprietary owned—and, as such, not open to modification or control by consumers—and ultimately serve to monetise behaviours, relations and emotions (Van Dijck, 2014). While adding to the growing datafication of everyday life, the Internet of Things also contributes to surveillance capitalism (Zuboff, 2015), which is a new business model based on the monetisation of data. As their personal data are consequently attributed economic value, individuals are positioned as both consumers of a service/product and the very product of this service/product. Couldry and Hepp (2017, p. 132) call the new relationship between human actors and artefacts "*tool reversibility*", to emphasise how users themselves are being used by the data-based, Internet-connected tools embedded in their everyday lives, which give shape to a seamless environment of dataveillance. The Internet of Things, then, transforms "its users into a resource that creates data" (Bunz & Meikle, 2018, p. 31).

As a growing part of the market of connected things for children (which also includes wearable devices), IoToys amplify the quantity and value of children's data within such a surveillance capitalism economy (Zuboff, 2015). In this new economic logic, children's play, learning and communicative practices become the object of algorithmic surveillance, aimed at calculating and predicting future (consumption) behaviour. The datafication of children's everyday lives and practices raises serious concerns among researchers, educators, policymakers and parents, because this development poses substantial privacy risks. Children's privacy is already under threat from data hacking and other security failures occurring over the last three years. For instance: the Vtech data breaches and Hello Barbie hackings that occurred in late 2015 (Holloway & Green, 2016); the security breakdowns of Genesis i-Que Intelligent Robot and My friend Cayla discovered and reported by the Norwegian Consumer Council #toyfailcampaign (author removed); and the leaking of over two million messages between children and parents that were recorded by CloudPet and over 800,000 user account details (Franceschi-Bicchierai, 2017). The longer-term implications of datafied childhoods include the so-called predictive privacy harms (Crawford & Schultz, 2014) and the emergence of new, or the reinforcement of, existing inequalities in children's access to opportunities and resources, such as education, health and credit, as we will further elaborate through the contributions in the fourth part of the book.

The increasing diffusion of connected toys and things for children also contributes to the normalisation of surveillance within society (Lyon, 2017) on a number of levels. This includes the level of parent–child relations, through the legitimisation of practices of intimate surveillance (Leaver, 2017) or caring surveillance (Holloway, in press a), where parents surveil their own children in order to monitor and/or care for them and the level of economic relations, with the new positioning of children as both consumers and objects of economic activity (as digital labourers) (Holloway, in press b).

What results from a surveillance economy, deeply embedded into everyday life, is ultimately a profound commodification of childhood, and its increasing datafication, whose consequences should be understood in the context of the broader surveillance of citizens' data (Barassi, 2017). The contributions to this volume will further examine the meaning, practices and consequences of the datafication of children's play, learning and communicative practices through their engagement with IoToys.

The Contributions of This Book

The book is organised into four sections, which engage with IoToys from a multidisciplinary approach, drawing on a wide range of theories and methodologies.

The first section, *New Toys, New Play, New Childhood?*, reflects on theories of robotification, connected and post-digital play and the uncanny and provides a set of conceptual tools to make sense of the emerging play and communicative practices that IoToys open up. In the first chapter, Jochen Peter, Rinaldo Kühne, Alex Barco, Chiara de Jong and Caroline van Straten examine the relationship between IoToys and social robots on a conceptual level and identify six characteristics (interactivity, energy, sensors, software control, movement, embodiment) that help to classify and distinguish social robots and Internet-connected toys along three dimensions: horizontal, vertical and spatial integration. Inherent to this classification, connected toys and social robots differ gradually rather than categorically, thus posing similar conceptual, methodological and techno-ethical issues to researchers. On this basis, the authors identify three common theoretical (absence or heterogeneity of theory, lacking developmental perspective, insufficient attention to intercultural differences) and three methodological issues (lack of standardised measures, study design issues, dominance of cross-sectional studies) that research on both social robots and IoToys needs to address. In the following chapter, Jackie Marsh draws on data from a study of young children's technological play in the home and suggests a complementary theoretical perspective, posthumanism, as a way to counterbalance the potential over-focus on risks that characterise media representations as well as much literature in the field. Focusing on children's interaction with a robotic toy, Furby, she considers the ways in which humans and machines interact in play. Drawing on the concepts of the uncanny valley and the anthropomorphic, the way in which the affective relationship between child and Furby is established is then analysed. In the final part of the chapter, posthuman philosophy is drawn upon to move beyond a human-centric perspective of this play in an attempt to understand the role of the toy itself in play episodes. It is argued that this approach allows for an account of play with the IoToys that pays heed to the opportunities such activities present. Seth Giddings also notes the importance of the need to pay attention to the layered relationships of material technology and intangible imagination, if we want to grasp the emerging possibilities of new developments in the IoToys. His chapter explores children's imaginative and playful engagement with robots and virtual pets, i.e. toys that demonstrate AI or autonomous behaviour. It takes a workshop on the design of a new robotic gaming platform as a central case study and shows how close descriptive and analytical attention to moments of interaction with such toys is essential in order to fully grasp the complex relationships between global technological imaginaries—in this case of AI and artificial life—and the material and embodied workings of imagination in play. The final chapter of the section, by Bjorn Nansen, Benjamin

Nicoll and Thomas Apperley, interrogates the evolving intersection of cross-media products and children's cultures of play using Amiibo Figurines as a case study and points to emerging questions around children's data literacies. Amiibo Figurines are based on characters from various Nintendo franchises, such as Super Mario Bros., and use NFC tags to connect wirelessly to Nintendo's Switch, 3DS and Wii U platforms. The authors show how, in their production, promotion and everyday use, the figurines solicit playful practices that cut across physical objects and digital spaces. Drawing on interface analysis, promotional discourses and videos of play on YouTube, their analysis highlights how Amiibo are framed as a means to envelop children in Nintendo's cross-media ecosystem by reinforcing a physical connection between child, toy, software, platform and intellectual property. Their line of argument is informed by the concept of post-digital play, through which they account for the reciprocal dynamic between children's everyday play and the branded world of IoT products.

The following section, *Domesticating the Internet of Toys: Practices and Contexts*, includes three chapters that provide empirical evidence on the appropriation of IoToys in both the domestic and school contexts. Rita Brito, Patricia Dias and Gabriela Oliveira analyse the findings from a qualitative exploratory study which involved 21 families and combined interviews, activities and non-participant observation. They adopt a domestication of technology approach to investigate the early stages of the domestication of new playthings and show how IoToys become part of an "ecosystem" of other toys and activities, while maintaining a "novelty" status. Their findings also reveal that parents have mixed perceptions about IoToys: they value their educational potential but fear an excess of technological play and consider them expensive. Lorna Arnott and Ioanna Palaiologou explore children's everyday use of Internet-connected toys in both home and early education through a socio-ecological model. Their chapter builds on data collected via a case study approach, which considers both children and practitioners' agency in their use of IoToys. Their findings show that digital childhoods are messy, multifaceted, multi-modal and ultimately complex, and that digital childhoods cannot be compartmentalised across various bounded systems. Instead, IoToys (as new technology still developing) are creating a synergy between digital and non-digital. Similarly, children's interactions with IoToys and with other children around IoToys are inseparably linked across the individual, the interpersonal and the community (Rogoff, 2008) in digital and non-digital spaces. Katriina Heljakka and Pirita Ihamäki also report on an empirical study conducted in a Finnish preschool context. Focusing especially on hybrid, connected play practices, they conclude that IoToys foster opportunities for playful formal and informal learning. However, they also note the importance of imaginative play, along with the relevance of the materiality and aesthetics of the toy. They also highlight the policy and design implications of the new, hybrid playthings: from an educational perspective, IoToys demand a multi-literacy approach; from a design perspective, they require consideration of their cultural appropriateness (e.g. which languages the toys include or whether they are capable of guiding play through universally recognised forms of communication).

Their considerations open the way to the third part of the book, dedicated to *Design and Research Methodologies*. Martin Van Mechelen, Bieke Zaman, Lizzy Bleumers and Ilse Mariën critically reflect on a participatory design (PD) approach that was used by an interdisciplinary team to design new IoToys applications for the home and school environments (the WOOPI project). The authors emphasise PD's aim to empower people in the design of technology that will have an impact on their lives and environments. Therefore, the chapter discusses the extent to which the case study adhered to the three core principles of PD, those being: (1) having a say (i.e. enabling people to voice their opinions and share decision-making power), (2) mutual learning (i.e. a two-way learning process in which the design team learns about users' experiences and viewpoints, and users learn about technological possibilities from the design team) and (3) co-realisation (i.e. people taking an active part in the visualisation and prototyping of ideas). They conclude by identifying six guidelines that can increase users' participation in the design of hybrid playful products. In the following chapter, Dylan Yamada-Rice draws on three different research projects in which children have been considered in relation to the design of digital products aimed at them and advocates that there are benefits in considering children as knowledgeable partners in the design process. Through the first case study, she shows how children have knowledge different to that of makers and designers of smart toys. Second, she demonstrates that young children have a range of expertise related to their own digital play, as well as skills for critiquing digital content and toys that could be fruitfully employed as part of the design process. The third study shows how including children in the design of connected toys and digital play might aid their understanding of how such products work and as a result allow them to be critical of the technologies and content they are consuming. Stéphane Chaudron, Dimitrios Geneiatakis, Ioannis Kounelis and Rosanna Di Gioia focus, instead, on the security issues of Internet-connected toys, addressing questions such as: What data can Internet-connected toys exchange? With whom? What are the possible threats and what are possible improvements to the technology to avoid them? The authors describe the usual data flow of IoToys architecture and introduce a threat model that highlights the possible threats that can be expected from this architecture. The results of the privacy and security tests indicate that personal data can be exposed in different points of the architecture, thus violating data confidentiality, and consequently end-users' privacy. The chapter concludes with specific recommendations to enhance the security and trust level of Internet-connected toys by end-users. Thomas Enemark Lundtofte and Stine Liv Johansen present the video ethnographic "Points-of-View" (POV) methodology, which provides audio-visual data from both ends of the interactions thanks to a dual camera set-up. The authors critically reflect on examples of empirical data created using this methodology in order to show its benefits—namely, how the POV method grants access to the sociomaterial practices between children and digital toys—and discuss critical issues and limitations of POV. In the next chapter, Giovanna Mascheroni and Donell Holloway propose a methodological toolkit to approach the digital-material configurations of connected play as situated in the context of everyday life, and they account for the complex and varied ways in which the interactions between children and IoToys—as media and material objects—emerge through play practices. With this aim, the authors outline a combination of methods, including an adaptation of the walkthrough method to the study of the affordances of robotic Internet-connected toys, and combine it with both traditional and innovative discourse-based and observational methods of research with young children. Theoretically, the chapter is informed by materialist-phenomenological approaches to practices in media studies, "more-than-representational" frameworks in digital ethnography, and novel theorisations of affordances.

The final and concluding section of the volume takes a closer look at the political economy of IoToys, and its social, political, economic and legal implications. Ingrida Milkaite and Eva Lievens offer an exploration of key fundamental rights and data protection legislation that is relevant to the IoToys context in the USA and the European Union. Adopting a children's rights perspective, the authors conduct an analysis of the US Children's Online Privacy Protection Act, the EU General Data Protection Regulation and the future ePrivacy Regulation and reflect on their implementation and enforcement in practice. Finally, they make a number of practical recommendations for IoToys actors, policymakers and regulators. Esther Martínez Pastor and Patricia Núñez focus on the practice of hidden advertising by analysing YouTube toys review videos in which young YouTubers review the "Hello Barbie Dream House". The aim of their critical analysis is twofold, namely a better understanding of (1) how brands use smart connected toys to promote their brands and (2) how they use YouTube channels to promote their IoToys through entertainment. Due to the fact that entertainment and sponsored content are not differentiated in such videos, the authors conclude that toy reviews constitute clear violations of Directive 2010/13/EU on audio-visual media services and Directive 2005/29/EC on unfair commercial practices. Vilmantė Liubinienė and Ana Jorge combine a framework of the political economy of children's media and leisure with a cultural and creative industries approach in the context of the increasing commercialisation of children's culture in order to discuss the implications of the structure of production of smart toys and local linguistic and cultural possibilities. Their chapter is based on media and advertising content analysis from 12 countries, linguistic analysis of smart toys' websites, analyses of start-up case studies from Lithuania and Portugal and secondary data on children, technology and digital literacy. The authors show how the production and promotion of smart toys are largely dependent on global market logics and how national incentives to software companies are not governed by the intention to support smaller linguistic cultures. Finally, Giovanna Mascheroni and Donell Holloway conclude the volume by revisiting the concepts of datafication and surveillance capitalism. In doing so, they emphasise the social, political and economic consequences of IoToys as data-based technologies and simultaneously aim to define critical questions and map out possible trajectories that future research in the field should address and pursue.

References

Barassi, V. (2017). BabyVeillance? Expecting parents, online surveillance and the cultural specificity of pregnancy apps. *Social Media + Society, 3*(2). https://doi.org/10.1177/2056305117707181.

Belpaeme, T., Baxter, P., De Greeff, J., Kennedy, J., Read, R., Looije, R., … Zelati, M. C. (2013). *Child-robot interaction: Perspectives and challenges*. Paper presented at the International Conference on Social Robotics.

boyd, d., & Crawford, K. (2012). Critical questions for big data. *Information, Communication & Society, 15*(5), 662–679.

Breazeal, C. (2003). Toward sociable robots. *Robotics and Autonomous Systems, 42*(3–4), 167–175.

Breazeal, C., Harris, P. L., DeSteno, D., Kory Westlund, J. M., Dickens, L., & Jeong, S. (2016). Young children treat robots as informants. *Topics in Cognitive Science, 8*(2), 481–491.

Bunz, M., & Meikle, G. (2018). *The internet of things*. Cambridge: Polity Press.

Chaudron, S., Di Gioia, R., Gemo, M., Holloway, D., Marsh, J., Mascheroni, G., … Yamada-Rice, D. (2017). *Kaleidoscope on the internet of toys—Safety, security, privacy and societal insights*. Ispra: Joint Research Centre. Retrieved from http://publications.jrc.ec.europa.eu/repository/bitstream/JRC105061/jrc105061_final_online.pdf.

Connected Toys. (n.d.). *Trends*. Retrieved from http://www.ala.org/tools/future/trends/connectedtoys.

Couldry, N., & Hepp, A. (2017). *The mediated construction of reality*. Cambridge: Polity.

Coulton, P. (2015). Playful and gameful design for the internet of things. In A. Niholt (Ed.), *More playful user interfaces* (pp. 151–173). Singapore: Springer.

Crawford, K., & Schultz, J. (2014). Big data and due process: Toward a framework to redress predictive privacy harms. *Boston College Law Review, 55*(1), 93–128.

Cukier, K. N., & Mayer-Schoenberger, V. (2013). The rise of big data how it's changing the way we think about the world. *Foreign Affairs*. Retrieved February 7, 2018, from https://www.foreignaffairs.com/articles/2013-04-03/rise-big-data.

Daily, S. B., James, M. T., Cherry, D., Porter, J. J., Darnell, S. S., Isaac, J., & Roy, T. (2017). Affective computing: Historical foundations, current applications, and future trends. In M. Jeon (Ed.), *Emotions and affect in human factors and human–computer interaction* (pp. 213–231). Amsterdam: Elsevier.

Demir, K. A., Caymaz, E., & Elci, M. (2017). *Issues in integrating robots into organizations*. Paper presented at the The 12th International Scientific Conference "Defence Resources Management in the 21st Century", Brazov.

Duffy, B. (2004). Robots social embodiment in autonomous mobile robotics. *International Journal of Advanced Robotic Systems, 1*(3), 17.

Ford, M. (2015). *Rise of the robots: Technology and the threat of a jobless future*. New York: Basic Books.

Franceschi-Bicchierai, L. (2017, February 27). Internet of things teddy bear leaked 2 million parent and kids message recordings. *Motherboard*. Retrieved December 22, 2017, from https://motherboard.vice.com/en_us/article/pgwean/internet-of-things-teddy-bear-leaked-2-million-parent-and-kids-message-recordings.

Haddon, L., & Silverstone, R. (2000). Information and communication technologies and everyday life: Individual and social dimensions. In K. Ducatel, J. Webster, & W. Herrman (Eds.), *The information society in Europe: Work and life in an age of globalization* (pp. 233–258). Lanham: Rowman and Littlefield.

Hartmann, M. (2006). The triple articulation of ICTs. Media as technological objects, symbolic environments and individual texts. In T. Berker, M. Hartmann, Y. Punie, & K. Ward (Eds.), *Domestication of media and technology* (pp. 80–102). Berkshire: Open University Press.

Hinske, S., Langheinrich, M., & Lampe, M. (2008, February 25–27). Towards guidelines for designing augmented toy environments. In *Proceedings of the 7th ACM Conference on Designing Interactive Systems*. Cape Town, South Africa.

Holloway, D. (in press a). *Children's digital lives: The parent factor*. Bingley, UK: Emerald Publishing.

Holloway, D. (in press b). The Internet of Toys and Things (IoTTs) for children: Surveillance capitalism and children's data. *Media International Australia*.

Holloway, D., & Green, L. (2016). The internet of toys. *Communication Research and Practice, 2*(4), 506–519.

Ihamäki, P., Pori, S., & Heljakka, K. (2018, January 10–12). *Smart, skilled and connected in the 21st century: Educational promises of the Internet of Toys (IoToys)*. Paper presented at the Hawaii International Conference on Arts and Humanities, Honolulu.

Kahn, P. H., Jr., Kanda, T., Ishiguro, H., Freier, N. G., Severson, R. L., Gill, B. T., … Shen, S. (2012). "Robovie, you'll have to go into the closet now": Children's social and moral relationships with a humanoid robot. *Developmental Psychology, 48*(2), 303–314.

Leaver, T. (2017). Intimate surveillance: Normalizing parental monitoring and mediation of infants online. *Social Media + Society, 3*(2). https://doi.org/10.1177/2056305117707192.

Lievrouw, L. A., & Livingstone, S. (2006). Introduction to the first edition (2002): The social shaping and consequences of ICTs. In L. A. Lievrouw & S. Livingstone (Eds.), *Handbook of new media* (pp. 15–32). London: Sage.

Livingstone, S. (2007). On the material and the symbolic: Silverstone's double articulation of research traditions in new media studies. *New Media & Society, 9*(1), 16–24.

Lyon, D. (2017). Surveillance culture: Engagement, exposure, and ethics in digital modernity. *International Journal of Communication, 11*, 824–842.

Marsh, J. (2017). The internet of toys: A posthuman and multimodal analysis of connected play. *Teachers College Record, 119*(15). Retrieved December 20, 2017, from http://eprints.whiterose.ac.uk/113557/.

Marsh, J., Mascheroni, G., Carrington, V., Árnadóttir, H., Brito, R., Dias, P., … Trueltzsch-Wijnen, C. (2018). *The online and offline digital literacy practices of young children: A review of the literature*. Sheffield: COST Action IS1410 DigiLitEY. Retrieved July 17, 2018, from http://digilitey.eu/wp-content/uploads/2017/01/WG4-LR-jan-2017.pdf.

McReynolds, E., Hubbard, S., Lau, T., Saraf, A., Cakmak, M., & Roesner, F. (2017, May 6–11). Toys that listen: A study of parents, children, and internet-connected toys. In *Proceedings of the 2017 CHI Conference on Human Factors in Computing Systems* (pp. 5197–5207). Denver, Colorado. Retrieved from https://www.franziroesner.com/pdf/ToysThatListen-CHI2017.pdf.

Paradeda, R., Ferreira, M. J., Martinho, C., Dias, J., & Paiva, A. (2016). *A persuasive storyteller robot: Pilot study*. Retrieved July 17, 2018, from https://r4l.epfl.ch/files/content/sites/r4l/files/proceedings_hri2017/R4L_HRI_2017_paper_6.pdf.

Payne, M. T., & Steirer, G. (2014). Redesigning game industries studies. *Creative Industries Journal, 7*(1), 67–71.

Rogoff, B. (2008). Observing sociocultural activity on three planes: Participatory appropriation, guided participation, and apprenticeship. In K. Hall, P. Murphy, & J. Solet (Eds.), *Pedagogy and practice: Culture and identities* (pp. 58–74). London: Sage.

Ruis, E. (2016). *The New Ludic City: From hybrid play towards embedded play within urban spaces*. Retrieved from https://www.researchgate.net/publication/305367984_The_New_Ludic_City_From_hybrid_play_towards_embedded_play_within_urban_spaces.

Serholt, S. (2017). *Child-robot interaction in education*. Ph.D., University of Gothenburg, Gottenburg.

Silverstone, R. (1994). *Television and everyday life*. London: Routledge.

Silverstone, R., Hirsch, E., & Morley, D. (1992). Information and communication technologies and the moral economy of the household. In R. Silverstone & E. Hirsch (Eds.), *Consuming technologies: Media and information in domestic space* (pp. 13–28). London: Routledge.

Soltano, E. (2008). How to evaluate what students have learned about cognition. *AP® Psychology*, 25.

Van Dijck, J. (2014). Datafication, dataism and dataveillance: Big data between scientific paradigm and ideology. *Surveillance and Society, 12*(2), 197–208.

Zuboff, S. (2015). Big other: Surveillance capitalism and the prospects of an information civilization. *Journal of Information Technology, 30*(1), 75–89.

Part I
New Toys, New Play, New Childhood?

2

Asking Today the Crucial Questions of Tomorrow: Social Robots and the Internet of Toys

Jochen Peter, Rinaldo Kühne, Alex Barco, Chiara de Jong and Caroline L. van Straten

Introduction

The past two decades have seen many technological changes (e.g. Eberl, 2016; Ross, 2016; Van Bergen, 2016; for a summary, see Peter, 2017a, 2017b): Computers have become ever more powerful and computing has turned into a mobile activity, at least where stable mobile networks

J. Peter (✉) · R. Kühne · A. Barco · C. de Jong · C. L. van Straten
Amsterdam School of Communication Research (ASCoR), University of
Amsterdam, Amsterdam, The Netherlands
e-mail: j.peter@uva.nl

R. Kühne
e-mail: r.j.Kuhne@uva.nl

A. Barco
e-mail: a.barcomartelo@uva.nl

C. de Jong
e-mail: c.dejong@uva.nl

C. L. van Straten
e-mail: c.l.vanStraten@uva.nl

© The Author(s) 2019
G. Mascheroni and D. Holloway (eds.), *The Internet of Toys*,
Studies in Childhood and Youth, https://doi.org/10.1007/978-3-030-10898-4_2

are available. In addition, digital information has become easily available via large information networks, notably the Internet. Much computing to date takes place in the cloud, which has disassociated information and software on the one hand from hardware devices on the other. At the same time, the cost of many technical devices, especially sensors, cameras and audio devices, has dropped sharply. Finally, insights from machine learning keep on advancing artificial intelligence (AI) and, as a consequence, the increasingly autonomous functioning of hitherto heteronomously operated devices (Thrun, 2004).

The technological changes of the past 20 years come together in current social robots, which are often predicted to have a major impact in the future (Barnatt, 2015; Ross, 2016). Robots have been around more than 50 years, but mainly as industrial and service robots (Thrun, 2004). These types of robots are typically designed to do work that is too dangerous or repetitive for human beings (e.g. Winfield, 2012). Although industrial and service robots usually operate autonomously in a particular environment, they are unable to engage with human beings in even the most basic way (industrial robots) or beyond the very restricted service tasks they are programmed to do (service robots) (Thrun, 2004). Social robots, in contrast, are designed to interact in a meaningful way with human beings and act and react autonomously in a variety of social situations (e.g. Breazeal, 2003; Dautenhahn, 2007; Fong, Nourbakhsh, & Dautenhahn, 2003; Lee, Peng, Jin, & Yan, 2006; Zhao, 2006).

To date, social robots have primarily been used in care for the elderly and as devices for children with an autism spectrum disorder, i.e. developmentally atypical children (e.g. Cabibihan, Javed, Ang, & Aljunied, 2013; De Graaf, Ben Allouch, & Klamer, 2015). However, social robots may also be relevant to developmentally typical children, notably when it comes to the Internet of Toys (Wang, Kuo, King, & Chang, 2010). Drawing on Holloway and Green's (2016) work, the Internet of Toys has been defined as "a set of software-enabled toys that: (1) are connected to online platforms through WiFi and Bluetooth, but also, potentially, to other toys; (2) are equipped with sensors; and (3) relate one-on-one to children" (Mascheroni & Holloway, 2017, p. 5).

The Internet of Toys is itself part of the Internet of Things, which is "a network of entities that are connected through any form of sensor, enabling these entities, which we term as Internet-connected constituents, to be located, identified, and even operated upon" (Ng & Wakenshaw, 2017, p. 4, emphasis removed from original).

Although social robots have been emphasized as an important part of the Internet of Toys (e.g. Future of Privacy Forum & Family Online Safety Institute, 2016; Mascheroni & Holloway, 2017; Peter, 2017b), it is still unclear how social robots and the Internet of Toys relate to each other on a conceptual level. The above definitions of the Internet of Toys and the Internet of Things highlight, for example, networked connectivity and sensor technology. These characteristics also appear in definitions of, and discussions about, (social) robots (e.g. Van Bergen, 2016; Winfield, 2012). Robots, however, include many more technological features (Winfield, 2012) and we do not know to what extent these features are relevant to the Internet of Toys. The first goal of this chapter is to address this issue.

As research on social robots and the Internet of Toys responds to recent fast-paced technological changes, both fields are still in a nascent state. Moreover, with their inherently interdisciplinary character, both fields attract attention from a diverse range of disciplines, from the engineering sciences and robotics, to law and philosophy, to the humanities and social sciences (for robots, see, e.g., Baxter, Kennedy, Senft, Lemaignan, & Belpaeme, 2016). As a result, we face—even when researchers ask the same questions—diverging foci and emphases in theoretical and conceptual frameworks as well as in methodological approaches and standards, certainly in research on social robots (e.g. De Jong, Peter, Kühne, & Barco, 2018; Eyssel, 2017; Van Straten, Peter, & Kühne, 2018). Against this background, it is important that, today, we are asking crucial questions about theoretical and methodological issues that are common to research on both social robots and the Internet of Toys. The second goal of this chapter is to identify and discuss theoretical and methodological problems that need to be solved to ensure progress in the two fields.

Social Robots, Smart Toys and Connected Toys

Although the literature on the Internet of Toys typically points out that toys with mechanical and electronic features have a long history (e.g. Future of Privacy Forum & Family Online Safety Institute, 2016; Wang et al., 2010), it also emphasizes that several current toys have new crucial features: They are unprecedentedly "smart" and they are "connected" to the Internet (Chaudron et al., 2017; Future of Privacy Forum & Family Online Safety Institute, 2016; Mascheroni & Holloway, 2017). Given the prominence of smart and connected toys in the literature on the Internet of Toys, in what follows we refer to these two rather than to the Internet of Toys, which also facilitates comparisons with social robots.

Smart toys are usually defined as toys that "contain embedded electronic features such that they can adapt to the actions of the user [...] [and] process more information from a greater variety of sensors. This may include the use of microphones or speech recognition, cameras for detection of patterns and visual cues, accelerometers, proximity sensors, gyroscopes, compasses, radio transmitters, or Bluetooth for communicating between various parts to [sic] the same toy" (Future of Privacy Forum & Family Online Safety Institute, 2016, p. 2). Smart toys, however, are only part of the Internet of Toys if they are *connected* toys (Future of Privacy Forum & Family Online Safety Institute, 2016). "Connected toys [...] incorporate Internet technologies that respond to and interact with children. They are sometimes equipped with speech recognition and activation and appear to react to the words of the user. They may also be controlled remotely across network infrastructure, for example via smartphones or tablets connected to the same network. These toys often use sophisticated sensor-based technologies to collect information from children and cloud-based platforms to process this information through real-time interactions. This cloud-based processing relies on sophisticated algorithms that can simulate human intelligence (AI) and deliver more personalised or individualised responses to children" (Mascheroni & Holloway, 2017, p. 5; see also Future of Privacy Forum & Family Online Safety Institute, 2016).

Defining Features of Smart Toys, Connected Toys and Social Robots

A smart toy does not have to be connected to the Internet and a connected toy does not have to be smart (Future of Privacy Forum & Family Online Safety Institute, 2016; Mascheroni & Holloway, 2017). Still, on a conceptual level, the above definitions of smart and connected toys include at least four common features, which Winfield (2012) has earlier also identified as defining functions of robots, as will be elaborated upon below. First, both smart and connected toys are electronic devices that need *energy* (from batteries or mains power). Second, both smart and connected toys tend to rely on one or more types of *sensors* (e.g. visual, audio, haptic) for input from their human and non-human environment. For smart toys, this input comes from their own, immediate environment and is unique to the particular toy. For connected toys, this input may in addition come from another, remote environment (e.g. in the form of information stored in the cloud). This input is thus unspecific to the particular toy. Third, smart and connected toys alike are *software-controlled*, which largely determines their "intelligence". Whereas, in smart toys, the software is embedded, it may be controlled remotely in connected toys. Fourth, both smart and connected toys *interact* with children; they thus not only process input from their human environment, but also respond to it.

The definition of smart toys includes, at least implicitly, two more conceptually important features that also merge with the functions of robots as outlined by Winfield (2012). The emphasis on accelerometers, gyroscopes and compasses suggests that smart toys may be able, or are intended, to *move* in the physical world. In addition, the above definition of smart toys highlights that smart toys have tangible material components. This points to the possibility that such toys may be embodied. *Embodiment* can be defined as "having a body in the physical world" (Looije, van der Zalm, Neerincx, & Beun, 2012, p. 719) (for an elaborate definition see Fong et al., 2003).

As mentioned above, the four features of smart and connected toys— energy, sensors, software control and interactivity—as well as the two potential additional features of smart toys—movement and embodiment—overlap with what Winfield (2012) considers the characteristic functions of robots. According to Winfield (2012, p. 4), "[s]ome of [the] five functions – sensing, signalling, moving, intelligence, and energy, integrated into a body – are present in all robots". Winfield (2012, pp. 4–7) defines the various functions as follows: Sensing includes vision, hearing, touch, relative and absolute orientation and location sensing, as well as short-range sensing (e.g. through infrared sensors) and long-range sensing (e.g. through laser sensors). Signalling refers to sounds, facial and body gestures, light and radio. Moving comprises motor-based wheeled, legged or flying movements. A robot's intelligence depends on its hardware—the microprocessor(s)—and its software, without which a robot is unable to operate because they are needed to process the sensors' input. The energy of a robot comes from mains power, batteries, solar panels or fuel cells (for an overview of the five functions, see Winfield, 2012, particularly Table 1, p. 7). The type and shape of a robot's body are related to its morphology (Winfield, 2012): It can be anthropomorphic and have human-like features; it can be zoomorphic and have animal-like features; it can be caricatured and look like animation figures; or it can be functional and have machine-like features (Fong et al., 2003). Anthropomorphic and functional robots currently dominate research (Riek, 2012).

Winfield's (2012) definition of robot functions refers to robots in general. As a result, interactivity with humans—in the sense of a meaningful exchange of symbols—is not explicitly included in his definition. Winfield does emphasize the signalling function of robots, broadly speaking the ability of robots to communicate in a textual/verbal or nontextual/nonverbal fashion. However, only when a robot is able to both act upon and react meaningfully to its (human) environment does it become interactive. Next to their capacity to adhere to the rules that belong to a particular social role ("Social Robot", n.d.), the ability of robots to both send and receive signals, or more specifically symbols, in a variety of interactions with human beings is essential for their social character (e.g. Breazeal, 2003; Dautenhahn, 2007; Fong et al., 2003; Zhao, 2006). The features of social robots (Winfield, 2012) thus resemble those of smart toys: Both (1) are interactive; (2) need energy to function; (3) use sensors to sense their social environment; (4) are controlled by software; (5) can move; and (6) are embodied. Connected toys differ from smart toys because their input may also come from other than their immediate environments and, notably, because their software can be remotely controlled. Connected toys differ from social robots because, in contrast to social robots, connected toys typically need to be connected to a network to function.

Horizontal, Vertical and Spatial Integration

Against this background, the question arises as to what distinguishes social robots from smart toys. In one of the first papers on the Internet of Toys, Wang et al. (2010, p. 265) classified smart toys (in the form of ePets), amongst other things, according to their level of integration, i.e. the extent to which smart toys "integrate more sensors, actuators [i.e. devices that control movements], mechanical parts, and comput-ing resources […] [to] make more sophisticated movements and expres-sions. They are closer to robots". In this classification, smart toys and social robots thus differ rather subtly. However, Wang et al. (2010) do not provide a theoretical rationale for the characteristics in which the integration of smart toys and social robots differs. Moreover, they do not define these characteristics explicitly.

To distinguish more precisely between smart toys and robots and, at the same time, include the connectivity of connected toys as a dimen-sion in its own right, it may be useful to rely on the aforementioned six features of social robots and to differentiate between vertical, hori-zontal and spatial integration. The terms are typically used in econom-ics and related fields and refer to the integration between companies (Colangelo, 1995) and regions (Van Oort, Burger, & Raspe, 2010). We use them here to explicate and extend Wang et al.'s (2010) notion of a device's integration. The notion that technological devices can be differ-entiated according to the number and complexity of their characteris-tics (which we explicate below) is inspired, for example, by the idea that media can be distinguished by their "richness" (through, for instance, immediate feedback and more modalities; e.g. Daft & Lengel, 1986).

Horizontal integration overlaps with Wang et al.'s (2010) definition of integration, but it relies on the six features of social robots identified above. It captures *how many* of the six features are present in a given device, where each feature is seen as a binary (present–absent) variable. The more of the six features a device has, the more horizontally integrated it is. It is, however, hard to think of smart toys and social robots that do not feature interactivity, energy, sensors and software control. Consequently, movement and embodiment play a crucial role in distinguishing smart toys and social robots in terms of their horizontal integration.

The concept of *vertical* integration goes beyond Wang et al.'s (2010) definition of integration. It refers to the *degree* to which each of the six features of social robots is present in a given device. Interactivity, energy, sensors, software control, movement and embodiment are thus each seen as a continuum. Consequently, smart toys and social robots can be distinguished by how interactive they are; how independent they are from an energy supply (e.g. through batteries); how many different sensors they have (e.g. vision, hearing, touch, location); how powerful their software control is (and thus their "intelligence"); how smoothly and robustly they can move in the physical world; and how embodied they are (e.g. from no body, to merely visible to tangible body). By and large, current social robots differ much more from smart toys in their vertical than in their horizontal integration: Not only do social robots have the highest level of embodiment as well as multiple sensors and actuators (for movement), but they also feature high levels of interactivity and advanced software control.

Finally, the concept of *spatial* integration theoretically explicates Wang et al.'s (2010) idea of the Internet of Toys: Spatial integration explicitly captures the connectivity of toys and social robots, thereby cutting through vertical and horizontal integration. High spatial integration means that a device needs to be continuously connected to function properly, whereas low spatial integration means that a device can incidentally be connected for (better) functioning (e.g. by downloading software updates). As connectivity currently plays a major role in the sensorial input to and software control of connected toys, it is possible that it will affect, in the future, their movement and interactivity.

It is important to note, however, that spatial integration does not have to go hand in hand with horizontal and vertical integration (Future of Privacy Forum & Family Online Safety Institute, 2016): A connected toy may be high in spatial integration but low in horizontal and/or vertical integration. Conversely, devices such as social robots may be high in horizontal and vertical integration but low in spatial integration. For example, as a connected toy, the digital smartphone-based toothbrush game/toy Grush (Grush) is higher in spatial integration than the social robot Nao (Softbank), as Grush, unlike Nao, needs to be connected to a network to function. Nao, in contrast, is higher in horizontal and vertical integration than Grush: Nao features energy, interactivity, motion sensors, software control, embodiment, and movement in the physical world, and all of them to an advanced degree. Grush lacks, in particular, both embodiment and movement in the physical world. The remaining four characteristics are less advanced in Grush than in Nao.

In sum, the relationship between the Internet of Toys—here: smart toys and connected toys—on the one hand and social robots on the other can be conceptualized according to six characteristics: interactivity, energy, sensors, software control, movement and embodiment (Winfield, 2012). Together with connectivity, these six characteristics help to classify smart toys, connected toys and social robots along three dimensions: horizontal, vertical, and spatial integration. It is inherent to this classification that smart toys, connected toys and social robots differ in rather subtle ways. As a result, it is conceivable that research on smart and connected toys, as well as on social robots, may face similar conceptual and methodological issues.

Conceptual and Methodological Issues

Research on both social robots and the Internet of Toys covers emerging fields. Still, research on social robots is currently more elaborate than research on the Internet of Toys (as of June 2018, a search for studies in the Web of Science elicits two hits for "Internet of Toys" and 311 for "social robots"). For the identification of conceptual and methodological issues, we therefore mainly rely on research on social robots.

Conceptual Issues

Broadly speaking, research on social robots can be divided into research on robot technology and research on human–robot interaction (HRI), which is most relevant to this chapter. In research on HRI in general and on child–robot interaction (CRI) in particular, at least three conceptual issues currently deserve attention. As others have also observed, these issues are the absence or heterogeneity of theoretical frameworks (Eyssel, 2017); the lacking focus on developmental differences between (child) robot users (Belpaeme et al., 2013); and the insufficient attention to intercultural differences in how humans deal with robots (Shahid, Krahmer, & Swerts, 2014).

Absence or heterogeneity of theoretical frameworks. Novel research fields typically lack unifying conceptual and theoretical frameworks; after all, fields usually build and test theories only when they mature (Kuhn, 1970). Social robotics, however, is an interdisciplinary field (Baxter et al., 2016) that can, in principle, draw on a variety of theoretical frameworks established in various disciplines. In this context, it is striking that, in a recent evaluation of research on HRI, Eyssel (2017, p. 365) concluded: "Browsing conference proceedings and even journal publications in the field, it becomes clear that many a paper lacks an actual theory section. While an introduction into the literature is commonly provided, one sometimes pauses to wonder what the just read 'Related Work' section would tell us about the study that has actually been conducted?" The need for more theory-driven research is echoed by other scholars (Dautenhahn, 2007; De Jong et al., 2018; Krämer, Eimler, von der Pütten, & Payr, 2011). In a recent review of what shapes children's acceptance of social robots, De Jong et al. (2018) more specifically pointed out that many of the studies on the determinants of children's acceptance of social robots remain theoretically somewhat ad hoc and are consequently difficult to compare. The authors, therefore, explicitly call for an overarching theoretical framework that can guide research on children's acceptance of social robots (see also Van Straten et al., 2018).

Even if studies are based on established theories, the approaches remain heterogeneous and scattered. For example, in a review of HRI, Broadbent (2017) identified multiple conceptual and theoretical frameworks used in research, such as evolutionary theory, realism inconsistency, psychoanalysis, media equation, anthropomorphism, perceptions of mind and emotional attachment. A cursory look at recent publications on HRI and CRI elicits several more approaches, e.g. uncertainty reduction theory and expectancy violation theory (Edwards, Edwards, Spence, & Westerman, 2016; Spence, Westerman, Edwards, & Edwards, 2014), self-determination theory (Looije, Neerincx, Peters, & Henkemans, 2016), theory of planned behaviour (De Graaf, Ben Allouch, & van Dijk, 2017) or attachment theory (Dziergwa, Kaczmarek, Kaczmarek, Kędzierski, & Wadas-Szydłowska, 2018) (for references to the origins of these theories, see the cited publications). The variety of theoretical frameworks used shows the dynamic character of the field but also calls for a more integrative, cumulative and overarching treatment of theories (Eyssel, 2017). Compared to research on HRI and CRI, research on the Internet of Toys is still *in statu nascendi*. Given the similarities between the two fields, however, it is important that research on the Internet of Toys commits to theory formation and integration right from the start. The distinction between horizontal, vertical, and spatial integration of devices may be a first tentative step in this direction.

Lacking focus on developmental differences. Research on the Internet of Toys and on the subfield of CRI in HRI inherently centres on children and adolescents. However, between childhood and adolescence—as well as within childhood and adolescence—enormous developmental differences occur. These developmental differences encompass cognitive, emotional, social, physical and psychological changes (e.g. Lightfoot, Cole, & Cole, 2013; Steinberg, 2008). From what we know about how young people select and use media (e.g. Valkenburg & Taylor Piotrowski, 2017), it is likely that developmental differences also affect how young people approach smart toys and social robots; how they interact with them; and what consequences this has (e.g. Beran, Ramirez-Serrano, Kuzyk, Fior, & Nugent, 2011; Kahn et al., 2012). Simply put, a smart toy that attracts a four-year-old may be boring for a seven-year-old. A talk with a social robot may lead a seven-year-old to believe he/she has made a friend, but this may seem ridiculous to a 12-year-old. And understanding the technological components of a social robot may overwhelm a 12-year-old, but may very well be possible for a 16-year-old (e.g. Beran et al., 2011).

Several studies on social robots have dealt with age differences between children, using a theoretically driven developmental perspective (e.g. Beran et al., 2011; Kahn et al., 2012). However, much research seems to focus on particular age groups of children based on pragmatic rather than developmental considerations (De Jong et al., 2018). To be clear, in several cases, it may be useless, or trivial, to compare different developmental groups when interacting with a social robot. For example, comparing four- and eight-year-olds regarding how particular robot features affect learning mathematical operations from a social robot seems futile because four-year-olds are cognitively not ready for such a task. Similarly, some smart or connected toys may target particular age groups; comparisons between developmental groups may thus make little sense. In contrast, a developmentally oriented approach to differences between young people's interaction with social robots and smart or connected toys may be appropriate when these devices are studied from a conceptual perspective. For instance, it is unclear to what extent different degrees of horizontal, vertical and spatial integration attract, or repel, different developmental groups and why this may be the case (De Jong et al., 2018). Similarly, many of the risks of connected toys regarding the privacy and security of young people (e.g. Holloway & Green, 2016) may be better understood on the basis of developmental theory.

Insufficient attention to intercultural differences. While several studies in HRI have dealt with intercultural differences (e.g. Bartneck, Suzuki, Kanda, & Nomura, 2007; Li, Rau, & Li, 2010), cross-cultural comparative studies are still rather rare in research on CRI (e.g. Kanngiesser et al., 2015; Shahid et al., 2014). Our knowledge about CRI is therefore limited to the specificities of the country where a particular study was done, which is typically in rich Western(ized) or Asian countries. As a result, we know little about how children in poorer and non-Western(ized) countries deal with social robots. It is, however, conceivable that a country's wealth, technological infrastructure and legal regulation of technology affect whether and how children (are able to) encounter advanced technologies, such as smart toys and social robots, and what consequences this has. As others have already pointed out (e.g. Li et al., 2010), more attention to intercultural differences is thus needed.

In this context, it is essential that the study of intercultural differences moves beyond a crude comparison of countries (Przeworski & Teune, 1970). On a theoretical level, we learn little by establishing that, for example, children in a Western European country may approach a social robot with somewhat more hesitation than children in Japan do. Following long-standing requests in comparative research, we need to abandon describing differences between countries in favour of explaining these differences with theoretically meaningful concepts (Przeworski & Teune, 1970). As children's play and interaction with smart and connected toys, as well as with robots, oscillate not only between the private and the public, but also between the local and the global (Marsh, 2017), research on intercultural differences seems more timely than ever.

Methodological Issues

With research on HRI and CRI coming from so many different disciplines, it is not surprising that methodological approaches and standards differ across studies. Although the methodological diversity across disciplines may foster cross-fertilization, it may also impair the quality of studies and the comparability of results. In line with Eyssel (2017) and Baxter et al. (2016), we focus on three issues in research on CRI: the lack of standardized measures, issues in the design of studies and the dominance of cross-sectional studies.

Lack of standardized, child-validated measures. The shortage of measures that have been standardized and validated for particular groups, for example children, is not limited to research on HRI or CRI and has also been observed in other interdisciplinary fields (e.g. Peter & Valkenburg, 2016). Still, the use of non-standardized measures not only questions the validity of measurement, but also impedes the comparability of findings. For example, a recent review of children's relationship formation with robots (Van Straten et al., 2018) concluded that key concepts, such as closeness with and trust in a robot, were sometimes operationalized in debatable ways. At the same time, observable behaviour, such as smiling, was used to capture different concepts. The lack of standardized measures was also noticed in a review of children's acceptance of robots (De Jong et al., 2018). The reviewed studies differed not only in their conceptual definitions of robot acceptance, but also in their operational definitions of the concept, which may contribute to the paucity of consistent patterns in current studies on children's acceptance of robots. The lack of standardized measures is particularly problematic in studies amongst children, who are the key user group of smart and connected toys. Ideally, measures should not only be standardized, but also appropriate for research with children. If we use non-standardized measures without evidence of their validation with children, some of our results may be imprecise.

The sparsity of standardized, child-validated measures in current research on CRI touches upon the more general issue of the quality of measurement. Eyssel (2017) has, therefore, called for more attention to be paid to physiological measures (e.g. reaction time, galvanic skin response, functional brain imagining) next to self-reporting measures, which may be plagued by cognitive and motivational biases (e.g. memory errors, social desirability tendencies in answering). Similarly, Bethel and Murphy (2010) have emphasized the need for the triangulation of measurement approaches in HRI research. While the advances in indirect, physiological measurement techniques are impressive, they may not be readily accessible to many researchers or may be inconvenient with children. In this context, observational measures may be a useful alternative, notably for studies that take place in children's natural habitats (e.g. Pellegrini, Symons, & Hoch, 2012), as seems likely for research on smart and connected toys.

Issues in the design of studies. Whether a study opts for an exploratory, correlational or experimental design depends on many considerations, ranging from the state of the art in a field through research ethics to feasibility. Against this background, researchers may sometimes have to take suboptimal decisions about their research design, especially when dealing with children. However, it remains important that research questions or hypotheses that make a causal claim be investigated in an internally valid way. Accordingly, Bethel and Murphy (2010, p. 347) have noted that "there is a growing need for strong experimental designs and methods of evaluation" in HRI (see also, Eyssel, 2017). Still, the aforementioned review of the influence of robot features on closeness with, and trust in, robots found that about one-third of the studies had a correlational design (Van Straten et al., 2018), a figure that also surfaced in another review on antecedents of children's acceptance of social robots (De Jong et al., 2018). This problem is exacerbated by the small number of participants in some studies and the pertinent lack of statistical power (e.g. Baxter et al., 2016; Bethel & Murphy, 2010; Eyssel, 2017). In line with others (e.g. Baxter et al., 2016; Bethel & Murphy, 2010; Eyssel, 2017), De Jong et al. (2018), for example, warn of imprecise effect estimates or type II errors because of underpowered studies. Despite the many complexities in research with children and their use of advanced technologies, such as connected toys and social robots, the issues of internal validity and statistical power deserve greater attention than they have hitherto received (see also Van Straten et al., 2018).

Dominance of cross-sectional studies. As mentioned before, new research fields need time to develop, not only in terms of their theoretical frameworks but also in terms of their methodological approaches. In this context, it seems understandable that the vast majority of studies on CRI are cross-sectional rather than longitudinal: In line with previous findings (e.g. Baxter et al., 2016), two recent review studies reported that 70% of studies on children's relationship formation with robots (Van Straten et al., 2018) and more than 80% of studies on antecedents of children's acceptance of social robots (De Jong et al., 2018) were cross-sectional. However, apart from not telling us anything about children's long-term use of robots and its consequences, the dominance of cross-sectional studies may create another, potentially more troublesome, problem. For children's use of social robots, several researchers have called for attention to novelty effects (e.g. Kanda, Hirano, Eaton, & Ishiguro, 2004; Leite, Martinho, & Paiva, 2013): Due to its novelty, a toy or device initially elicits children's interest and enthusiasm, but the interest wanes quickly once children have repeatedly played with the toy or device.

Novelty effects seem to be particularly problematic in CRI, where children's high expectations of social robots may be quickly disappointed by robots' still unstable and limited performance (e.g. Belpaeme et al., 2013). For cross-sectional studies, the novelty effect may imply that much of what we know from these studies may be snapshots of CRI in initial interactions, but may not apply to long-term interaction. As a result, it is crucial that more longitudinal research be conducted, preferably over a relatively long period (see also, e.g. Baxter et al., 2016; De Jong et al., 2018; Leite et al., 2013; Van Straten et al., 2018). Moreover, it is paramount that we do not extrapolate from cross-sectional studies how children approach, experience and appreciate social robots in general (e.g. De Jong et al., 2018). Finally, we also need to take seriously the possibility of novelty effects in studies on smart and connected toys. The design and engineering of market-ready smart and connected toys may try to avoid novelty effects, e.g. by increasing the horizontal, vertical and spatial integration of toys. Still, the question of how children's play with toys changes over time—and with play its consequences—needs more attention and appropriate integration in our research approaches.

Conclusion

With the fast-paced and far-reaching changes in children's technological environment, it is important that, today, we identify and ask questions that will matter tomorrow. Social robots and the Internet of Toys—(smart) toys connected to the Internet (Mascheroni & Holloway, 2017)—present two of these changes in children's technological environment. From a conceptual point of view, smart toys, connected toys and social robots differ only subtly, not categorically: Social robots are typically higher in horizontal and vertical integration than are smart or connected toys. Once connected to a network, both smart toys and social robots may resemble connected advanced toys. Differences in horizontal, vertical and spatial integration raise novel questions. For example, it may be worth studying on which levels of the three types of integration children find a device attractive and how this develops over time. Similarly, we need to know which levels of integration impair or facilitate children's attachment to a device—both to maximize the opportunities and to reduce the risks of children's interaction with the device. To study such questions rigorously, however, we need to tackle several theoretical and methodological issues, in research on both social robots and the Internet of Toys. More consistently applied theories, attention to developmental and intercultural differences, a commitment to standardized, child-appropriate measures, more internally valid designs and a longitudinal perspective may greatly help to start preparing today for what matters tomorrow.

Acknowledgements This research was funded by the European Research Council (ERC) under the European Union's Horizon 2020 research and innovation programme, under grant agreement No. 682733 to the first author.

References

Barnatt, C. (2015). *The next big thing: From 3D printing to mining the moon.* ExplainingTheFuture.com.

Bartneck, C., Suzuki, T., Kanda, T., & Nomura, T. (2007). The influence of people's culture and prior experiences with Aibo on their attitude towards robots. *AI & Society, 21*(1–2), 217–230. https://doi.org/10.1007/s00146-006-0052-7.

Baxter, P., Kennedy, J., Senft, E., Lemaignan, S., & Belpaeme, T. (2016). From characterising three years of HRI to methodology and reporting recommendations. In *2016 11th ACM/IEEE International Conference on Human-Robot Interaction (HRI)* (pp. 391–398). Piscataway, NJ: Institute of Electrical and Electronics Engineers (IEEE). https://doi.org/10.1109/HRI.2016.7451777.

Belpaeme, T., Baxter, P., de Greeff, J., Kennedy, J., Read, R., Looije, R., ... Zelati, M. C. (2013). Child-robot interaction: Perspectives and challenges. In *ICSR 2013 (Volume 8239)* (pp. 452–459). https://doi.org/10.1007/978-3-319-02675-6_45.

Beran, T. N., Ramirez-Serrano, A., Kuzyk, R., Fior, M., & Nugent, S. (2011). Understanding how children understand robots: Perceived animism in child-robot interaction. *International Journal of Human-Computer Studies, 69*(7–8), 539–550. https://doi.org/10.1016/j.ijhcs.2011.04.003.

Bethel, C. L., & Murphy, R. R. (2010). Review of human studies methods in HRI and recommendations. *International Journal of Social Robotics, 2*(4), 347–359. https://doi.org/10.1007/s12369-010-0064-9.

Breazeal, C. (2003). Toward sociable robots. *Robotics and Autonomous Systems, 42*(3–4), 167–175. https://doi.org/10.1016/S0921-8890(02)00373-1.

Broadbent, E. (2017). Interactions with robots: The truths we reveal about ourselves. *Annual Review of Psychology, 68*(1), 627–652. https://doi.org/10.1146/annurev-psych-010416-043958.

Cabibihan, J.-J., Javed, H., Ang, M., & Aljunied, S. M. (2013). Why robots? A survey on the roles and benefits of social robots in the therapy of children with autism. *International Journal of Social Robotics, 5*(4), 593–618. https://doi.org/10.1007/s12369-013-0202-2.

Chaudron, S., Di Gioia, R., Gemo, M., Holloway, D., Marsh, J., Mascheroni, G., … Yamada-Rice, D. (2017). *Kaleidoscope on the internet of toys: Safety, security, privacy and societal insights (EUR 28397)*. Ispra: Joint Research Centre. Retrieved from https://doi.org/10.2788/05383.

Colangelo, G. (1995). Vertical vs. horizontal integration: Pre-emptive merging. *The Journal of Industrial Economics, 43*(3), 323–337. https://doi.org/10.2307/2950583.

Daft, R. L., & Lengel, R. H. (1986). Organizational information requirements, media richness, and structural design. *Management Science, 32*(5), 554–571. https://doi.org/10.1287/mnsc.32.5.554.

Dautenhahn, K. (2007). Socially intelligent robots: Dimensions of human-robot interaction. *Philosophical Transactions of the Royal Society of London. Series B, Biological Sciences, 362*(1480), 679–704. https://doi.org/10.1098/rstb.2006.2004.

De Graaf, M. M. A., Ben Allouch, S., & Klamer, T. (2015). Sharing a life with Harvey: Exploring the acceptance of and relationship-building with a social robot. *Computers in Human Behavior, 43*, 1–14. https://doi.org/10.1016/j.chb.2014.10.030.

De Graaf, M. M. A., Ben Allouch, S., & van Dijk, J. A. G. M. (2017). Why would I use this in my home? A model of domestic social robot acceptance. *Human-Computer Interaction*, 1–59. https://doi.org/10.1080/07370024.2017.1312406.

De Jong, C., Peter, J., Kühne, R., & Barco Martelo, A. (2018). *Children's acceptance of social robots: A narrative review of the research 2000–2017*. Manuscript submitted for publication.

Dziergwa, M., Kaczmarek, M., Kaczmarek, P., Kędzierski, J., & Wadas-Szydłowska, K. (2018). Long-term cohabitation with a social robot: A case study of the influence of human attachment patterns. *International Journal of Social Robotics, 10*(1), 163–176. https://doi.org/10.1007/s12369-017-0439-2.

Eberl, U. (2016). *Smarte Maschinen. Wie künstliche Intelligenz unser Leben verändert* [Smart machines. How artificial intelligence changes our lives]. Munich, Germany: Hanser.

Edwards, C., Edwards, A., Spence, P. R., & Westerman, D. (2016). Initial interaction expectations with robots: Testing the human-to-human interaction script. *Communication Studies, 67*(2), 227–238. https://doi.org/10.108 0/10510974.2015.1121899.

Eyssel, F. (2017). An experimental psychological perspective on social robotics. *Robotics and Autonomous Systems, 87,* 363–371. https://doi.org/10.1016/j. robot.2016.08.029.

Fong, T., Nourbakhsh, I., & Dautenhahn, K. (2003). A survey of socially interactive robots. *Robotics and Autonomous Systems, 42*(3–4), 143–166. https://doi.org/10.1016/S0921-8890(02)00372-X.

Future of Privacy Forum, & Family Online Safety Institute. (2016). Kids and the connected home: Privacy in the age of connected dolls, talking dinosaurs, and battling robots. Retrieved from https://fpf.org/wp-content/uploads/2016/11/Kids-The-Connected-Home-Privacy-in-the-Age-of-Connected-Dolls-Talking-Dinosaurs-and-Battling-Robots.pdf.

Holloway, D., & Green, L. (2016). The internet of toys. *Communication Research and Practice, 2*(4), 506–519. https://doi.org/10.1080/22041451.2 016.1266124.

Kahn, P. H., Kanda, T., Ishiguro, H., Freier, N. G., Severson, R. L., Gill, B. T., … Shen, S. (2012). "Robovie, you'll have to go into the closet now": Children's social and moral relationships with a humanoid robot. *Developmental Psychology, 48*(2), 303–314. https://doi.org/10.1037/a0027033.

Kanda, T., Hirano, T., Eaton, D., & Ishiguro, H. (2004). Interactive robots as social partners and peer tutors for children: A field trial. *Human-Computer Interaction, 19*(1), 61–84. https://doi.org/10.1207/s15327051hci1901&2_4.

Kanngiesser, P., Itakura, S., Zhou, Y., Kanda, T., Ishiguro, H., & Hood, B. (2015). The role of social eye-gaze in children's and adults' ownership attributions to robotic agents in three cultures. *Interaction Studies, 16*(1), 1–28. https://doi.org/10.1075/is.16.1.01kan.

Krämer, N. C., Eimler, S., von der Pütten, A., & Payr, S. (2011). Theory of companions: What can theoretical models contribute to applications and understanding of human-robot interaction? *Applied Artificial Intelligence, 25*(6), 474–502. https://doi.org/10.1080/08839514.2011.587153.

Kuhn, T. S. (1970). *The structure of scientific revolutions.* Chicago, IL: University of Chicago Press.

Lee, K. M., Peng, W., Jin, S.-A., & Yan, C. (2006). Can robots manifest personality?: An empirical test of personality recognition, social responses, and social presence in human-robot interaction. *Journal of Communication, 56*(4), 754–772. https://doi.org/10.1111/j.1460-2466.2006.00318.x.

Leite, I., Martinho, C., & Paiva, A. (2013). Social robots for long-term interaction: A survey. *International Journal of Social Robotics, 5*(2), 291–308. https://doi.org/10.1007/s12369-013-0178-y.

Li, D., Rau, P. L. P., & Li, Y. (2010). A cross-cultural study: Effect of robot appearance and task. *International Journal of Social Robotics, 2*(2), 175–186. https://doi.org/10.1007/s12369-010-0056-9.

Lightfoot, C., Cole, M., & Cole, S. R. (2013). *The development of children* (7th ed.). New York: Worth Publishers.

Looije, R., Neerincx, M. A., Peters, J. K., & Henkemans, O. A. B. (2016). Integrating robot support functions into varied activities at returning hospital visits. *International Journal of Social Robotics, 8*(4), 483–497. https://doi.org/10.1007/s12369-016-0365-8.

Looije, R., van der Zalm, A., Neerincx, M. A., & Beun, R.-J. (2012). Help, I need some body: The effect of embodiment on playful learning. In *2012 IEEE RO-MAN: The 21st IEEE International Symposium on Robot and Human Interactive Communication* (pp. 718–724). Piscataway, NJ: Institute of Electrical and Electronics Engineers (IEEE). https://doi.org/10.1109/ROMAN.2012.6343836.

Marsh, J. (2017). The internet of toys: A posthuman and multimodal analysis of connected play. *Teachers College Record, 119*(12), 1–32. Retrieved from http://eprints.whiterose.ac.uk/113557/.

Mascheroni, G., & Holloway, D. (Eds.). (2017). *The internet of toys: A report on media and social discourses around young children and IoToys.* DigiLitEY.

Ng, I. C. L., & Wakenshaw, S. Y. L. (2017). The internet-of-things: Review and research directions. *International Journal of Research in Marketing, 34*(1), 3–21. https://doi.org/10.1016/J.IJRESMAR.2016.11.003.

Pellegrini, A. D., Symons, F., & Hoch, J. (2012). *Observing children in their natural worlds: A methodological primer* (3rd ed.). New York: Taylor & Francis Group. https://doi.org/10.4324/9780203101759.

Peter, J. (2017a). New communication technologies and young people: The case of social robots. In R. Kühne, S. E. Baumgartner, T. Koch, & M. Hofer (Eds.), *Youth and media: Current perspectives on media use and effects* (pp. 203–217). Baden-Baden, Germany: Nomos. https://doi.org/10.5771/9783845280455-203.

Peter, J. (2017b). Social robots and the robotification of childhood. In S. Chaudron, R. Di Gioia, M. Gemo, D. Holloway, J. Marsh, G. Mascheroni, … D. Yamada-Rice (Eds.), *Kaleidoscope on the internet of toys: Safety, security, privacy and societal insights (EUR 28397)* (pp. 14–16). Ispra: Joint Research Centre. http://doi.org/10.2788/05383.

Peter, J., & Valkenburg, P. M. (2016). Adolescents and pornography: A review of 20 years of research. *The Journal of Sex Research, 53*(4–5), 509–531. https://doi.org/10.1080/00224499.2016.1143441.

Przeworski, A., & Teune, H. (1970). *The logic of comparative social inquiry.* New York: Wiley.

Riek, L. D. (2012). Wizard of Oz studies in HRI: A systematic review and new reporting guidelines. *Journal of Human-Robot Interaction, 1*(1), 119–136. https://doi.org/10.5898/JHRI.1.1.Riek.

Ross, A. (2016). *The industries of the future.* New York: Simon & Schuster.

Shahid, S., Krahmer, E., & Swerts, M. (2014). Child-robot interaction across cultures: How does playing a game with a social robot compare to playing a game alone or with a friend? *Computers in Human Behavior, 40,* 86–100. https://doi.org/10.1016/j.chb.2014.07.043.

Social Robot. (n.d.). Retrieved February 12, 2018, from https://en.wikipedia.org/wiki/Social_robot.

Spence, P. R., Westerman, D., Edwards, C., & Edwards, A. (2014). Welcoming our robot overlords: Initial expectations about interaction with a robot. *Communication Research Reports, 31*(3), 272–280. https://doi.org/1 0.1080/08824096.2014.924337.

Steinberg, L. (2008). *Adolescence* (8th ed.). Boston: McGraw Hill.

Thrun, S. (2004). Toward a framework for human-robot interaction. *Human-Computer Interaction, 19*(1), 9–24. https://doi.org/10.1207/s15327051hci1901&2_2.

Valkenburg, P. M., & Taylor Piotrowski, J. (2017). *Plugged in: How media attract and affect youth.* New Haven, CT: Yale University Press. https://doi.org/10.1080/17482798.2017.1341116.

Van Bergen, W. (2016). *De robots komen eraan! Feit en fictie over de toekomst van intelligente machines* [The robots are coming! Fact and fiction about the future of intelligent machines]. Amsterdam and Antwerp: Business Contact.

Van Oort, F., Burger, M., & Raspe, O. (2010). On the economic foundation of the urban network paradigm: Spatial integration, functional integration and economic complementarities within the Dutch Randstad. *Urban Studies, 47*(4), 725–748. https://doi.org/10.1177/0042098009352362.

Van Straten, C. L., Peter, J., & Kühne, R. (2018). *Child-robot relationship formation: A narrative review of empirial research*. Manuscript submitted for publication.

Wang, W.-N., Kuo, V., King, C.-T., & Chang, C.-P. (2010). Internet of toys: An e-Pet overview and proposed innovative social toy service platform. In *2010 International Computer Symposium (ICS2010)* (pp. 264–269). Piscataway, NJ: Institute of Electrical and Electronics Engineers (IEEE). https://doi.org/10.1109/COMPSYM.2010.5685507.

Winfield, A. (2012). *Robotics: A very short introduction*. Oxford: Oxford University Press. https://doi.org/10.1093/actrade/9780199695980.001.0001.

Zhao, S. (2006). Humanoid social robots as a medium of communication. *New Media & Society, 8*(3), 401–419. https://doi.org/10.1177/1461444806061951.

3

The Uncanny Valley Revisited: Play with the Internet of Toys

Jackie Marsh

Introduction: Post-humanist Perspectives on Play

Play in the digital world is becoming increasingly complex due to children's use of technologies. What is central to contemporary play practices is that they take place across a range of digital and non-digital domains and make connections across various axes (e.g. between online and offline, digital and non-digital, local and global, public and private dimensions) (Marsh, 2014, 2017). This chapter focuses on an analysis of one type of this connected play, play with an Internet-enabled toy, drawing on data from a study undertaken in the UK of young children's engagement with tablet apps (Marsh et al., 2015).

The chapter considers the data in the light of a number of different perspectives on the interaction between humans and machines. It is argued that more recent moves to analyse such interaction from

J. Marsh (✉)
University of Sheffield, Sheffield, UK
e-mail: j.a.marsh@sheffield.ac.uk

© The Author(s) 2019
G. Mascheroni and D. Holloway (eds.), *The Internet of Toys*,
Studies in Childhood and Youth, https://doi.org/10.1007/978-3-030-10898-4_3

a post-human perspective offer a means of de-centring the human, leading to an enhanced understanding of play with robots and other Internet-connected toys. Karen Barad (2007, p. 332) has argued for a focus on the 'ontological entanglements' that occur between human and non-human entities, and she emphasises the significance of the 'intra-action' between matter. In these intra-actions:

> The relationship between the material and the discursive is one of mutual entailment. Neither discursive practices nor material phenomena are ontologically or epistemologically prior. Neither can be explained in terms of the other. Neither is reducible to the other. Neither has privileged status in determining the other. Neither is articulated or articulable in the absence of the other; matter and meaning are mutually articulated. (Barad, 2007, p. 152)

This has implications for analyses of children's play. The study of play research that focuses on 'play with objects' or 'playthings', and which outlines the kinds of play that take place using a wide range of objects, both natural and non-natural (Opie and Opie, 1997) does not normally provide insights into the roles that the objects themselves have in play episodes. Traditional approaches to analysing play with objects place the central emphasis on the human and focus on explaining what happens in relation to human cognition and development when interacting with toys (e.g. Goldstein, 1994). The flat ontology associated with a post-humanist approach to understanding human–machine interaction instead suggests that the roles of each participant in the encounter should be understood.

Post-humanist accounts of play are now emerging. Tesar and Arndt (2016, p. 196) suggest that 'Thing-matter-energy-child assemblages with power and forces arise in early childhood entanglements through toy-things and thing-stories'. They draw on an abstract discussion of the wooden doll Pinocchio, related to the story of the same name, to illustrate their argument, but Harwood and Collier (2017) bring the concept of 'thing-matter-energy-child-assemblages' to life with an account of children's play with sticks in a forest. They describe how sticks became a range of things in the play, such as weapons, wands, tools to draw with and so on. At times, the shape/texture of the stick shaped the play, and in these instances, they argue that the 'stick is agential, seemingly calling to the children to be held, ridden, swung and so on' (Harwood & Collier, 2017, p. 345). Post-humanism, therefore, offers a framework for understanding play that traces the intra-actions between children and the material objects of play, and it provides insights into the role of the objects themselves in play episodes. This theoretical perspective is drawn upon in an analysis of a child's play with a robot toy, Furby.

Play and Technology

The aim of the wider study that formed the backdrop to the data analysed in this chapter was to explore young children's play and creativity with tablets and apps. In the first phase of the study, an online survey was undertaken with 2000 parents of 0–5-year-olds who had access to a tablet. In the second phase of the study, six children aged from 6 months to 4 years and 11 months were visited in their homes over a three-month period and were observed and interviewed as they played with tablets. Their parents were also interviewed. In addition, three of the children wore GoPro Chestcams in order to collect data on themselves using tablets. The chapter focuses on two of the six children who took part in the case studies, Angela and Amy, both two years old at the start of the study.

A range of types of children's play with technology were identified in the study (see Marsh et al., 2016), including play that connected apps with physical toys. These toys could be characterised as part of the 'Internet of Toys' (IoToys) (Wang, Kuo, King, & Chang, 2010), which enable, according to Mascheroni and Holloway 2017, p. 6), the interaction of three elements: Internet connectivity, simulation of human interaction and programmability by the user. There have been a range of concerns raised about these toys, largely relating to their capacity to collect data on children's use, with all of the attendant issues with regard to data privacy (Chaudron et al., 2017a; Holloway & Green, 2016; Manches, Duncan, Plowman, & Sabeti, 2015; Mascheroni & Holloway, 2017).

Whilst acknowledging that these are significant concerns that deserve attention, this chapter does not address these issues. Rather, the focus is on attempting to understand play episodes in which children encounter the IoToys. What happens when children engage with these kinds of playthings? How might we conceptualise the exchanges that take place, and what implications does this analysis have for research, policy and future practice? These questions are addressed through an analysis of Angela's and Amy's encounters with the Internet-connected toy 'Furby'.

Furby is a socio-robotic toy developed by Hasbro and first released in 1998. It is frequently described as being owl-like or hamster-like, and it has a furry body with large eyes and ears. The robot was the first successful robotic toy to penetrate the domestic market (Cuddihy & Metcalfe, 2005), selling millions across the globe, with 40 million units sold in its first three years of production (Grossberg, 2012). The toy is programmed to encourage its user to look after it from the beginning of ownership, inciting him or her to pet it, stroke its tummy, feed it and so on. The Furby speaks its own language, Furbish, but can learn English over time. The toy is programmed to let its owner know it is hungry, and it can signal to the owner that it is sick if it does not get fed. The Furby also dances and goes to sleep, sometimes snoring as it does so.

Following a drop in sales after its first years of production, the Furby was re-introduced in 2005 and then again in 2012, this time with flashing LCD eyes and the ability to adapt its behaviour according to how the user interacted with it. Additional sensors were added to the toy to enhance its lifelike and intelligent interactions, according to the patent application of its producers (Judkins, Paulson, Han, Cameroon, & Pale, 2017, p. 7). In the patent application, the producers also describe how the Furby can now be hatched from an egg, using an app:

> …The virtual character may begin as an egg that a player earns from the physical toy character, a friend's physical toy character, or from a virtual toy character. A player may store several eggs in a virtual cartoon and selectively choose eggs to 'incubate'. The player will then incubate the eggs until it is ready to hatch. When the egg hatches, it has certain personality traits imprinted on it. These personality traits come from the physical toy character. The player then nurtures the baby virtual character by feeding it, cleaning it and playing with it. (Judkins et al., 2017, p. 8)

The latest version of Furby, 'Furby Connect', engages with the 'Furby Connect World' app, which enables it to undertake a wide range of activities, including hatching virtual baby Furblings, as described above, and collecting items that can be purchased in order to grow the user's Furbling virtual village into a paradise. The Furby can be taught to remember a name that is given to it by the user, learn song lyrics from videos and chat to other Furbies. Enabling the Furby to link to the Furbies of the user's friends is a deliberate move to create communities of players.

The toy is programmed to have a range of behaviours, including making lots of noise and laughing almost hysterically at times. The toy can be received by users in a range of ways, and Chesher, in a review of YouTube videos created by Furby users, demonstrates how Furbies are both celebrated as cute pets that deserve loving and demonised as crazed robots that require destroying in some way. Chesher reviews a number of videos that, for example, celebrate a Furby in some way, perhaps by carefully 'unboxing' it (unwrapping it when first purchased), or portray a Furby dancing and/or chatting away whilst someone tries to destroy it. Chesher comments:

> When it is 'awake', Furby is at work with autonomous affective labour. As there are historically few conventions about how human-robot inter-actions should be scripted, the designers overloaded it with affective cues: a writhing body, snapping beak, animated eyes and relentless chatter. It is engineered to entertain, interesting enough to circulate and cute and zany enough to be destroyed. (Chesher, 2017, p. 6)

This range of responses to the Furby, whilst exaggerated for the purposes of humour in relation to the production of some of the YouTube videos described by Chesher, was evident in the study drawn upon in this chapter. In the first section of the chapter, the negative response of two-year-old Angela to a Furby is analysed in relation to the concept of the uncanny (Jentsch, 1906). In contrast, the second part of the chapter outlines the play of another two-year-old, Amy, who plays in a more positive way with the toy than Angela. In the final part of the chapter, the play of both children is discussed through the lens of post-humanist philosophy in order to understand the role of the toy itself in interactive play.

Furby the Uncanny

Angela lived with her mother, father and older brother, Zach, and was 2 years and 2 months old at the start of the project. Angela has a great interest in technology and in particular enjoyed playing on a tablet. She did not play with robotic toys, perhaps because of an early experience of Furby. Angela's mother described how Angela's Zach had owned a Furby, but Angela did not like it:

Mother: I think that's because it was evil. We got an evil one.
Father: Yeah, it was.
Interviewer: It sounds like you didn't feel it was a very successful toy anyway.
Father: No.
Mother: No, we ended up selling it actually.
Interviewer: Oh, right.
Father: Yeah, because Zach didn't like it either really.
Interviewer: No. Was it one of those that interacts with the iPad or anything?
Mother: It was. But I think each one's set to have a different personality or something, and Zach's was evil.
Father: Yeah, it were.
Mother: Its eyes used to roll round and it used to go like, "Ugh… ugh…"
Interviewer: Yeah. So what was their reaction to it then? Just not wanting to… ?
Father: If Angela saw it she'd leave the room.

This short extract from an interview with Angela's parents highlights an issue that has been discussed extensively with regard to human inter-actions with robots—their potential 'uncanny' nature, which creates feelings of unease and anxiety in humans.

The 'uncanny' is a concept first introduced by the German psychologist Jentsch (1906), which was then developed further by Sigmund Freud, to characterise 'intellectual uncertainty' (Freud, 1919/2003, p. 125). Freud, in his work on the notion of the uncanny, drew on

Jentsch's essay, in which the latter used the word 'usicherheit', translated as 'unsureness', to describe this intellectual uncertainty. Holmes (2010, n.p.) notes that Freud 'etymologically assessed the German word and found that the meaning of the former had been pushed to the extreme such that it finally coincided with its negative form; familiar-*cum*-intimate-*cum*-secret-*cum*-strange'. The significant point about the uncanny, then, is that it registers familiarity and strangeness at the same time.

The concept found its way into the robotics field, given the extent to which robots can be both familiar and alienating. The term 'uncanny valley' was first developed by Mori (1970), who developed a graph (with the vertical axis labelled 'familiarity' and the horizontal axis labelled 'human likeness') that mapped responses to robots. He suggested that as robots' appearances become more human-like, the viewers'/users' sense of familiarity increases. However, when a robot is both human-like and non-human-like, the viewer/user experiences the 'uncanny valley'. Mori gives the example of a prosthetic hand that looks very human-like in appearance, but is cold to the touch. He suggests this is at the bottom of the uncanny valley (human-like, but unfamiliar), in contrast to bunraku puppets that look similar to humans (but are not as lifelike as the prosthetic hand) and are familiar in terms of their eye and hand movements being similar to humans, and so sit at the top of the uncanny valley on Mori's (1970) graph.

The extent to which children experience the uncanny valley is of interest in relation to the study reported in this chapter. Brink, Gray, and Wellman (2017) studied the concept of the uncanny valley in relation to age. They tested 240 children's (aged 3–18) responses to a variety of robots, which ranged from more human-like to more machine-like. They found that the uncanny valley develops with age, in that younger children were less likely than older children to find human-like robots creepy, with the uncanny valley emerging in middle childhood. Uncanniness emerges 'when a human-like machine violates our learned expectations of how a machine should look or behave' (Brink et al., 2017, p. 2) and, as for young children, they expect robots to have intelligent features. Brink et al. (2017, p. 9) found that 'young children found robots to be more pleasing (less uncanny) when they perceived the robots to have more mental abilities'. For young children, therefore, it may be the case that it is only when robots exhibit fewer mental abilities than expected, or display anti-social behaviours, that they experience the uncanny valley. This certainly appeared to be the case for Angela (and her family), as the Furby looked like a cute and cuddly toy, but they experienced it as exhibiting strange behaviour, making rough grunting sounds and rolling its eyes. Indeed, Hasbro deliberately program the Furby to resort to such behaviours so that its owners will play music to it, or stroke it to sooth it, bringing it back to more serene behaviour, but the Internet is replete with accounts of how this did not happen in many families as the uncanny feelings produced by the unsociable behaviour caused them to get rid of the toy.[1]

The concept of uncanny has been used in studies which have suggested that the phenomenon can account for adults' unease with many of the technologies encountered by children and young people today (Carrington, 2005). Certainly, robotic toys have received a range of negative reviews, including suggestions that such toys restrain imaginative play. Eberle (2009, p. 183), for example, stated that 'a doll that stands at the brink of the uncanny valley will also likely sap play and undermine creativity'. These kinds of statements lack substantive evidence, however, and further research needs to be undertaken before such conclusions can be drawn with any surety. Much more credible are the concerns about data privacy and the datafication of play mentioned previously (Holloway & Green, 2016; Mascheroni & Holloway, 2017), as there is evidence of data-hacking of toys, reported on in Manches et al. (2015). These matters are discussed elsewhere in this book. In this chapter, the focus is on understanding the nature of the child/toy interaction. In order to examine the way in which the IoToys can foster play, therefore, the chapter moves on to consider Amy's more positive experiences with a Furby.

The Anthropomorphic Furby

Amy was 2 years and 11 months old when the project began. She was an only child and lived with her parents in a northern city in the UK. Amy's mum, Gaynor, reported that her child loved robotic toys, although recently she noted that, '...we've had to sort of try and curb it now a bit though because there's a whole range of these cats, baby ones...', and the expense became prohibitive. Amy received her first robot toy, a dog, on her second birthday as a present from her grandmother. Gaynor felt that she was a little young at that age to receive such a toy and, indeed, she commented that:

> ...she didn't like it for about 5 or 6 months after we got it, she really was scared of it. So it went away for a while until she was older, and then one day she just asked for it out and she's started enjoying it. But at first she didn't like it. But it was seeing it, and I don't know, she's always shown an interest in sort of robotic toys and things like that. (Amy's mum)

Amy's mum stated that Amy now played with her robotic toys about once or twice a week, which was much less frequently than previously. Gaynor noted that some of the apps that came with the robotic toys were not designed for young children, and so Amy had had to work out for herself how to use them. In addition, Amy's father had helped out by finding out how the toys worked through YouTube.

> ...so she got these robots and she was ... we actually watched a video on how to work the robots. Her dad's very into ... won't follow instructions, but we'll YouTube it. So he'll YouTube it to find out how to work it. So we did look at this and how to use these robots.

Once the family worked out how to use the robots using these means, Amy became proficient herself in controlling her robot dog and dinosaur through voice commands and hand movements. Whilst Amy did become proficient in the use of the apps that related to the toys, she experienced technical difficulties in controlling them due to the unreliability of the Bluetooth connection and interference from other household noises:

> ...she doesn't have to control them with the app, she can just play with them, and she can talk to them actually as well and she can control them with her voice, which is what she started doing at first, and with her

hands. So the apps, she didn't start using them actually for quite a while after. And she didn't like them at first because like she didn't really know what to do with them. It is difficult but they're not really aimed for her age … I don't even think they're aimed for pre-school, but she just really showed interest in them … and yeah, she can control them now and she knows what she's doing. But they're quite temperamental actually, they don't tend to listen … Sometimes she gets a bit fed up with them, because you have to … if she wants to control them with the app she has to be the right distance away, it has to be turned up loud and with no other noise, so it's quite hard to control with the app. But sometimes she does do it.

Amy's family appeared to be supportive of her interest in the IoToys, and they did not raise any concerns about the potentially negative aspects of the toys mentioned above. This may have been because they were not aware of these issues; in this study as a whole, parents of young children did not seem to be aware of a number of safety aspects regarding children's uses of technology (Marsh et al., 2015), as has been found to be the case in other studies (Chaudron et al., 2017b).

The latest addition to Amy's robot family was her Furby, which she had received for her third birthday, celebrated part-way through the study. Gaynor commented:

She actually wanted it for Christmas but I thought she was a bit young really for Furby, it's more … it's aimed at older children. But … I mean she can navigate and use the app quite well really so … well sort of knew what it did really, what they were really, Furbies, … I think they were around when I was a child, Furbies.

The fact that the Furby brand had been around in Gaynor's own childhood made her feel more comfortable with its purchase. Indeed, Amy's parents sometimes played alongside her as she engaged in play with the Furby, as outlined in the following section.

In the following extract from a transcript of play in Amy's home, recorded by a researcher using a voice recorder as she observed the play, Amy is engaging with a Furby alongside her mum. Amy is using an app on a tablet to interact with the toy as her mother observes and comments.

Mum: What are you going to do to him first? What are you going to do?
Amy: Shower.
Mum: Give him a shower. Go on then. Make sure it's not too cold. That's it. You need to turn the water on don't you … that's it. Oh look the water's dirty because he's filthy. Is he all clean now?
Amy: Yes.
Mum: Yay! He had food. Food, what are you going to feed him today?
Amy: A sock.
Mum: A sock! You don't feed him a sock. Oh he doesn't like that.
Amy: Ha, ha, ha.
Mum: Give him something nice now. What are you going to give him?
Amy: A bubble.
Mum: Oh he's being sick … oh, that's disgusting. He's been sick, that was horrible. Right choose him something nice this time.
Amy: He'll like it—a car.
Mum: Well that's disgusting! Right I think we've had enough of being sick, let's try it again. Right feed him something nice this time … Feed him something nice. Some sweeties! Let's wipe your nose. Oh he'll like that Amy.
Amy: What's he doing. He's … and he's…
Mum: You've got a snotty nose haven't you, duck? Does he like that?
Amy: Yeah. He likes.
Mum: He likes it?
Amy: An ice lolly.
Mum: An ice lolly.
Amy: Yes.
Mum: Oh he's eaten it all hasn't he?…
Amy: Huh? Another drink? Another drink.
Mum: Oh he's giving you some money because he said it's nice.
Amy: That was nice.
Mum: Are you going to choose something different this time? Just ice cream? An ice cream drink?
Amy: It's blue. It's a blue drink.
Mum: Oh Amy.
Amy: Oh he's running, so he's loved it.
Mum: It is lovely.
Amy: Now let's try again. Want another? Let's put…
Mum: Why don't you play another game with him now?

Amy: Maybe this one. He's watching.
Mum: Why don't you give him some fruit this time? No? Just bad stuff.
Amy: Here you go.
Mum: What would you like to have in a drink?
Amy: I want to have a drink … he likes it.

The first point to note about this extract is that Gaynor begins the play episode by immediately attributing a gendered identity to the toy ('What are you going to do to him first?'). One way of understanding this is to view it as a reflection of the tendency for people to anthropomorphise non-human entities, that is, to view non-human phenomena as having human attributes, which also occurs in relation to the uncanny valley. Since the beginning of humankind, the dynamic between ánthrōpos (human) and morphē (form) has been apparent, with some arguing that the process of ascribing human attributes to non-human entities is innate, leading to people creating gods in their own image (Guthrie, 1993). It is argued that the process of anthropomorphising helps individuals to make sense of an uncertain world and occurs, according to Epley, Waytz, and Cacioppo (2007, p. 864), in relation to three motivating factors, which are, 'the accessibility and applicability of anthropocentric knowledge (elicited agent knowledge), the motivation to explain and understand the behaviour of other agents (effectance motivation), and the desire for social contact and affiliation (sociality motivation)'.

The first factor relates to the fact that the knowledge that an individual has about humans is developed earlier and more fully than knowledge about non-human entities, and therefore, it is drawn upon when encountering non-human entities. The second factor signals the extent to which humans are motivated to try and understand and explain to themselves other agents when they encounter them, and Epley et al. (2007, p. 874) suggest that this factor explains the fact that children are more likely to anthropomorphise than adults, a phenomenon supported by other research (e.g. Bering & Bjorklund, 2004). It is also the case that younger children are likely to possess less knowledge about both human and non-human entities than older children and adults, and therefore, they are more likely to anthropomorphise because of that factor also. The third motivating factor that Epley et al. (2007) outline is the desire for social engagement, pointing out that not only do humans actively seek out human-like social cues even from non-human agents, but also actively seek social connections with others. The three psychological determinants interact, and social and cultural contexts will shape them in different ways.

In this episode, it is the adult who anthropomorphises the toy first, perhaps due to a shared history of play in which this process occurs, as this does not take place in the same way with Angela's family (who, whilst they do attribute an 'evil' disposition to the toy, refer to the Furby as 'it'). Amy, throughout the episodes of play with her Furby, always refers to it using the pronouns he/him. The second issue of note in the play is that Gaynor begins by asking, 'What are you going to do *to* him first?' (author's italics). She does not ask, 'What are you going to do *with* him first?' This indicates that the pattern of play with the Furby is one in which, when the app is used, the nurturing element is paramount. Gaynor did relay to the researcher that Amy sometimes played with her robotic toys without apps, thus engaging in a wider range of play activities than was observed in this episode. However, in this instance, the play was proscribed by the app, although Amy did demonstrate agency in the face of her mum's endeavours to engage the Furby in healthy eating. Her transgressive play (Marsh et al., 2016) involved feeding Furby items that she knew the toy was programmed not to like, enjoying the responses it made (e.g. of being sick). She eventually adheres to her mum's entreaties to feed the toy sweeties by giving the Furby an ice lolly, but then goes back to giving it, from her mum's point of view, 'just bad stuff'.

There is a long history of children engaging in this kind of nurture play with technological objects, such as the Tamagotchi. The difference between that history of play and contemporary children's engagement with the IoToys is that children are now connected to an online network in which they can engage with, and be directed to, new products. In the case of Furby, children can watch videos in a theatre on the app, and the producers update this element with new content now and again, which is signalled by the Furby's antennae changing colour. New content is unlocked by additional play with Furby and the

Furblings that are hatched from eggs. In-app purchases can be made by adding credit card details, and the ability to disable this element is not widely publicised. The toy, therefore, is set up to encourage continuous engagement, which may then lead to additional purchases. The nurturing of these types of robot toys thus becomes big business, with toys designed to encourage anthropomorphising as quickly, and as fully, as possible.

The process of anthropomorphising offers one way to understand what happens in play with the IoToys. However, this perspective emerges from a humanist philosophy in which human and non-human are seen as a binary, with the human at the centre of the action. An alternative reading of the data may be undertaken from a post-humanist perspective, which enables an understanding to be developed of the way in which non-human objects themselves operate in these episodes. In order to move beyond a human-centric approach, therefore, the final section of the chapter draws on key tenets of post-human philosophy.

The Post-human Furby

Post-humanism, as outlined in the introduction, fosters insights into the intra-actions between material objects and humans. Returning to Angela's family's experiences with the Furby, it is clear that the toy itself had a role to play in its reception:

> *Mother*: …I think each one's [Furby] set to have a different personality or something, and Zach's was evil.
> *Father*: Yeah, it were.
> *Mother*: Its eyes used to roll round and it used to go like, "Ugh…ugh…"

In this case, the toy's activities led to an emotional response from the family members and, as Barad (2007, p. 152) suggests, 'the relationship between the material and the discursive is one of mutual entailment'. The intra-action between the toy and the humans led to an outcome that is, arguably, not one Hasbro had planned. They hope that the users will respond to the Furby's programmed demonic behaviour by engaging in the kind of nurturing practices described previously, thus ensuring continued engagement with the brand. It is clear that the inventors of the toy designed it to have agency within the human-toy dynamic in this way, as they state in the patent that, 'The physical toy character is a driving force behind the game...' (Judkins et al., 2017, p. 27). In the case of Angela and her family, the toy was certainly a driving force in that it quickly drove them to disengage with it, an outcome that is caricatured in some of the YouTube memes that Chesher (2017) outlines, in which Furbies are shot at, set on fire and microwaved, amongst other actions.

The intra-action between Furby and child is also of interest in Angela's play episode. Ash (2015) identifies the role of 'inorganically organised objects' in human-technology encounters. These are non-human objects that are embedded in interfaces, which are 'a point of contact between separate types and categories of beings' (Ash, 2015, p. 23). In this case, the interface in question is the screen of the tablet that Amy uses to engage with her Furby, and the inorganically organised objects are the representations of food that appear as pixelated images on the screen, along with the inorganically organised object of the Furby itself. These objects have a key role to play in the 'thing matter energy child assemblage', with the vivacious response of the Furby, in which the toy moves from side to side after receiving a virtual blue drink, causing Amy to state, '*Oh he's running, so he's loved it*'. In Marsh (2017), an extended play episode of another encounter Amy had with the Furby is outlined, this time featuring video film of the play from a GoPro camera that Amy wore on her chest as she used the tablet and toy. In that analysis, it is suggested that the transduction of modes that occurs as the toy's sensors receive relevant data from the app signalling that the user has fed it, which then triggers movement, noise and light in the Furby, creates an effective response in the user. This can also be seen in the data discussed in this chapter. The toy has a strong role in this encounter, as its producers intended, leading the child to engage further with the toy, as she says, '*Now let's try again. Want another?*'

A post-humanist approach to understanding play with the IoToys thus leads to recognition that the relationship between children and toys in any one play encounter is complex and the toy themselves may have agency in such an encounter, if one views agency as an action leading to a further action (rather than agency as intentional). This is not to suggest, however, that the toys dictate the play. Children still move beyond the scripts embedded in toys to engage in free, imaginative play with them, which Gaynor acknowledged was the case with Amy. In this extract from the data, however, Amy's transgressions from the producers' intentions were for humorous effect and, indeed, it cannot be said that these kinds of play with Furby were unanticipated by the producers— they did programme the toy to be sick when users tried to feed it something that was non-digestible, after all.

Conclusion

This chapter has considered the play of two children with a robotic toy, Furby, as an example of interactions with the IoToys. It is acknowledged that this is a limited sample to draw on, but the aim of the chapter is not to generalise about such play, but rather to delve into ethnographic data on IoToy play that offer insights into the meanings and motivations of this activity. The analysis suggests that, for these children, the Furby itself had a strong part to play in how it was received and, in the case of Amy, shaped the play episode itself. There are a number of implications of this analysis for further research, policy and practice.

First, this study has examined the play of only two children, and both were female, White, aged two at the start of the study and living with heterosexual parents who are located under the same roof. This lack of diversity is a concern. There is a need to consider how the IoToys is taken up in all kinds of different families, including by children who are not as technologically engaged in general as both Amy and Angela are. Second, research needs to be undertaken on the conditions under which children's play becomes far removed from the play scripts embedded in the toy, to take on an imaginative and creative life of its own. Third, further studies are required in relation to the different kinds of toys that can be purchased from the IoToys category. How does the play cohere or diverge across these different types? Are children more or less likely to engage in nurture play with a robot dog than a robot dinosaur, for example? Finally, there are lessons to be learned for policy and practice. Policymakers should acknowledge the pleasures and creativity that can be embedded in the IoToys experience, instead of focusing almost exclusively on the risks discourse. In terms of practice, the designers of such toys would do well to consider the ways in which their toys might be developed further to enhance play. Can, for example, children be provided with apps that enable them to program the toys to undertake certain activities, thus being creators as well as consumers of such products?

To conclude, there is much that we can learn about children's playful encounters with the IoToys through careful observation and analysis. It is important that we do so, otherwise we run the risk of new toys, and data policies for that matter, being developed that do not build effectively on established knowledge, but are based on assumptions and beliefs. This could lead to impoverished play practices and restrictive approaches that limit the possibilities of play with playthings related to the IoToys. The future in this area holds much promise; let us, collectively, help children to access such a future, whilst also ensuring they are effectively safeguarded from harm.

Note

1. See, for example http://www.amommystory.com/2013/01/what-happens-when-your-furby-becomes-evil.html.

References

Ash, J. (2015). *The interface envelope: Gaming, technology, power*. New York, London, New Dehli, and Sydney: Bloomsbury.

Barad, K. (2007). *Meeting the universe halfway: Quantum physics and the entanglement of matter and meaning*. Durham and London: Duke University Press.

Bering, J. M., & Bjorklund, D. F. (2004). The natural emergence of reasoning about the afterlife as a developmental regularity. *Developmental Psychology, 40*, 217–233.

Brink, K. A., Gray, K., & Wellman, H. M. (2017). Creepiness creeps in: Uncanny valley feelings are acquired in childhood. *Child Development,*

99999

999999999999999

1–13. Published online ahead of print 13 December 2017. http://onlinelibrary.wiley.com/doi/10.1111/cdev.12999/abstract;jsessionid=1FB78152B-8DC1BBF0A0D4BAC70F9E69B.f02t02.

Carrington, V. (2005). The uncanny, digital texts and literacy. *Language and Education, 19*(6), 467–482.

Chaudron, S., Di Gioia, R., Gemo, M., Holloway, D., Marsh, J., Mascheroni, G., … Yamada-Rice, D. (2017a). *Kaleidoscope on the internet of toys—Safety, security, privacy and societal insights.* Luxembourg: Publications Office of the European Union. Retrieved from http://publications.jrc.ec.europa.eu/repository/bitstream/JRC105061/jrc105061_final_online.pdf.

Chaudron, S., Marsh, J., Navarette, V. D., Mascheroni, G., Smahel, D., Cernikova, M., … Soldatova, G. (2017b). Rules of engagement: Family rules on young children's access to and use of technologies. In S. Danby, M. Fleer, C. Davidson, & M. Hatzigianni (Eds.), *Digital childhoods.* Singapore: Springer.

Chesher, C. (2017). Toy robots on YouTube: Consumption and peer production at the robotic moment. *Convergence,* 1–13. https://doi.org/10.1177/1354856517706492.

Cuddihy, K., & Metcalfe, P. (2005). *Christmas's most wanted: The top 10 book of Kris Kringles, merry jingles and holiday cheer.* Washington, DC: Potomac Books.

Eberle, S. G. (2009). Exploring the uncanny valley to find the edge of play. *American Journal of Play, 2,* 167–194.

Epley, N., Waytz, A., & Cacioppo, J. T. (2007). On seeing human: A three-factor theory of anthropomorphism. *Psychological Review, 114*(4), 852–864.

Freud, S. (1919/2003). *The uncanny* (D. McLintock, Trans.). London: Penguin Books.

Goldstein, J. (1994). *Toys, play and child development.* Cambridge: Cambridge University Press.

Grossberg, J. (2012). Furby's coming back! Five things to know about this iconic toy. *E!.* Retrieved April 12, 2012, from http://uk.eonline.com/news/308423/furby-s-coming-back-five-things-to-know-about-this-iconic-toy.

Guthrie, S. E. (1993). *Faces in the clouds: A new theory of religion.* New York: Oxford University Press.

Harwood, D., & Collier, D. R. (2017). The matter of the stick: Storying/(re)storying children's literacies in the forest. *Journal of Early Childhood Literacy, 1*(3), 336–352.

Holloway, D., & Green, L. (2016). The internet of toys. *Communication Research and Practice, 2*(4), 506–519.

Holmes, E. (2010). Strange reality: Glitches and uncanny play. *Eludamos. Journal for Computer Game Culture, 4*(2), 255–276.

Jentsch, E. (1906). Zur psychologie des unheimlichen. *Psychiatrisch-Neurologische Wochenschrift, 8.22* (August 25, 1906), 195–198 & *8.23* (September 1, 1906), 203–205.

Judkins, D., Paulson, K., Han, A., Cameroon, D., & Pale, J. (2017, June 13). *United States Patent US 9,675,895 B2.* https://patentimages.storage.googleapis.com/70/03/e4/24a0732cd192a5/US9675895.pdf.

Manches, A., Duncan, P., Plowman, L., & Sabeti, S. (2015). Three questions about the internet of things and children. *TechTrends, 59*(1), 76–83.

Marsh, J. (2014). Online and offline play. In A. Burn & C. Richards (Eds.), *Children's games in the new media age: Childlore, media and the playground.* London: Ashgate.

Marsh, J. (2017). The internet of toys: A posthuman and multimodal analysis of connected play. *Teachers College Record, 119.* Retrieved November 2017, from http://www.tcrecord.org/Content.asp?ContentID=22073.

Marsh, J., Plowman, L., Yamada-Rice, D., Bishop, J. C., Lahmar, J., Scott, F., … Winter, P. (2015). *Exploring play and creativity in pre-schoolers' use of apps: Final project report.* Retrieved from http://www.techandplay.org.

Marsh, J., Plowman, L., Yamada-Rice, D., Bishop, J. C., & Scott, F. (2016). Digital play: A new classification. *Early Years: An International Research Journal, 36*(3), 242–253.

Mascheroni, G., & Holloway, D. (Eds.) (2017). *The Internet of Toys: A report on media and social discourses around young children and IoToys. DigiLitEY.* http://digilitey.eu/wp-content/uploads/2017/01/IoToys-June-2017-reduced.pdf

Mori, M. (1970). The uncanny valley. *Energy, 7*(4), 33–35.

Opie, I., & Opie, P. (1997). *Children's games with things.* Oxford: Oxford University Press.

Tesar, M., & Arndt, S. (2016). Vibrancy of childhood things: Power, philosophy, and political ecology cultural studies. *Critical Methodologies, 16*(2), 193–200.

Wang, W., Kuo, V., King, C., & Chang, C. (2010). *Internet of toys: An e-pet overview and proposed innovative social toy service platform.* Computer Symposium, Tainan, December 16–18. https://doi.org/10.1109/compsym.2010.5685507.

4

Toying with the Singularity: AI, Automata and Imagination in Play with Robots and Virtual Pets

Seth Giddings

Introduction

Five 8-year-old children sit around a large table in a primary school classroom. Asked to draw and talk about their experience of and ideas about robots, they talk excitedly:

- It could be a household robot … a microwave here, and a washing machine there!
- Mine looks like a snail!
- I'm thinking of Droidius from Star Wars…
- Brian! The Confused.com robot! [two of the children recite in unison the words of a recent TV advertisement for this price comparison website featuring a comic robot]
- None of the robots in adverts are proper robots.

S. Giddings (✉)
University of Southampton, Southampton, UK
e-mail: S.Giddings@soton.ac.uk

© The Author(s) 2019
G. Mascheroni and D. Holloway (eds.), *The Internet of Toys*,
Studies in Childhood and Youth, https://doi.org/10.1007/978-3-030-10898-4_4

The workshop leader picks up on this last statement. 'So what's a proper robot'?

- Uses proper technology, not just wires.
- You can program it!
- Brian's probably just remote-controlled.
- R2D2!
- Mine's like a snail…

This chapter will explore the various and layered ways in which imagination and imaginative processes intersect with the development, promotion and everyday reception of and play with new playful technologies for children. As commodities and consumer technologies, smart, automated, networked and hybrid toys emerge from the commercial and technical systems and processes of design, manufacture and dissemination that foster the introduction of all new technological devices, their design shaped by imaginative processes that are inextricably industrial, technical and cultural (Balsamo, 2011; Oudshoorn & Pinch, 2003). As consumer technologies, their reception is heralded by speculative and ideal visions of their future place in everyday lives presented in advertising, marketing and packaging, visions that aim to capture consumers' imaginations (du Gay, Hall, Janes, Mackay, & Negus, 1997). Theorists of technoculture paint broader canvases of global imaginaries, technological imaginaries and new ontologies of virtual, hybrid, cyborgian or post-human near-futures of which individual artefacts, systems or relationships might be either evidence or symptoms (Allison, 2006; Flichy, 1999; Haraway, 1990).

Toys, however, are a distinctly ambiguous type of consumer technology, and they track ambivalent paths through these layered imaginaries. For my argument here, they are distinct among industrially produced artefacts in their mobilisation of imaginative processes in three significant ways. First, as industrially produced commodities and technologies, toys are by and large not instrumental: they are designed *for* imagination to foster imaginative play. Second, over centuries, they have served as microcosmic models of social, cultural and technological orders and attitudes, or have been regarded as a kind of training or education of young imaginations in the skills and values of the adult world (from building blocks to toys soldiers and dolls houses) or the forces and phenomena of the natural world (optical toys, scientific toys). And third, recent developments in the use of advanced networked, interactive, virtual and mechanical technologies in toy design add to longer-established commercialisation, franchising and 'mediatization' of toys (Bak, 2016). From themed LEGO sets to transmedia systems such as Pokémon, from videogames to children's virtual worlds, global media corporations attempt to engineer and monetise imaginative play. This has led to intense popular and academic debate over whether we are seeing a withering of imaginative potential in children's lives in the twenty-first century (e.g. Giddings, 2014b; Hjarvard, 2004; Kline, 1993; Wasko, 2010).

In this chapter, I will argue that to grasp the emerging possibilities of new developments in the Internet of Toys, paying critical attention to these layered relationships of material technology and intangible imagination is needed. Moreover, taking toys that demonstrate AI or autonomous behaviour as a central example, I will argue that paying close descriptive and analytical attention to moments of interaction with such toys is essential to fully grasp the complex relationships between global technological imaginaries—in this case of AI and artificial life—and the material and embodied workings of imagination in play. Recent developments in robotic toys are integral to the broader category of the Internet of Toys as; on the one hand, they are often designed with networked capabilities and social media connectivity. On the other hand, they exemplify significant facets of digital toy technology that can be found across the range of Internet of Toys objects and systems, including sensors, cameras, autonomous behaviour and AI, interaction algorithms, augmented reality, game platforms and data storage. I include virtual pets (both physical and virtual) in this discussion, which further blurs the distinctions between categories of robots, 'bots, game characters, game worlds and toys.

My aim then is to acknowledge the importance of the imaginary in the design, dissemination and adoption/adaption of playful technologies, whilst arguing that this imaginary dimension needs to be anchored in the material and technical characteristics of the play objects and systems themselves and—importantly—in the embodied and imaginative playful relationships and events they engender. As Minna Ruckenstein notes, 'toys are designed both materially and semiotically [...] the materiality of toys intertwines with prominent ideologies and narratives' (Ruckenstein, 2010, p. 501). It is only by describing the intimate and contingent relationships between particular toys and technologies and their playful use that we can both resist overly optimistic or dystopian predictions of the near future of children's playful technoculture and explore the nature of play in that technoculture.

Introducing the Robot

> The robot twitched, then jerked into life, its front legs rearing up threateningly, something like a tarantula responding to a threat. Its servos whirred and the whole device clattered noisily against the melamine-topped table. With involuntary gasps and a collective 'whooaaa', the children started back from the object in front of them, which had instantly transformed from a boxy and technical looking assemblage of grey plastic elements, joints and wires into an uncannily lifelike creature. (Fig. 4.1)

There were two robots: a large grey animate one assembled from a proprietary robotic kit; and a smaller, palm-sized orange object. This smaller one was a 3D printed maquette produced to indicate the scale and eventual look of the toy under development. It had a distinct style and feel, an alien mix of an arthropod and a military vehicle from a science fiction film (Fig. 4.1). However, strictly speaking, there were *no* robots in the classroom. The small orange object was inanimate, non-mechanical, with no smart digital capacity. The grey tarantula's movement was remote controlled by Silas, the robot toy project's lead designer, as yet it had no autonomous or sensing capabilities, aspects often taken as key elements of a robot (Winfield, 2012). There was, however, a set of material objects, intangible ideas and excited imagination that added up to a range of ideas—expressed through talking, drawing and playing—about robots in general, robots past and present, fictional and actual robots and a robot toy to come.

Fig. 4.1   The prototype robot (top) and 3D printed model (below)

The children and virtual robot were gathered at a workshop run at an inner-city primary school in Bristol. The research was supported by a Prototype Funding award from REACT, a Knowledge Exchange Hub for the Creative Economy funded by the Arts and Humanities Research Council (UK). The start-up robotics company, Reach Robotics, was developing a robot-based computer-game platform, in which physical robots would be controlled by an app. This stage of the research looked to explore the balance between technology and user experience, focusing on the everyday and popular contexts of play with technology.

The discussion quoted at the start of this chapter demonstrates how, in just a few seconds of talk and play, children's ideas about new technologies can be seen to be woven together from popular cultural and media characters and narratives (here from advertising and popular film) and scientific and technical knowledge (the significance of programming and autonomous behaviour in robotics), and affected by whatever playful and/or educational setting pertains at that moment. The workshop leader was supported by the robot toy's lead designer, with the author recording the event with video cameras and audio recorders. This video and audio material formed the basis of a microethnographic analysis, a thick description of the interactions between children's speech, gestures, drawings, prototype technologies and workshop environment (Giddings, 2007, 2014a).

The workshop was structured into two main sections. Before revealing the prototype objects, we asked the children to talk about their experience and knowledge of robots. The resulting chatter was marked by a collective fascination with Brian, a comical robot from a series of TV advertisements for a price comparison website. Two children were able to recite the dialogue from one of these adverts in full and in unison. Disney/Pixar's WALL-E featured very briefly, and Star Wars was mentioned, but with little reference to the names, characters or characteristics of particular droids within the films, beyond a fleeting reference to Droidius.[1] It was clear that the first associations that sprang to mind were from popular media culture and not actual robots, nor, interestingly, toy robots. One girl pointed out, however, that none of these were real robots, and that Brian was probably remote-controlled. Others concurred, suggesting an understanding of some specific features of actual robotic technology, notably the distinction between remote control by a human operator and pre-programmed behaviours. Two of the children had recent experience of actual robots, at a popular science centre in Bristol. They had taken part in a workshop in which they programmed a robot to use sensors to distinguish between coloured balls. No further detail was offered at this point, but the notion of sensors—and these children's hands-on experience of them—was to affect the children's imaginary future scenarios for the robot from then on.

We asked the children to draw robots as we talked. Most of these imagined robots were boxy, with screens for faces, perhaps a mix of Wall-E and Brian (the simple graphic eyes of Wall-E and two had caterpillar tracks, rather than legs, like Brian). One drawing was even labelled 'sort of Brian' (Fig. 4.2). Another, however, was more rocket-like in shape and inspired by R2D2, and one had a dome-like body above caterpillar tracks—its creator announced repeatedly, apparently no less surprised than everyone else, that it had turned out to be a snail robot.

There was no evidence at this point of the anxieties prevalent in adult discourse on developments in robotics, in job losses due to automation and artificial intelligence and notions of robots 'taking over' or the 'singularity', the putative future point at which artificial intelligence exceeds the capacities of human intelligence and control. Nor, it seemed, had the children picked up on more benign developments and predictions for everyday robots, such as vacuum cleaners or pets. It was clear that whatever these children's understanding was of an everyday life of robotic interaction, it was imagined primarily in terms of characters from popular media entertainment, and even then only those very recently experienced.

However, the children's imaginative engagement with and exploration of the possibilities of a robotic toy shifted significantly once they had seen and played with the actual prototype. I will return to this and its implications. First though, it will be useful to open up the broader conceptual frameworks that articulate ideas of imagination, technological design and lived experience.

The Technological Imaginary

The role of imagination and the imaginary in the anticipation, design and reception of new technologies (both instrumental and for entertainment/consumption) has been explored across a number of disciplines concerned with technological development and consumer culture.

Fig. 4.2 Children's robotic imaginary (top), with 'Sort-of Brian' (below)

Producers and marketers of new consumer devices spin what William Boddy called 'instrumental fantasies' of their future place in consumers' lives, 'an implicit fantasy scenario of its domestic consumption, a polemical ontology of it as a medium, and an ideological rationale for its social function' (Boddy, 1999, in Lister, Dovey, Giddings, Grant, & Kelly, 2009, p. 254). These are facets of what has been called the 'technological imaginary'. The concept of the technological imaginary draws attention to the ways in which visions of emerging or speculative technologies are deployed to promise a better society, to overcome existing social, political or environmental challenges. It 'refers us to the way that new technologies are taken up within culture and are hooked into, or have projected onto them, its wider social and psychological desires and fears' (Lister et al., 2009, p. 70) and 'draws attention to the way that […] dissatisfactions with social reality and desires for a better society are projected onto technologies as capable of delivering a potential realm of completeness' (Lister et al., 2009, p. 67). Thus, a technological imaginary might envision idealised, utopian visions, whereas a similar imaginary and symbolic operation drives anxious and dystopian predictions for current and emergent technologies.

The Tamagotchi Imaginary

Sherry Turkle's pioneering work on children's imaginative engagement with computer technology and media is key here. Her observations of children's negotiation of ideas about life, consciousness and the animate in smart toys in the late 1970s and early 1980s remain pertinent for the study of Internet of Toys today. Importantly, she documents children's philosophical interpretation of the nature of the artificial intelligences with which they are playing. These are synthetic and machinic enough for the children to be clear they are not conversing or playing with an actual intelligence, but sophisticated and responsive enough to be regarded as acting 'as-if' they were intelligent. Children playing with interactive electronic toys such as Simon know they are not alive in the same way that a child or a pet is alive. But they are, as one nine-year-old girl said, 'sort of alive' (Turkle, 1984, p. 41). In their degree of autonomous behaviour (asking questions, responding to answers, competing with the child in games), they are quite different to other toys, ones that are, by and large, imbued with life and intelligence only by the imaginative and manual action of the child himself or herself. In addition to the long-established as-if realities of play with toys, these toys and devices bring a new degree of sort-of life and to play with them is by necessity to respond to them as if they were alive, again in new ways.

Turkle's articulation of the philosophical and psychological concepts of consciousness, human–machine relations and life with empirical observation of actual technological encounters produced a nuanced and sensitive model of the operations of imagination in digital technocul-ture. As smart toys, and virtual pets in particular, hit the toyshops and public consciousness in the late 1980s, they were met with a distinctly dystopian technological imaginary in both the popular press and aca-demic cultural critique. They represented the 'technological erosion of emotion' (Kritt, 1999). Others saw in the Tamagotchi craze a meta-phor of our times, representing the blurring of boundaries, between real reciprocal relationships and surrogate, one-way imaginary ones. It high-lights the dominant role of technology in our lives; no longer simply a tool for use in science and industry, but now a substitute for human relationships (Bloch & Lemish, 1999, p. 295).

Here, a late twentieth-century technocultural imaginary of postmod-ernist illusion and ennui finds in Tamagotchi play a dangerous blurring of people and artefacts, subjects and objects, and a waning of loving and caring relationships in an era of disposability and artifice.

For Anne Allison, the Tamagotchi epitomises a (less pessimistic) 'global imaginary', a transnational cultural economy of Japanese hard-ware and media products, embraced by children around the world. For her, the new intimacies between the human and (newly animate) non-human epitomised by the Tamagotchi are less catastrophic but no less revolutionary: they are driven by increasing virtuality and a concomi-tant 'cyborgian fantasy' (Allison, 2006, p. 164). The Tamagotchi's play at 'the boundaries of the imaginary is symptomatic of the social reality we inhabit: one in which virtuality is becoming increasingly integrated into everyday life and movement' (Allison, 2006, p. 179). For Allison, these toys are not the harbingers of an unsettling virtualised world, rather they are an imaginative palliative to it, they 'both reflect and shape an imagination that not only fits these post-industrial times but also helps kids adjust to a world where the border between the imagi-nary and the real is shifting so quickly' (Allison, 2006, p. 179).

What neither of these commentaries does, however, is consider the ways in which these overarching sets of ideas about an imminent post-human (children's) technoculture actually drive or shape chil-dren's imaginative play with technologically sophisticated toys—or indeed whether they do so at all. Importantly, they do not fully account for the very particular contexts of play, neither the often ironic, phantasmagorical inversions of imaginative play (evident throughout the examples here) (Sutton-Smith, 1997) nor the particular mechanisms of games themselves as technocultural phenomena. So, the Tamagotchi is presented and marketed as offering a loving and caring relationship, but close attention to play with smart toys, robots or virtual pets, however, reveals a more nuanced and complex interplay of affect, mechanics and instrumentalism, imagination augmented with patterns that are schematic, algorithmic and procedural (Apperley & Heber, 2015).[2] The child must learn which buttons to press in response to particular virtual events and prompts, as much for ludic as affective purposes (to level up the character, gain rewards, expend points or virtual commodities and so on). And of course, as with computer games, this is implicitly and entirely understood by the child, that it is a software system as well as an imagined companion.

So, without attention to the technical characteristics, possibilities and limitations in moments of actual everyday play, and the nuanced and nonlinear set of relationships between ideas, imagination, technologies and media characters they generate, critical work on the Internet of Toys runs the risk of perpetuating idealist assumptions. Indeed, from government policy to the home and classroom, this adult idealism can be a source of conflict or negotiation over values and anxieties. Minna Ruckenstein's ethnographic study of young children and Tamogotchi in Finland, for instance, emphasises the complex interrelationships between the material characteristics and capacities of technological toys and their cultural framing as articulated in children's play. She notes a small but significant battle between young girls and their teachers over a technological and affectual imaginary of official approval. The teachers were invested in ideas that cuddly, animal-shaped toys were socially and pedagogically far superior to digital games and battery-operated toys, actively intervening in discussions about toys to encourage 'bonding' with their preferred toys. As one girl showed both her Tamagotchi and cuddly dog to the class, she was asked which was best. 'This one', she said, holding up the Tamagotchi, 'because it can be fed'. The teacher resisted, 'It is a bit cold, like a machine. Beautiful soft doggy: such a cute face' (Ruckenstein, 2010, p. 506).

Jackie Marsh's observations of a three-year-old girl's play with her (app-augmented) Furby is an excellent example of the articulation of a meta-level technological imaginary with an ethnographic eye for the details and textures of the lived moment. She teases out what we might call micro-imaginaries—contingent on and spun into existence by the intersection of the material affordances of the toy and the fleeting images, dramas, gestures and concerns that characterise young children's imaginative play:

> ...she always plays a number of times with the toilet feature of the app, in which Furby is encouraged to use the toilet, and then she flushes it by pressing the button in the app and creating clouds of air freshener around the toilet. At one point, Amy pretends that she has Furby's feces on her hands. (Marsh, 2017)

Marsh notes that here 'the AR technology of the app has promoted imaginative play that moves beyond the inorganic organized objects contained within the play. This shifts the imaginative play experience onto a different plane' (Marsh, 2017). My interpretation of this is that whilst the app and toy play are no doubt predicated by an imaginative acceptance of artificial intelligence and autonomous behaviour, this dimension is not reflected on by Amy (as it was with Turkle's informants). Rather, it is taken for granted and the interactive and gamelike aspects of the app pull her into a much more hands-on engagement with virtual life—here hands-on in both actual and virtual terms, with the latter having a distinctly tactile quality.

Marsh accounts for these tiny but vivid technocultural events through theories of post-humanism. In these terms, this encounter is as much a material instantiation of broader technocultural change as is an imaginary one. Citing Karen Barad's notion of post-humanism and the 'ontological entanglement' of human and nonhuman entities, Marsh sees in the moment-by-moment contingencies of the co-constitution of Amy, the app and the Furby in play a manifestation of this post-human condition, a deep and complex meshing of domains (Marsh, 2017). In the micro-event above, the global strategies of Hasbro, the design and programming of a particular toy system and the playful, scatological and embodied imagination of a child collude in the simulation of a pungent dimension of (artificial) life. Thus, while Allison's cyborgian fantasy projected a post-human future from emergent popular techno-cultural products, here it is lived in the here-and-now, fully contemporaneous, everyday and generally unremarkable.

Revealing the Robot

This complex tangle of the material and the immaterial, the tangible and the intangible, the technical and the imaginary were evident too in our robot workshop. In the first half of the session, then, the children's robotic imaginary was largely shaped by popular media, inflected with some scientific knowledge. It changed markedly once they had actually seen, touched and controlled the 3D printed model and the animatronic prototype:

- Those look like lasers! [shooting noises] It could twist its head and kill you!
- I would build a Lego city and make it destroy it! It would be like Godzilla! It doesn't look nice and kind!
- If it was mine, I would make it walk first. Then I would make its front legs come [gestures it rearing up with her arms].
- [responding to a question about playing with friends with two robots] They could work together to destroy a city.
- Or battle together with their front legs! Ninja!
- If I had one on my own, I would make a park for it to go through, to follow and path and turn corners [one of the children who had been to the robot workshop]. Sensors.
- If it was that size [points to the small 3D printed model] I'd make a spider costume for it to use to trick people—I'd send it into my sister's room.

On the one hand, unsurprisingly, the children immediately began to imagine how the robot might be played with, what features might be added and what playful possibilities they might afford. As I watched the video back later, it became evident that the children's imaginative engagement with the physical and moving robots was kinaesthetic and bodily expressive, as well as simply cognitive or symbolic. As they excitedly invented possible scenarios and events for the future robots in their everyday play, they gestured—the dramatic motion of the robot's front legs was performed, forearms held up with hands bent down at the wrist, moving rapidly up and down as a large spider or praying mantis might attack its prey.

Once the children were familiar with the form and interactive movement of the proposed robot toy, we asked them again to draw as we talked. This time the drawing activity was framed as a design exercise and they were asked to work with photocopied outlines of the proposed robot—to suggest ways in which it could be coloured, patterned and augmented as a physical object. Unsurprisingly, the constraints and framing of the drawing activity drove a more precise and concrete set of ideas about what the toy might look like, what its capabilities might be and what future playful events and scenarios it might bring about. Lights and power sources were drawn on screens/faces added and sensors incorporated. This second drawing activity and its attendant conversations were characterised by a mix of dramatic scenarios and technical practicalities. Here, a girl drawing yellow flames shooting from her robot's feet shared ideas with the boy next to her:

- [quietly] Jetpacks.
- Yeah! Jetpacks would be epic! On its feet
- [both gesture and vocalise the sound and motion of a rocket-like take off].
- It could land on the sky!
- It could land on the ceiling!
- Oh yeah, a charger input.
- A charger input should be in its bottom [they giggle conspiratorially] (Fig. 4.3).

On the other hand, though—and the sneaky spider costume hints at this—much of the conversation was shot through with a distinct unease about aspects of the proposed toy. The insect- or alien-like and combative-looking character of the design did not alarm them, but something about its potential autonomous capabilities caught the collective imagination in ways both exciting and unsettling. This became particularly evident when Silas explained a key feature of the planned toy:

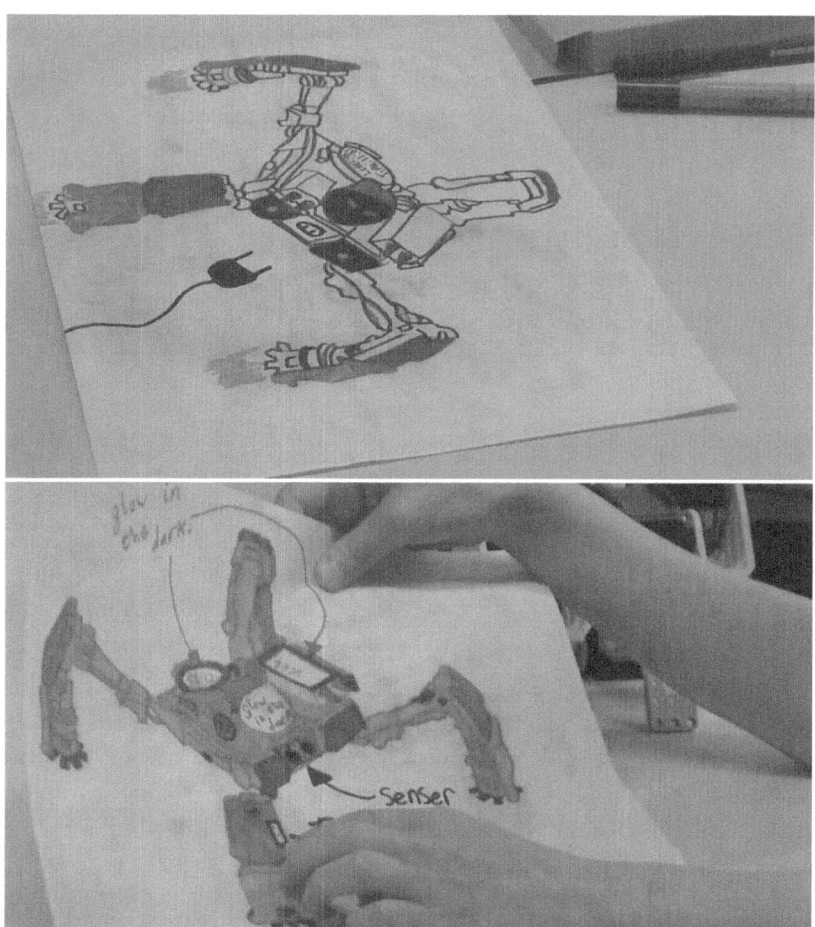

Fig. 4.3 Robot design drawings, with jet packs (top), and sensors (below)

- (Silas) Something else about these robots that I forgot to tell you. If you leave them by themselves, they can just walk around and have fun by themselves. Is that a good thing or not?
- (All) No!
- If you go on holiday, it could move around and break things and then when you get back it could have gone or gone outside and you can't find it.
- Or it could just be walking on a table and just fall off and break.
- It's creepy—if you're reading in a room and it comes up to you [laughs].
- I think it would be scary if you just left it at the end of your bed, in the middle of the night it was just crawling on top of you.

One girl imagined another nocturnal, near-nightmarish, scenario:

- If they were like at the bottom of your stairs and they somehow climbed up the stairs to your closed door and started banging on your door because they wanted to come in. They know it's the door to your bedroom, because they want that person to start playing with them.

Silas asked her if it would be better if it didn't crawl, but moved like a different animal.

- No, I like it to crawl, but only when I want it to.

Surprised by these misgivings, Silas suggested adding a switch that would let the owner decide whether the robot can go off by itself or not. This was generally seen as a good idea. It also reminded one of the children about her experience with a Furby toy, and there followed a number of rather implausible anecdotes about family travails with Furbys that would not turn off and would talk and sing in the night, or that needed to be put in a cupboard under the stairs because they woke up in the light.

- It just does its own stuff, and annoys you at night, so you couldn't get to sleep.

One child compared another toy favourably with Furby:

- I have a toy called a Blue Nose Friend, a teddy. It doesn't move around but it talks and it's got a switch, so it doesn't just go off and talk by itself and be really annoying.

This collective anxiety about nonhuman intelligence and autonomous movement was generated not by a general dystopian technological imaginary of robot supremacy and AI singularity, but by the specific technical characteristics of the proposed toy and their imagined place and activity within the safety of the children's homes and bedrooms. The robot's material, mechanical and behavioural aspects are inseparable from imaginative response and speculation: here, the unsettling possibilities of an animate and autonomous creature were ameliorated with a set of ideas for technical solutions that reinstated a reassuring degree of control over the machine (see also Hilu, 2016).[3]

The anxiety about the toy's potential autonomy manifested itself more subtly as well, influencing ostensibly practically-driven ideas about its design and possible behaviours. As noted earlier, two of the children had recently participated in a workshop in which they programmed a robot to sense and respond to its environment. Probably as a result of their explanations, sensors appeared as salient technical features in the drawings (Fig. 4.3). A grasp of robotic sensing also shaped a recurrent theme in the children's imagining of the robot's movement in their domestic space. This began with one girl's answer to a question about how the children imagined they might play with the robot:

- If I had one on my own I would make a path for it to go through, to follow, and turn corners.
- Like sensors!

After Silas had discussed the toy's worrying capacity for autonomy, the affordances of sensors seemed to inflect further less-nightmarish but still anxious scenarios. Early on, one of the children who had attended the programming workshop imagined the robot walking about on a table, its sensors maybe keeping it on the table or perhaps failing, resulting in the robot falling. This image of the robot falling off furniture appeared repeatedly thereafter, a mix, perhaps, of the underlying disquiet about artificial movement with more familiar worries about dropping and breaking delicate and expensive toys:

• It should be smart, really smart, but not too smart. Not smart enough to not jump off the table, then obviously if you put it on the table it could be your fault if it breaks because it's your responsibility.
• When it's walking around it could have sensors on it so that if there was a step it could sense the step and go off somewhere else.
• [...]
• I'd like sensors ... so if it was on a table it wouldn't just walk off the end. Even if you did try to control it off the edge it wouldn't do it.

So now the physical and behavioural capacities of the projected robotic toy were salient in a set of more or less anxious micro-imaginaries. These scenarios and designs were partly technical, practical speculations about the ways in which the robot might behave and the behaviours it might be capable of depending on actual components, and partly a much more detailed and collectively generated vision of how it might exist within and interact with their domestic space, family relationships, play and dreams.

Conclusion

Even after 40 years of smart and interactive toys, videogames, virtual pets and more recent developments in robotic and networked toys, it appears that concepts and dramas of artificial life and nonhuman autonomy persist in children's play with them. However, close ethnographic studies of children's play with toys and other consumer technologies have demonstrated that these ideas about life and nonhuman agency vary significantly according to the particular toy or system in play, the backgrounds, relationships and even recent TV viewing of the children playing. They warn against simply assuming playful behaviour from the instrumental fantasies of the toys' marketing and instruction, and they challenge ideal (utopian or dystopian) imaginaries of virtuality, simulation, cyborgian or globalised subjectivity. But the broader technological imaginaries are no mere abstractions or illusions, they shape the design and reception of toys as technologies, facilitating and scaffolding certain kinds of play whilst never fully determining it. They mesh the material characteristics and operations of the technology, the culture and sociality of the play environment and images and dramas from the children's media environment and—not least—with the phantasmagorical imaginations of children themselves. Imagination and materiality interact and co-constitute with and across each other at global and extremely local intersections.

And play itself affects distinct cultural and technical environments and attitudes. A 'lusory attitude' to materials, spaces, objects and ideas is never far away in children's interactions and conversations. The ideal completeness of the toy's advertisement and packaging is rarely if ever realised. In imaginative play, anxieties and excitement blur and flip, agency and control are surrendered and inverted, subjects become willing objects and objects come to life.

Acknowledgements The robot workshop was part of a project with Reach Robotics to prototype their Mecha Monsters toy (now marketed as MekaMon) and was funded by REACT, a Knowledge Exchange Hub for the Creative Industries. REACT ran from 2012 to 2016 and was funded by the Arts and Humanities Research Council, UK: http://www.react-hub.org.uk/. Thanks to Silas Adekunle, CEO of Reach Robotics, for his enthusiastic cooperation; and many thanks to Penny Giddings for setting up, planning and running the workshop.

Notes

1. As far as I am aware, there is no 'Droidius' in the Star Wars narrative universe. This could possibly be a conflation of the droideka robots and General Grievous.
2. This overlooks the long history of mechanical and clockwork toys for children, construction toys and the sophisticated engineering of pop-up and interactive books that date back at least to the first commercial toy

production in Germany in the late eighteenth century (see Opie, Opie, & Alderson, 1989).

3. There are issues here with the nature of 'animation' in play with toys. Children have always brought their toys to life, and a possible delegation of that control to nonhuman agency is clearly not necessarily seamless. Moreover, there are echoes here of a much longer imaginary about toys—children's stories and cinema are full of stories of toys that come to life, particularly at night, stories that can be both reassuring (a favourite toy as friend, from Starewicz's *The Mascot* (1933) to the Pixar/Disney *Toy Story* films) or unsettling and scary (the *Child's Play* films, *Pinocchio*).

References

Allison, A. (2006). *Millenial monsters: Japanese toys and the global imagination*. Berkeley: University of California Press.

Apperley, T., & Heber, N. (2015). Capitalizing on emotions: Digital pets and the natural user interface. In J. Enevold & E. Macallum-Stewart (Eds.), *Game love: Essays on play and affection* (pp. 149–161). Jefferson, NC: McFarland.

Bak, M. (2016). Building blocks of the imagination: Children, creativity, and the limits of *Disney Infinity*. *The Velvet Light Trap, 78*, 53–64.

Balsamo, A. (2011). *Designing culture: The technological imagination at work*. Durham, NC: Duke University Press.

Bloch, L., & Lemish, D. (1999). Disposable love: The rise and fall of a virtual pet. *New Media & Society, 1*(3), 283–303.

Du Gay, P., Hall, S., Janes, L., Mackay, H., & Negus, K. (1997). *Doing cultural studies: The story of the Sony Walkman*. London: Sage.

Flichy, P. (1999). The construction of new digital media. *New Media & Society, 1*(1), 3–39.

Giddings, S. (2007). Playing with nonhumans: Digital games as technocultural form. In S. de Castell & J. Jensen (Eds.), *Worlds in play: International perspectives on digital games research* (pp. 115–128). Frankfurt, Germany: Peter Lang.

Giddings, S. (2014a). *Gameworlds: Virtual media and children's everyday play*. New York: Bloomsbury.

Giddings, S. (2014b). Bright bricks, dark play: On the impossibility of studying LEGO. In M. J. P. Wolf (Ed.), *LEGO studies: Examining the building blocks of a transmedia phenomenon* (pp. 241–267). New York: Routledge.

Haraway, D. (1990). A manifesto for cyborgs: Science, technology, and socialist feminism in the 1980s. In L. J. Nicholson (Ed.), *Feminism/postmodernism* (pp. 190–234). London: Routledge.

Hilu, R. (2016). Girl talk and girl tech: Computer talking dolls and the sounds of girls' play. *The Velvet Light Trap, 78*, 4–21.

Hjarvard, S. (2004). From bricks to bytes: The mediatization of a global toy industry. In I. Bondebjerg & P. Golding (Eds.), *European culture and the media* (pp. 43–64). Bristol, UK: Intellect.

Kline, S. (1993). *Out of the garden: Toys and children's culture in the age of TV marketing*. New York: Verso.

Kritt, D. (1999). Loving a virtual pet: Toward the technological erosion of emotion. *Journal of American and Comparative Cultures, 23*(4), 81–87.

Lister, M., Dovey, J., Giddings, S., Grant, I., & Kelly, K. (2009). *New media: A critical introduction* (2nd ed.). London: Routledge.

Marsh, J. (2017). The internet of toys: A posthuman and multimodal analysis of connected play. *Teachers College Record, 119*(2). Retrieved from http://eprints.whiterose.ac.uk/113557/.

Opie, I., Opie, P., & Alderson, B. (1989). *A treasury of childhood: Books, toys, and games from the Opie collection*. London: Pavilion Books.

Oudshoorn, N., & Pinch, T. (2003). Introduction: How users and non-users matter. In T. Pinch & N. Oudshoorn (Eds.), *How users matter: The co-construction of users and technology* (pp. 1–25). Cambridge, MA: MIT Press.

Ruckenstein, M. (2010). Toying with the world: Children, virtual pets and the value of mobility. *Childhood, 17*(4), 500–513.

Sutton-Smith, B. (1997). *The ambiguity of play*. Cambridge, MA: Harvard University Press.

Turkle, S. (1984). *The second self: Computers and the human spirit*. New York: Simon & Schuster.

Wasko, J. (2010). Children's virtual worlds: The latest commercialization of children's culture. In T. Vebjørg & D. Buckingham (Eds.), *Childhood and consumer culture* (pp. 113–129). New York, NY: Palgrave Macmillan.

Winfield, A. (2012). *Robotics: A very short introduction*. Oxford: Oxford University Press.

5

Postdigitality in Children's Crossmedia Play: A Case Study of Nintendo's Amiibo Figurines

Bjorn Nansen, Benjamin Nicoll and Thomas Apperley

Introduction

Children's media spaces and practices are becoming increasingly complex arrangements as devices, screens and toys are digitally integrated to enable the mobility and flow of both content and data (Holloway & Green, 2016). Nintendo's 'Amiibo' figurines are exemplary of these burgeoning 'crossmedia' infrastructures. They represent the dual trajectories of industry production and user participation in assembling and dispersing entertainment and franchises across multiple media platforms (Lomborg & Mortensen, 2017). They are, then, part of a broader

B. Nansen (✉)
University of Melbourne, Melbourne, VIC, Australia
e-mail: nansenb@unimelb.edu.au

B. Nicoll
Queensland University of Technology, Brisbane, Australia
e-mail: b2.nicoll@qut.edu.au

T. Apperley
Tampere University, Tampere, Finland

© The Author(s) 2019
G. Mascheroni and D. Holloway (eds.), *The Internet of Toys*,
Studies in Childhood and Youth, https://doi.org/10.1007/978-3-030-10898-4_5

industry of the Internet of Toys (IoT). Amiibo figurines are physical toys based on characters from various Nintendo franchises. Amiibos work by 'interacting' with Nintendo hardware and software via wireless near-field communication (NFC) technology. In their production, promotion and everyday use, the figurines solicit playful practices that cut across physical objects and digital spaces. For companies such as Nintendo, this type of crossmedia play—sometimes referred to as 'toys to life'—is a desirable commercial activity. It nurtures a physical bond between children, software and the intellectual property (IP) of characters from various game franchises. Yet, as researchers have long recognised, children's media practices often exceed or confound the activities prescribed by media industries and promotional discourses (Giddings, 2014; Kline, 1995), and Amiibos are no exception.

This chapter explores how Nintendo Amiibo figurines circulate in and through children's crossmedia practices. We draw on three sites of analysis: first, interface analysis of how Amiibo products operate with the Wii U and Nintendo Switch platforms; second, the promotional messages and discourses surrounding Amiibo figurines; and finally, video content and user comment analysis of Amiibo unboxing and play on YouTube. This analysis highlights how Amiibos are clearly framed as a means to envelop children in Nintendo's crossmedia ecosystem. This is achieved through the software affordances of the figurines—which are capable of storing data corresponding to personal game experience and progress—as well as through marketing and promotional materials. However, YouTube videos of children's Amiibo play also highlight a tension in such crossmedia ecosystems. Although Amiibos are designed to reinforce the interaction between the child and the branded world of Nintendo, the toys often enter the messy reality of children's everyday play in ways that exceed prescription through alternative forms and meanings of play.

This analysis connects with IoT research by building on the concept of 'postdigital' play (Apperley, Jayemanne, & Nansen, 2016), which describes how the historical distinction between the digital and the non-digital has become increasingly blurred through mobile, pervasive, locative and augmented media (Berry, 2014). Previously, we conceptualised postdigital play through an 'aesthetics of recruitment', which involves an enrolment of player bodies and sensations that moves beyond the screen. In an article on the 'ontological entanglement' of 'the physical and virtual domains' of children's play with smart toys, Jackie Marsh (2017, n.p.) similarly suggests that children's IoT play should be considered hybrid and co-constitutive. She calls for further research on the political economy of internet-enabled toys—that is, how data are extracted and mobilised by toy companies, and for what purposes. Marsh (2017, n.p.) also reflects briefly on the possibilities of transgressive play with smart toys and considers the ways in which 'a young app user might be compliant with, and resistant to' the data collection strategies of smart toys. Our chapter aims to address both of these concerns. In this chapter, we use the Amiibo to interrogate the evolving intersection of crossmedia products and children's cultures of play. Informed by game studies' material turn (Apperley & Jayemanne, 2012), we explore the intersection of the political economy and everyday practice in configuring such forms of postdigital play. We account for the reciprocal dynamic between children's everyday play (which often encompasses the appropriation and repurposing of toys) and the branded world of IoT products in which transgressive forms of play are reincorporated back into a branded environment. In turn, these dynamics point to emerging questions around children's data literacies within the environments and economies of postdigital play—how the 'mundane data' (Lupton, 2017; Pink, Sumartojo, Lupton, & Heyes La Bond, 2017) produced within these everyday contexts of play are felt, experienced and understood.

Postdigital Ecologies of Domestic Play

This chapter contributes to a long tradition of household media research that has sought to understand how new technologies are domesticated within physical spaces, family relations and social practices, as well as how these practices become physically, socially and symbolically located within the home (Silverstone & Hirsch, 1992). This tradition of research began with broadcast media, such as television and its reception in the home (e.g. Morley, 1986), and later evolved to consider digital technologies such as the home computer (Lally, 2002), the

Internet and the mobile phone (Haddon, 2011) and videogame systems (e.g. Aarsand & Aronsson, 2009). This research reveals that as successive waves of media technologies are domesticated—spreading spatially throughout the house and temporally around the clock—the places and patterns of leisure and play undergo changes. A key example is the shift from collective family television viewing, once organised around a single and immobile broadcast box (Morley, 1986), to the emergence of more distributed and individualised media practices (Turkle, 2011), based on the affordances of multiple and portable devices connected to the Internet via household Wi-Fi. This steady accretion and dispersal of media throughout the home has created dense household ecologies of media.

These ecologies have become further intensified through emerging technologies in which computation and play spread beyond the screen through Internet-connected toys. In game studies, this has been described as a 'postdigital' phase of play, wherein play is no longer a singular activity contained by one digital device at a time (Giddings, 2014; Jayemanne, Apperley, & Nansen, 2016). In a postdigital environment, play multiplies across digital infrastructures and environments, and media companies are thus incentivised to broaden their interface 'envelopes' to capture increasingly unruly and transgressive forms of digital/physical play. The concept of 'postdigital' (Berry, 2014; Berry & Dieter, 2015) is used to refer to the widely distributed digital connectivities and mobilities that have become characteristic of contemporary devices and apps. In videogaming, postdigital play is best illustrated in Internet-enabled collectible figurines such as those associated with *the Skylanders* (Toys for Bob, 2011–) series, the *Disney Infinity* (Disney Interactive Studios, 2013) series, the *Lego Dimensions* (Traveller's Tales, 2015) series and Nintendo Amiibos. These toys use NFC to facilitate the mobility and storage of data between games and consoles. Postdigital forms of play can also be understood to include non-videogame-connected toys, augmented reality apps and computer-augmented board games, each of which is adding new material elements and contexts to videogame play.

Elsewhere, we have characterised the ludic devices and arrangements of postdigital play in terms of an 'aesthetics of recruitment' (Apperley et al., 2016; Jayemanne et al., 2016). This conceptualisation has been useful for thinking through the reconfigurations of play within such postdigital videogaming contexts, in which emergent and often unstable relations are produced through the enrolment and redistribution of various toys, devices, bodies, interfaces, data and spaces in the formation of play. We are not the first to deploy the notion of 'recruitment' in political economic analyses of digital games. Scholars such as Scott Lash and Celia Lury (2007, pp. 54–55), for example, argue that FIFA digital games function to recruit consumers to the broader FIFA brand. In the context of the postdigital, however, crossmedia franchises such as Amiibo figurines recruit different elements into an assemblage of play, cutting across the physical and digital to recruit a larger set of objects and practices into the branded space of play. This crossmedia configuration reinforces the connection to the brand by enrolling physical toy figurines based on characters from various Nintendo franchises into the space of play. This extends the digital brand out into the physical spaces of children's physical play spaces and, in turn, reincorporates extensive forms of play back into a branded environment through attachment to both a physical object and the data it embodies. The Amiibo-player relationship is quantified through personalised histories of gameplay and reward and qualified through an affective interaction based on an 'ecotechnics of care' (Ash, 2015, p. 109). In this arrangement, 'care' for characters and progress is bolstered through an expanded interface 'envelope' that reinforces a physical connection between child, toy, software, platform and IP.

The Amiibo Interface

Amiibo play attempts to establish a postdigital videogaming ecosystem in which integration of the physical and the digital is designed to reinforce the branded world of the franchise. In software studies, interfaces are understood as arrangements that assemble and decompose in dynamic relations and through a suite of different elements, including bodies, devices, peripherals, software, IP and so on (Ash, 2015; Cramer & Fuller, 2008). Amiibo figurines are designed after characters from various Nintendo franchises, such as the crossmedia 'mascots' Mario and Luigi, who appear in a range of Nintendo games. Amiibo figurines harbour NFC tags that can connect wirelessly to Nintendo's Switch, 3DS and Wii U videogame platforms. They can be differentiated from similar 'hybrid' toy/videogame franchises such as *Skylanders, Disney Infinity* and *Lego Dimensions* to the extent that their functions multiply across platforms and games; they are not designed with one, specific technology or game in mind. This significantly reinforces the crossmedia appeal of Amiibos. An Amiibo based on Nintendo's *Zelda* franchise, for example, is compatible with any NFC-enabled Nintendo platform, and it will perform different functions depending on the software in use when the Amiibo is scanned. Amiibos are designed to interface directly with Nintendo hardware, so they are also distinct in not requiring additional plug-in hardware, like the USB 'Toy-Pad' that was necessary to play Traveller's Tales' *Lego Dimensions*.

In mediating such platform relations, Amiibo figurines operate as coded software objects (Kitchin & Dodge, 2014) for data storage and transmission. For some games, Amiibos operate on a read-only basis—that is, they merely 'unlock' pre-existing content in the software when detected by the platform's NFC reader. For other games, such as *Super Smash Bros. for Wii U* (Bandai Namco Games & Sora Ltd., 2014), Amiibos function as data storage devices that keep track of player profiles and character progress. Amiibos are often connected within the Nintendo crossmedia environment in multiple ways, which allows for different qualities of data to be shared. For example, in *Super Smash Bros.* for the *Wii U*, players can develop the strengths and abilities of the Zelda avatar, store this data on the Amiibo and transfer it between Wii U and 3DS devices. This feature is similar to the limited data storage that Nintendo introduced on its Wii remote controller or 'Wiimote', which allowed for the storage of up to ten player-created 'Mii' (which refer to personalised player avatars on the Nintendo Wii), which could then be used if the Wiimote was connected to a different Nintendo Wii console.

Additionally, each Amiibo that is scanned to a device unlocks additional material. The promotional game *Amiibo Touch & Play: Nintendo Classics Highlights* (Nintendo, 2015) (also known as *Amiibo Tap: Nintendo's Greatest Bits*) allowed users to play one three-minute demo of a classic Nintendo game for each Amiibo they scanned. At the end of the demo, players would be directed to the Virtual Console area of the Nintendo e-shop where the full version of the game could be purchased. Many of these classic games—such as *The Legend of Zelda* (Nintendo R&D4, 1986) and *Punch-Out!!* (Nintendo R&D3, 1987)—contain early incarnations of characters now featured on Amiibo figurines. These features situate Amiibos in an elaborate crossmedia promotional culture (Kinder, 1991; Kline, Dyer-Witheford, & de Peuter, 2003), which connects the postdigital present of the Amiibo figure to the repackaging of past Nintendo content. This connection suggests a palpable enactment of an affective pedagogy of taste, where the toy becomes the access point to a curated database of 'classic' experiences that are available to enrich people's affective experience of contemporary content and Amiibos themselves.

The distributed interface of Amiibos can, then, not only be understood through its expanded envelope of branded interaction and relationality, but also as a further development of video gaming's current 'achievement' culture, wherein player performance, cultural capital and gamer 'credentials' are made publicly available across an ecosystem of platforms. Examples of this include Microsoft's 'achievement' and 'gamertag' systems and Sony's 'public trophy' system. These systems function not only as personal profiles for Xbox One and PlayStation 4 owners, but also as publicly viewable 'gamer CVs' of sorts. They display data on users' achievements and awards earned within specific games, and they do so as a means of aggregating an individual player's skill, performance and cultural capital. James Ash (2012, p. 16) notes that, while these systems 'have absolutely no exchange value in themselves', their political economy lies in their 'affective value'. That is, players seek out achievements and trophies because they have been purposefully engineered—graphically and sonically—to be aesthetically pleasurable and rewarding, and also because they bolster the player's public reputation. In turn, these systems generate 'interface envelopes' (Ash, 2015), or affective spaces that establish player allegiances to particular IPs and platforms, connect individual gameplay experiences to a wider platform ecosystem and ultimately make players want to play more and longer, thus generating economic profit.

Nintendo is aiming to create a similar system with its Amiibos, except that rather than cultivating affective value solely through a screen interface, the whole system is externalised into the physical world of collectible toys and figurines. This greatly expands the interface envelope to encompass a broader 'aesthetics of recruitment', wherein players may (unintentionally) enrol themselves in the Amiibo universe (and, by extension, the Nintendo platform ecosystem) through a simple physical encounter—either by handling or playing with a figurine—which may then translate into digital play somewhere down the line. This is an especially effective strategy when it comes to enrolling children in the Nintendo ecosystem, as children are arguably more likely to develop an affective connection to a physical toy, which can then serve as an entry point into Nintendo's crossmedia ecosystem. As Stephen Kline et al. (2003, p. 126) note, Nintendo has long been concerned with generating a sense of brand loyalty among its child consumer base as a means of developing a lifelong feeling of belongingness and commitment to Nintendo products. Amiibo figurines can be seen as an extension of this long-standing business philosophy.

When it comes to Amiibo figurines, brand loyalty cuts across physical and digital spaces, and it may emerge through a messy combination of online or offline play practices, memories and experiences. As will be discussed in the following section, the collapse of physical and digital play enabled by the figurines is constantly referenced in Amiibo promotional discourses. This is further reinforced by the digital representation of Amiibo content in the videogames themselves. For example, the fictional universe of the Nintendo game *Super Smash Bros.* for *Wii U* is premised on the concept that Nintendo figurines are coming to life and doing battle. Likewise, Nintendo's recent Switch game *Splatoon 2* (Nintendo EPD, 2017) features a digital recreation of an Amiibo box—complete with branding and plastic packaging—in the game's main foyer area. If the player scans a *Splatoon* Amiibo on the Switch controller, an Amiibo figurine appears in the digital box and pops into life, and the player is rewarded with bonus content.

Nintendo's Promotional Discourses

Unsurprisingly, the first Wii U game to feature Amiibo compatibility was *Super Smash Bros. for Wii U*—a crossover fighting game that had already established itself as an explicitly crossmedia product through its transposition of characters from other Nintendo franchises, such as Mario and Pikachu, into a new game. This transposition of characters figured prominently in the initial marketing surrounding Amiibos. In the *Smash Bros.* series, various Nintendo figurines come to life and battle against each other, with the in-game representation of figurines predating the release of Amiibo toys. Amiibo figurines were, then, marketed as objects that physically externalised this game universe. Players can 'train' and 'level up' their favourite characters in the game world and store their experience and progress on corresponding Amiibo figurines.

Nintendo's initial marketing for Amiibo figurines focused on naturalising the concept of a crossmedia figurine ecosystem. In an early promotional video first shown at the 2014 Electronic Games Expo (E3), Nintendo of America's product and marketing manager, Bill Trinen, explains that Amiibo figurines offer 'new ways to interact with your favourite Nintendo characters' and 'each figure contains the spirit of the character they represent' (Nintendo, 2014a). He goes on to explain their functionality through the example of *Super Smash Bros. for Wii* U. In the video, the figurines are presented almost as a 'remediation' of the concept behind the *Smash Bros.* series itself, as well as an articulation of an (allegedly) long-standing childhood fantasy of seeing Nintendo characters come to life and do battle. Trinen also emphasises the affective value of Amiibo toys. He explains that 'no two Amiibos will be the same' and repeatedly emphasises the 'unique' and 'personal' nature of the player-Amiibo relationship: 'collect your favourite figures, then battle, train, level up, and form your own unique bond with them'.

Amiibo figurines' affective value is the focus of another 2014 promotional video entitled 'Gameplay & Quest for the amiibo!' (Nintendo 2014b). In this video, a young *Smash Bros.* player ('Jack') seeks to beat his sibling's older friends in the game (and thus win their respect) by purchasing, training and levelling up his own Mario Amiibo. In order to do this, Jack is portrayed developing an affective bond with the toy both inside and outside the digital world of the game, at the dinner table, at the park, in his bedroom and so on. Once Jack has dedicated the necessary affective commitment to the toy, he is shown upstaging his sibling's older friends in a competitive match. This promotional video neatly illustrates the discursive instructions that Nintendo seek to impart to consumers for how to integrate these toys in both online and offline play. First, it attempts to illustrate that 'proper' usage of Amiibos entails a unique, personal and above all affective attachment to be forged between player and toy. The interface envelope generated by the game 'follows' Jack into the messy reality of everyday life through the Amiibo figurine, thus producing an aesthetics of recruitment that cuts across digital and physical spaces.

The promotional video also reinforces and extends an 'ecotechnics of care' (Ash, 2015, p. 109), insofar as the Amiibo literally functions to minimise the discouragement felt by the player when he loses at the game. In fact, after Jack loses a match early on, a competing player consoles him with the following advice: 'he hasn't even levelled up yet – but see, that's the fun part; you'll train [the Amiibo] and do better'. The Amiibo functions to mitigate Jack's feeling of discouragement by making him focus less on the present loss and instead on abstract player statistics that, with proper care and development, will help him succeed in the future. Thus, Jack's feelings of frustration and anger are converted into an ecotechnics of self-care and self-quantification, which ensure he remains enrolled in Nintendo's platform ecosystem, and less likely to 'back out'. This, of course, feeds into the notion of gamer 'credentials' raised earlier. In the advertisement, Jack wins the respect of his sibling's friends by virtue of his gamer 'capital', which he accrues through extensive affective investment in his relationship with the Amiibo.

YouTube Videos and Amiibo Play

Beyond the Amiibo's interface and product advertising, the representation, understanding and use of Amiibos extend into everyday postdigital practices of play, which are accessible in some sense through video content and comments of Amiibo unboxing, review and play posted to YouTube by users. These videos contextualise and visualise different ways in which Amiibos are configured within everyday play and situated within domestic and family media ecologies, in which the complexity and messiness of digitally connected devices, screens and toys unfolds. Nintendo's Amiibo figurines are seen in these videos as exemplary of expanding crossmedia and postdigital infrastructures of play, whilst also pointing to tensions between design intent and acts of appropriation within everyday play spaces and practices.

In a review video posted by the FamilyGamerTV YouTube channel, entitled 'Super Smash Bros & Amiibo Get Toy Tested' (FamilyGamerTV, 2014a), the channel host introduces the newly released Amiibo figurines. The video involves the channel host interviewing and discussing Amiibos with a television games reviewer to explain to viewers how they work within the Nintendo platform and franchise ecosystem, providing demonstrations of game use and describing them in relation to other examples of postdigital toys:

> *Host*: As you play with them, they level up, which means they get stronger. But also, they unlock new moves, so they develop and they grow. But also, you get special items and you feed them to your character. And that gives them more powers and more abilities.
> *Reviewer*: It's almost Tamagotchi-esque, if that's even a word! You have to feed them, look after then, take care of them.
> *Host*: The more you do that, the more time you spend with them, the better they get.
> *Reviewer*: The other thing that really interested meyou're saying that you can play them in more than one game ... so you said super *Super Smash Bros.* and *Mario Kart 8*. So I'm assuming that as Nintendo bring out more games, these will be able to be put into different games. Now that is more interesting, because with *Skylanders* or *Disney Infinity*, you are playing the one game. Say you buy your *Mario*, you know that it's just not finished when they bring out *Super Smash Bros.* You know that you need to keep that, to look after that, because that's going to be useful to you next Christmas when I buy you the next game. So it has that longevity to it ... which all parents want.

The video, then, works as a piece of videogame review and pedagogy, highlighting the affective attachments or 'ecotechnics of care' that Amiibos engender through their cross-platform and software affordances for personalising player data and history, whilst also explaining how they operate by making connections to other familiar postdigital toys, like *Skylanders* figurines, and going further back, Tamagotchi. Such connections establish a legacy of digital toy play, whilst simultaneously attempting to overcome the affective limitations identified in toys such as Tamagotchis, which were critiqued for materialising 'disposable love' and therefore degraded ecotechnic relations of care (Bloch & Lemish, 1999; Turkle, 2011). *Skylanders* is an essential reference here, because it was the first franchise to popularise crossmedia NFC toys. Many children and parents are familiar with the *Skylanders* franchise, which released a multiplatform game and associated figures annually from 2011 to 2017.

In a separate video from the FamilyGamerTV YouTube channel, entitled 'Brothers and Sisters Play Super Smash Bros. & Amiibo Wii U' (FamilyGamerTV, 2014b), the channel host—clearly operating more in his role as a father—demonstrates the intergenerational pedagogy that is tied into the use of Amiibo figurines. He presents his three children with three Amiibos and asks them to identify them: Mario, Link and Pikachu. This is followed by a short lesson on the nomenclature of *Legend of Zelda*, carefully explaining the difference between the titular Zelda and the protagonist Link, in order to clarify the name of the Amiibo that one of his children is using. Nevertheless, this confusion continues throughout the video.

The parent/host then turns to the more practical matters of showing and teaching the children how to use the Amiibos with *Super Smash Bros.* for *Wii U* and *Mario Kart 8* (Nintendo EAD, 2014). The adult focuses particularly on the more nuanced engagement that Amiibos have *with Super Smash Bros.* for *Wii U*. In doing so, he appears to be fostering his children's data literacy by explaining how storing data will allow them to 'train' and 'level up' the Amiibo character for use as what Nintendo (2014a) calls 'your alter ego, partner, or rival' in *Super Smash Bros.* for *Wii U*. The levelling up creates scope for customisation of the Amiibo, which means that the children have to make decisions about how to develop their Amiibos as soon as they have registered the figurines on *Super Smash Bros.* for *Wii U.* Then, the host/parent gets his children to play Mario Kart, where the Amiibos unlock franchise-specific wearable content for the Mii drivers of vehicles in the game, allowing players to customise their appearance (e.g. by wearing a Yoshi-themed green and white helmet). The host reflects with his children on his initial comparison with *Skylanders* and points out how their integration into multiple games makes Amiibos distinct.

Throughout the video, the host comments on the toy-like elements of Amiibos, and how his children interact with them as toys, which he regards as a positive element of Amiibos: 'having this physical element to the game that brings them out of the game and into the living room'. His reflections emphasise the 'physicality' of the toy and how this extends the interface: 'you have that physical connection between the on-screen action and the physical toy', and attachment to the franchise/brand: 'there's that real connection created between the on-screen character and the physical Mario toy'. His comments also suggest that the interface envelope is permeable. Towards the end of the video, he discusses some footage of his children playing *Super Smash Bros.* for *Wii U*, noting that: 'with Tom playing in the background, Ollie's just happy to have that link character in his hand and treats it much like he would any other toy'. Not only does the physicality of the Amiibo create new opportunities for play, within practices of 'turn-taking' in social screen-based play (see Apperley, 2010), but it also means that it can be removed from the screen environment, only to be later reincorporated. This latter possibility is noted positively by the video host: '[the Amiibo] gives him a reason to do stuff away from the screen'.

It is conceivable, then, that crossmedia play with Amiibo toys can move outside the branded world of the franchise and into the messy reality of children's everyday play worlds, where data are less reliably tracked. In fact, the interface envelope established by the Amiibo facilitates the movement between these two forms of play, which are not necessarily understood as 'separate' as children recruit different objects into their play practice and imbue them with new significance outside of their everyday context (Benjamin, 1999, p. 390). While the way that the physical characteristics of the Amiibo facilitate this shift between spheres of play is noted clearly by the presenter of FamilyGamerTV, Nintendo's official position is that Nintendo's goal for Amiibos is to use them to 'tie' people 'back to the game experience' (Peckham, 2015, n.p.) and 'to forge a better connection between gameplay and Amiibo itself' (Peckham, 2017, n.p.). In the aforementioned video, for example, the parent describes how his child fostered an attachment to the figurine much like any other toy, which seemed to occur independently of the software or platform (FamilyGamerTV, 2014b). Many children are also more interested in the figurines as collectors' items rather than objects that augment the experience of Nintendo software. Nintendo's president, Tatsumi Kimishima, has openly stated that this is a 'challenge' for the company to overcome, as their main intention for the figurines is to create a more fully integrated media ecosystem that cuts across the physical and the digital, rather than a 'regular' line of toys that children can collect and play with (Peckham, 2015, n.p; 2017, n.p.). For Kimishima (Peckham, 2015, n.p.), Nintendo's aim with the Amiibos is to 'tie [the Amiibo experience] back to the game experience, and then we're creating a stronger connection with general knowledge of our IP and that fun experience they have'.

In the second video, the crossmedia element is speculated as leading to a deeper 'affective investment' in the Amiibo figure, as it has a 'life' beyond individual gameplay, software or hardware. This affective investment in the Amiibo is created by the open-ended sequence of gamified and affectively constructed acts of data exchange. These data exchanges enact an ecotechnics of care, in which the process of caring for the Amiibo enhances the child's gaming experience. There is a clear tangible benefit to Amiibo play by enacting this data exchange. But there is also a palpable experience of personal data produced through Amiibo play—it is made meaningful through such everyday contexts (Pink et al., 2017), in which data are sensed or 'felt' (Lupton, 2017) through their storage within the embodied materiality of the figurine and transmission into gameplay personalisation and progression. These data are personal insofar as they record player statistics and behaviour, rather than identifiable personal information. Nonetheless, the Amiibo offers a possibility for young children to gain a sense or understanding of personal data and data exchange within the context of crossmedia play. The process through which young people develop a rich and informed understanding of everyday data exchange is an underexplored area of digital literacy. Amiibos and the Nintendo crossmedia system imply an ostensibly 'safe' and bounded circuit for data exchange. Given that Nintendo is a seemingly 'trusted' brand, and there are no personally identifiable information in the data, parents appear to be comfortable with letting their children engage in the datafied play guided by the prompts from the software and hardware. In this respect, Amiibos offer children access to basic data literacies in an informal context.

Data literacy competencies are often difficult for young people to informally acquire, and they are often shaped by the more deliberate and didactic pedagogies of families and schools with their emphasis on security and safety, in which data exchange is seen as a risk. In one sense, play may normalise data exchange, but the Amiibo crossmedia system also makes these often-invisible exchanges explicitly tangible by demanding a haptic engagement. Rather than being a configuration of settings on the software interface, Amiibos require the coordination of hand, toy and device to produce data exchange, foregrounding it as an activity by making it a momentary focus within a game, rather than relegating data exchange to a more invisible or ambient experience (Hjorth & Richardson, 2014). However, in another sense, the play ethos and reward system of the Amiibo crossmedia system runs startlingly contra to everyday understandings of the 'risks' associated with the collection and sharing of children's data. As it stands, the enclosed circuits of data exchange of the Amiibo promulgate an informal data pedagogy of assumed safety that may not serve young people as a useful model if deployed in a context where data exchange has wider privacy ramifications. In particular, the relationship of trust, care and reward that shapes the experience of Amiibo use could create vulnerabilities if young people do not also develop a critical and discerning platform-specific understanding of data sharing; to be able to evaluate whom, when and what to share. This highlights the need for more research on the informal data literacies of children; a better understanding of this area could help parents, teachers and policymakers develop a pedagogy of data that supports young people from the safe data exchanges of these kinds of crossmedia ecologies to more connected, risky and data-diverse environments.

Conclusion

Studies of 'postdigital' play have acknowledged that children's play with digital media is increasingly messy and unpredictable. Postdigital play flexibly accommodates physical and digital experiences, leading to imaginative and potentially transgressive practices that 'cannot necessarily be predicted before they emerge in the process of play' (Jayemanne et al., 2016, p. 51). Internet-enabled toys such as Nintendo's Amiibos can be seen in a similar light; however, they also point to recent developments in videogame interfaces wherein the 'messiness' of postdigital play is spatially co-opted and accounted for. In this chapter, we have argued for a need in digital games research and crossmedia studies to account for this reciprocal dynamic.

Our analysis of Nintendo's commercial ambitions for the Amiibo—which are laid bare in the advertisements, the in-game content and the interfacing techniques involved in Amiibo play—reveals that postdigital forms of play are often reincorporated into a branded environment. Amiibos naturalise the process of data collection, generation and sharing. They expand Nintendo's interface 'envelope' to encompass physical activities that would normally go unnoticed or 'uncaptured' by traditional videogame hardware or software. Amiibos facilitate an 'eco-technics of care', wherein the difference between success and failure in videogame play is a product of the amount of 'care' one invests in one's Amiibo toy. By extension, Amiibos also suggest that one's personal data can be endlessly groomed to better accommodate individual tastes and desires, thereby inculcating children in a digital environment where self-governance is mediated through 'user-friendly' software (Chun, 2011). Crucially, these interface 'effects' take place in familiar environments for children—in physical play spaces, with toys and IPs that children recognise, trust and personally connect with.

However, our analysis of YouTube videos suggests that children often appropriate and repurpose branded IoT products into everyday play practices. Nintendo explicitly acknowledges the 'challenge' of getting children to treat Amiibos as more than just a 'regular' line of toys; to encourage children to develop the necessary connections between software, IP, data and 'fun'. Interestingly, however, when conducting our YouTube search for videos of children playing with and using Amiibo toys, the majority of videos we encountered portrayed children participating in very prescriptive modes of play. Granted, this could be an effect of the YouTube platform and the types of videos users seek to create, which are now less vernacular and more professionalised (Nansen & Nicoll, 2017). It could also be an effect of parental mediation, in that parents often feature in the videos and provide instructions to children about the 'right' way to play with the toys. However, children in these videos often follow Nintendo's instructions for their Amiibos quite closely and only rarely play in unintended or unpredictable ways. In a sense, perhaps this illustrates that Nintendo's commercial ambitions for the Amiibo—which have been repeatedly emphasised in advertisements and in-game content—are slowly filtering into the ostensibly 'messy' world of children's postdigital play.

Ultimately, Amiibo and other toys-to-life figurines imply that sharing data is a fun and rewarding play experience. This suggests a need for a better understanding of how toys that involve the storage and transfer of personal data are experienced and understood by children, and how such playful data practices may translate into wider values and norms of data sharing. While Amiibo data transfer takes place in a playful environment, characterised by trusted iconic figures and multiple small rewards, we need to consider the broader implications of such mundane postdigital play data for shaping children's data literacies.

Acknowledgements This work was supported through funding from the Australian Research Council (ARC): Discovery Early Career Researcher Award grant DE13010073 and Discovery Project grant DP140101503.

References

Aarsand, P., & Aronsson, K. (2009). Computer gaming and territorial negotiations in family life. *Childhood, 16*(4), 497–517. https://doi.org/10.1177/0907568209343879.

Apperley, T. (2010). *Gaming rhythms: Play and counterplay from the situated to the global.* Amsterdam: Institute of Network Cultures.

Apperley, T., & Jayemanne, D. (2012). Game studies' material turn. *Westminster Papers in Communication and Culture, 9*(1), 5–24. https://doi.org/10.16997/wpcc.145.

Apperley, T., Jayemanne, D., & Nansen, B. (2016). Postdigital literacies: Materiality, mobility and the aesthetics of recruitment. In B. Parry, C. Burnett, & G. Merchant (Eds.), *Literacy, media and technology: Past, present and future* (pp. 203–218). New York: Bloomsbury.

Ash, J. (2012). Attention, videogames and the retentional economies of affective amplification. *Theory, Culture & Society, 29*(6), 3–26. https://doi.org/10.1177/0263276412438595.

Ash, J. (2015). *The interface envelope: Gaming, technology, power.* New York: Bloomsbury.

Benjamin, W. (1999). *The arcades project* (H. Eiland & K. McLaughlin, Trans.). Cambridge: Belknap Press.

Berry, D. (2014, June 6). The Post-digital ornament, stunlaw [blog post]. Retrieved from http://stunlaw.blogspot.com.au/2014/06/the-post-digital-ornament.html.

Berry, D., & Dieter, M. (Eds.). (2015). *Postdigital aesthetics: Art, computation and design.* London: Palgrave Macmillan.

Bloch, L., & Lemish, D. (1999). Disposable love: The rise and fall of a virtual pet. *New Media & Society, 1*(3), 283–303. https://doi.org/10.1177/14614449922225591.

Chun, W. (2011). *Programmed visions: Software and memory.* Cambridge: MIT Press.

Cramer, F., & Fuller, M. (2008). Interface. In M. Fuller (Ed.), *Software studies: A lexicon* (pp. 149–152). Cambridge: MIT Press.

FamilyGamerTV [FamilyGamerTV]. (2014a, December 3). *Super Smash Bros & Amiibo Get Toy Tested* [video file]. Retrieved from https://www.youtube.com/watch?v=BXzyyHFlFmg.

FamilyGamerTV [FamilyGamerTV]. (2014b, November 28). *Brothers and Sisters Play Super Smash Bros. & Amiibo Wii U* [video file]. Retrieved from https://www.youtube.com/watch?v=oyyFiqOhXoY.

Giddings, S. (2014). *Gameworlds: Virtual media and children's everyday play*. New York: Bloomsbury.

Haddon, L. (2011). Domestication analysis, objects of study, and the centrality of technologies in everyday life. *Canadian Journal of Communication, 36*, 311–323. https://doi.org/10.22230/cjc.2011v36n2a2322.

Hjorth, L., & Richardson, I. (2014). *Gaming in social, locative and mobile media*. London: Palgrave.

Holloway, D., & Green, L. (2016). The internet of toys. *Communication Research and Practice, 2*(4), 506–519. https://doi.org/10.1080/22041451.2016.1266124.

Jayemanne, D., Apperley, T., & Nansen, B. (2016). Postdigital interfaces and the aesthetics of recruitment. *Transactions of the Digital Games Research Association, 2*(3), 145–172. https://doi.org/10.26503/todigra.v2i3.56.

Kinder, M. (1991). *Playing with power in movies, television, and video games: From Muppet Babies to Teenage Mutant Ninja Turtles*. Berkeley: University of California Press.

Kitchin, R., & Dodge, M. (2014). *Code/space: Software and everyday life*. Cambridge: MIT Press.

Kline, S. (1995). *Out of the garden: Toys, TV, and children's culture in the age of marketing*. London: Verso.

Kline, S., Dyer-Witheford, S., & de Peuter, G. (2003). *Digital play: The interaction of technology, culture, and marketing*. Montreal: McGill-Queen's University Press.

Lally, E. (2002). *At home with computers*. Oxford: Berg.

Lash, S., & Lury, C. (2007). *Global culture industry*. Cambridge: Polity.

Lomborg, S., & Mortensen, M. (2017). Users across media: An introduction. *Convergence: International Journal of Research into New Media Technologies, 23*(4), 343–351. https://doi.org/10.1177/1354856517700555.

Lupton, D. (2017). Feeling your data: Touch and making sense of personal data. *New Media & Society, 19*(10), 1599–1614. https://doi.org/10.1177/1461444817717515.

Marsh, J. (2017). The internet of toys: A posthuman and multimodal analysis of connected play. *Teachers College Record, 119*(15), n.p. Retrieved from http://eprints.whiterose.ac.uk/113557/.

Morley, D. (1986). *Family television*. London: Routledge.

Nansen, B., & Nicoll, B. (2017). Toy unboxing videos and the mimetic production of play. In *Proceedings of Annual Conference of the Association of Internet Researchers (AoIR)*.

Nintendo [Nintendo] (2014a, June 10). *Nintendo—Amiibo E3 2014 trailer* [video file]. Retrieved from https://www.youtube.com/watch?v=odUjMhc6 YgU&t=3s.

Nintendo [Nintendo] (2014b, October 23). *Super Smash Bros. Gameplay & Quest for the Amiibo!* [video file]. Retrieved from https://www.youtube.com/ watch?v=C3c_JDDp99k&t=114s.

Peckham, M. (2015, December 3). Exclusive: Nintendo's new president on the icon's future. *TIME,* n.p. Retrieved from http://time.com/4129171/ nintendo-tatsumi-kimishima/.

Peckham, M. (2017, February 7). 19 things Nintendo's president told us about switch and more. *TIME,* n.p. Retrieved from http://time.com/4662446/ nintendo-president-switch-interview/.

Pink, S., Sumartojo, S., Lupton, D., & Heyes La Bond, C. (2017). Mundane data: The routines, contingencies and accomplishments of digital living. *Big Data & Society, 4*(1), 1–12. https://doi.org/10.1177/2053951717700924.

Silverstone, R., & Hirsch, E. (Eds.). (1992). *Consuming technologies: Media and information in domestic spaces.* London: Routledge.

Turkle, S. (2011). *Alone together.* New York: Basic Books.

Gameography

Bandai Namco Games, & Sora Ltd. (2014). *Super Smash Bros.* for *Wii U* [videogame]. Nintendo Wii U: Nintendo.

Nintendo. (2015). *Amiibo Touch & Play: Nintendo Classics Highlights* [videogame]. Nintendo Wii U: Nintendo.

Nintendo EAD. (2014). *Mario Kart 8* [videogame]. Nintendo Switch: Nintendo.

Nintendo EPD. (2017). *Splatoon 2* [videogame]. Nintendo Switch: Nintendo.

Nintendo R&D3. (1987). *Punch-Out!!* [videogame]. Family Computer Disk System [Nintendo Entertainment System]: Nintendo.

Nintendo R&D4. (1986). *The Legend of Zelda* [videogame]. Family Computer Disk System [Nintendo Entertainment System]: Nintendo.

Part II
Domesticating the Internet of Toys: Practices and Contexts

6

The Domestication of Smart Toys: Perceptions and Practices of Young Children and Their Parents

Rita Brito, Patrícia Dias and Gabriela Oliveira

Introduction

In our fast-evolving, tech-savvy and hyperconnected society, along with many other products and services, toys are becoming smarter. The Internet of Toys (IoToys) is an emergent and growing new category of phygital products (combining physical items with digital interfaces and content) (Llorente & Cuenca, 2017). It is important to mention that there are different conceptualizations of "smart toy" in the literature, and underlying assumptions and debates. In our study, we adopted the model presented by Mascheroni and Holloway (2017), which highlights as defining features the Internet connection and the embedding of

An earlier version of this work was published in the *British Journal of Educational Technology*.

R. Brito
Polytechnic Institute of Lisbon, Lisbon, Portugal

P. Dias (✉) · G. Oliveira
Catholic University of Portugal, Lisbon, Portugal
e-mail: pdias@fch.lisboa.ucp.pt

© The Author(s) 2019
G. Mascheroni and D. Holloway (eds.), *The Internet of Toys*,
Studies in Childhood and Youth, https://doi.org/10.1007/978-3-030-10898-4_6

sensors and self-learning algorithms that afford human interaction with children or other toys.

These new types of toys are entering the homes of contemporary families, which are already heavily mediatized (Hepp & Krotz, 2014). Contemporary children have been described as the touch-screen generation (Rosin, 2013) or "digitods" (Holloway, Green, & Stevenson, 2015), the first generation to be exposed to digital media since birth, and they start using them at a very young age, with no reference to predigital times (Marsh, 2005; Plowman, McPake, & Stephen, 2008).

Recent research into the use of digital technologies by young children has revealed that parents, the main mediators of digital media (Nikken & Jansz, 2014; Plowman et al., 2008), are navigating uncharted territory. Being frequent users of digital media themselves, they are the first generation of parents confronted with doubts about the risks and opportunities of the Internet for children (Chaudron et al., 2015), and particularly smart toys (Chaudron et al., 2017; Mascheroni & Holloway, 2017).

The Domestication Approach

The domestication approach is a relevant framework for understanding how families are adopting smart toys and integrating them into their daily practices, as "For twenty-five years, a domestication of technology approach has offered a fertile approach for the study of technologies in family contexts" (Holloway & Green, 2017, p. 16). Initially proposed in the 1990s (Silverstone & Haddon, 1996; Silverstone & Hirsch, 1992), it has developed and been applied to several digital media (e.g. Chambers, 2016; Haddon, 2006; Katz & Aakhus, 2002; Ling, 2004; Reuver, Nikou, & Bouwman, 2016). According to the domestication approach, the adoption and integration of technology into daily life in an ongoing process that results from a mutual shaping of the affordances of technology and of the social context (Haddon, 2011). In addition, it highlights the construction and negotiation of meaning, how this is affected by and affects the sociocultural context, and how it results in specific impacts on family relations and daily practices (Holloway & Green, 2017).

The domestication approach has been applied to the study and understanding of mobile devices, emphasizing their symbolic dimension (Ling, 2004), due to their personal and connected nature. There is a close relationship between mobile phones—currently smartphones—and their users, as they are always turned on and at hand. Also, they are personalizable, as users shape and tailor them to reflect their preferences, lifestyle and even identity. Also, these devices represent the possibility of "perpetual contact" (Katz & Aakhus, 2002) with the ones we love the most and are repositories of significant content, such as photos and messages. Mobile phones are, thus, affective technologies (Vincent, 2006). Smart toys, because of their human-like interaction affordance, are also likely to become objects of affective connection and to foster learning (Chen, Liao, Chien, & Chan, 2011).

Thus, the domestication approach conceives the adoption and appropriation of technology as an interactive and dynamic process that includes the materiality of technology itself, but also the social and cultural dimensions of a household (including the relationships between its members) and the symbolic meanings they attribute to technologies and usage practices (Silverstone & Haddon, 1996). It has four general stages (which are, however, not necessarily linear and may be renegotiated in re-domestication processes) (Berker, Hartmann, Punie, & Ward, 2006; Haddon, 2011; Silverstone & Hirsch, 1992):

1. appropriation, including perceptions, negotiations and choices concerning the purchase and adoption of a technology;
2. objectification, when the technology is integrated into the space and aesthetics of the home and also inti particular use practices and routines (thus being defined by its functionality but also gaining meaning);
3. incorporation, when users and the domestic context change due to the inclusion of the new technology, and this technology starts blurring into the background as it becomes familiar and taken for granted; and

4. conversion, when particular use practices become incorporated into the identity of users and into the dynamics of households, resulting in emerging market trends, and thus influencing subsequent technological development and innovation.

In our research, we use the domestication approach and its several stages to map how smart toys are entering the home (who is making the purchasing decisions, how and why), how they are being perceived by different family members and how they are impacting on play practices and family life.

Parental Mediation and the Importance of Perceptions

When it comes to young children (under 8) and digital media, parents play a key role as mediators (Kucirnova & Sakr, 2015; Plowman et al., 2008). At such ages, parents tend to determine or monitor not only access to the devices, but also the digital practices of children who, in their explorations and learning, often mimic their parents or ask them for help. In addition, it is usually parents that first "present" digital technologies to children, thus shaping their adoption, and children look up at them as examples and role models, tending to mimic their practices and preferences (Connell, Lauricella, & Wartella, 2015). There are different models of parental mediation styles (e.g. Nikken & Jansz, 2014; Valcke, Bonte, Wener, & Rots, 2010; Valkenburg, 2002), which Livingstone et al. (2017) grouped into two main sets of parental mediation patterns: "enabling" parents tend to "support" and "instruct" children's digital practices, thus teaching and helping them to overcome difficulties; while "restrictive" parents tend to "control" and "restrict" their digital practices.

According to Valcke et al. (2010), the authoritative parental mediation style is the most frequent when it comes to digital media, combining high parental control (including supervising and restricting) with high parental warmth (participating, supporting, co-using, teaching). Chaudron et al. (2015) found similar results in their European-scale comparative study. Some rules are common in many homes, such as only being allowed to play after finishing homework and not being allowed to play for long periods of time or just before bedtime (Dias & Brito, 2016). Parental control focuses more on screen-time than on content (Wang, Kuo, King, & Chang, 2010).

Previous research on the parental mediation of digital technologies has revealed that the perceptions and attitudes of parents towards digital media have a significant influence on the mediation style adopted (Livingstone et al., 2015; Valcke et al., 2010). Parents with positive perceptions and attitudes are more likely to adopt enabling parental mediation styles, acting as scaffolders for the development of digital (and others) skills in children, while parents with negative perceptions and views about digital media are more likely to monitor, restrict and limit the digital practices of children (Livingstone et al., 2017; Nikken & Jansz, 2014). Also, research shows that perceptions and attitudes are interwoven with experiences, as parents who have higher education, higher incomes and are intense and skilled users of digital media themselves are more likely to have positive views (Brito, Francisco, Dias, & Chaudron, 2017; Dias et al., 2016; Livingstone et al., 2015).

The Adoption of Smart Toys

Prior to domestication, there is a decision to adopt a certain technology. The concepts of consumer journey and consumer decision-making provide interesting insights for exploring the adoption of smart toys (Kotler, Kartajaya, & Setiawan, 2017). Toys, in general, target a double public: children and parents. Children are the users of toys, but the decision to purchase them or not is usually up to the parents. However, most advertising of toys is directed at children, so they act as influencers by expressing their preferences and wishes to parents. The expressions "pester power" and "nag factor" are used in the marketing literature to describe the effectiveness of the influence exerted by children (Lawlor & Prothero, 2011). A study by Mitskavets (2015) revealed that parents are more vulnerable to pester power, as they nurture closer and open relationships with their children. On the other hand, because of their contact with digital media, children are more informed and start to influence decisions about all types of consumer goods, not just toys and food. Also, children are more impatient and eager for new consumption. Parents are more or less resistant to pester power, depending on the object of desire, its affordability for the family, and to what extent it is considered beneficial for the child by the parents. Thus, this dynamic between children and parents as counterparties of consumer choices is a relevant perspective for exploring the adoption of smart toys.

Methodology

We conducted an exploratory study following an interpretivist approach (Charmaz, 2004).

We addressed the following research questions, related to the different stages of domestication:

1. Who, in the home, decides on the adoption (purchase) of smart toys and why? (appropriation);
2. How are smart toys perceived by parents and children? (appropriation and objectification);
3. How are smart toys used in the home, and how are that affecting family life and the play practices of young children? (objectification and incorporation); and
4. Is it possible to identify emergent patterns and trends concerning the domestication of smart toys? (conversion).

For our study, we selected a purposive sample, which aims to be representative of the themes being studied, instead of the population it refers to (Charmaz, 2004; Ray, 2012). Thus, we looked for families with young children (under 8) who owned smart toys and searched for variety in the following criteria:

- Gender of the child(ren);
- Diversity of family composition (including divorced parents, older and younger siblings, no siblings);
- Geographical diversity;

- Income and education of the parents;
- Penetration of digital media in the home.

After some initial recruitment contacts, using our personal networks and also schools, kindergartens and parishes, we concluded that there were very few families who owned smart toys. Thus, we decided to focus on medium–high income families, where the children used digital media daily, as these were more likely to own smart toys. We also decided to set the upper age limit to 10 years old and to adopt a broad definition of "smart toy". The visits took place between November 2016 and March 2017. We interviewed a total of 21 families, 11 from the Lisbon metropolitan area and 10 from the Oporto metropolitan area, in Portugal. Table 6.1 presents a detailed description of our sample.

We adapted the research protocol from the project "Young Children (0–8) and Digital Technologies" (Chaudron et al., 2015), thus combining interviews, activities and participant observation (Denscombe, 2007). Also, we developed activities to conduct with the parents and children separately. They were designed to collect relevant information, to validate the data collected using triangulation of methods and prevent parents from influencing the spontaneous participation of children and to motivate children to participate and make them more at ease (Mukherji & Albon, 2010).

Our visits to the homes were structured as four moments:

i. Introduction and presentation of the study (5–10 minutes): Presentation, explanations about our research and signing of consent forms.
ii. Ice-breaker activities (20–30 minutes): One of the researchers interviewed the parents in the living room while the other interviewed the child(ren) in the bedroom. With the children, we used sets of app icons and emojis and asked them to pair the apps that they had already used with how they made them feel. With the parents, we gave them a set of keywords (boring, anti-social, risky, family fun, with mum, with dad, curious, challenge, difficult, discussion, distraction, fun, educational, explore together, easy, informative, interesting, annoying, necessary, need skills, social,

Table 6.1 Socio-demographic information about the families which participated in the study[a]

Family	Members	Income	Age	Education	Occupation of parents
F1	Joana	High	40	Degree	Computer engineer
	António		40	Master	Speech therapist
	Edgar		8	Primary	
	Maria		**6**	**Primary**	
F2	Telmo	Medium	43	Degree	Civil engineer
	Francisca		40	Degree	Notary's helper
	José		**8**	**Primary**	
F3	Vasco	Low	41	Degree	Tech consultant
	Cristina		40	Degree	Export manager
	Madalena		**6**	**Primary**	
F4	Luís	High	39	Degree	Entrepreneur
	Mariana		38	Degree	Housekeeper
	Armanda		**8**	**Primary**	
F5	Isabel	High	41	Degree	Economist
	Adriana		38	Master	Manager
	Mónica		8	Primary	
	Bárbara		**6**	**Primary**	
	Marco		3	Kindergarten	
F6	Mateus	Low	38	Degree	Nurse
	Sónia		36	Secondary	Shop assistant
	Afonso		**8**	**Primary**	
	Xavier		3	Kindergarten	
F7	Daniel	Medium	40	Degree	Teacher
	Rosa		39	Degree	Teacher
	Joaquim		8	Primary	
	Bernardo		**5**	**Primary**	
F8	Vasco	High	45	Degree	Manager
	Sandra		42	Degree	Project manager
	Pedro		11	Primary	
	Manuel		**5**	**Kindergarten**	
F9	Bruno	Medium	45	Degree	–
	Nádia		43	Degree	Project manager
	Rodrigo		10	Secondary	
	Teresa		**6**	**Primary**	
F10	Oscar	Medium	40	Degree	Teacher
	Patrícia		39	Degree	Teacher
	André		8	Primary	
	Diogo		**5**	**Kindergarten**	
F11	Gonçalo	High	43	Degree	Biologist
	Carmo		42	Degree	Biologist
	Tiago		**8**	**Primary**	

(continued)

Table 6.1 (continued)

Family	Members	Income	Age	Education	Occupation of parents
F12	Soraia	Medium	37	Degree	Auditor
	César		7	Primary	
	Paulo		4	**Kindergarten**	
F13	Guilherme	Low	35	Secondary	Wine seller
	Lara		33	Degree	Unemployed
	Alice		6	**Primary**	
F14	Emília	Low	36	Ph.D.	Kindergarten teacher
	Fernando		8	**Primary**	
F15	David	Medium	36	Degree	Technology consultant
	Matilde		40	Degree	Product manager in
	Fátima		8	**Primary**	communications
F16	Ricardo	Medium	40	Degree	Consultant
	Inês		40	Degree	Consultant
	Marcelo		8	Primary	
	Nuno		4	**Kindergarten**	
F17	Joaquim	Low	39	Secondary	Plumber and fireman
	Sofia		29	Secondary	Unemployed
	Margarida		10	Primary	
	Adriano		8	Primary	
	Sebastião		7	**Primary**	
	Benjamim		3	Kindergarten	
	Jorge		1	-	
	Bianca		1	-	
F18	Bárbara	Low	42	Secondary	Health assistant
	Renato		8	**Primary**	
F19	Inês	Medium	43	Degree	Civil engineering
	Ricardo		39	Degree	Civil engineering
	Vicente		7	**Primary**	
	Tomás		2	-	
F20	Camila	Medium	36	Degree	Anatomical pathology
	Mafalda		8	**Primary**	technique
F21	José	High	60	Degree	Dentist
	Luciana		43	Degree	Psychologist
	Alda		8	**Primary**	

[a]*Notes* The children that were the focus of our research are signaled in bold; all the information included on this table was given by the families

solitude, tension, useful and addictive) and asked them to choose the ones that they associated with digital technologies, along with a brief explanation.

iii. Semi-structured interviews (20–30 minutes): We interviewed the parents and children separately, and we focused specifically on smart toys. We asked parents about their perceptions and opinions, about adoption decisions, and about the integration of smart toys into the routines of the family. We asked children about which smart toys they knew, owned or would like to have. We provided cardboard images of popular smart toys on the Portuguese market[1] and asked the children to mark them with coloured post-its according to these categories: green for "I own one"; pink for "I know it and I would like to have one"; yellow for "I know it but I wouldn't like to have one"; blue for "I don't know it". We used this game to explore the perceptions of the children, their interactions with their parents about buying decisions, and how they integrate smart toys into their daily play.

iv. Finalizing (10–15 minutes): Thanking the families for their participation.

A few months after the visits, we made follow-up phone calls to the families who owned smart toys (F1, F2, F4, F13 and F19), in April 2018. During these calls, we talked to one of the parents and to the children separately, and we asked them about their practices with their smart toys.

The audio of the interviews and phone calls was recorded and fully transcribed. The participants were anonymized using a coding system based on aliases. We applied thematic analysis to the transcripts, building categories from a preliminary reading of the interviews in order to discover patterns and development of themes, and also based on the theoretical framework presented and our research questions (Boyatzis, 1998). We worked with QSR NVivo 11 Plus software for Windows.

Findings and Discussion

Perceptions of Digital Media and of Smart Toys

As previous research shows (e.g. Chaudron et al., 2015; Dias & Brito, 2016, 2017), parents have mixed perceptions of digital technologies in general. This is relevant to our research because parents' general perceptions of digital technologies tend to be reflected in their particular views of smart toys.

Regarding positive views, our interviews revealed that parents value the educational benefits of digital media. They are considered useful for researching for school and some families get together to carry out school projects using digital resources. Technologies are also seen as an asset for learning English and programming. In addition, parents recognize that we live in a digital society that children are naturally immersed in technology and feel it is impossible to go back. Parents report that digital media stimulate children cognitively. In games, children have to use several senses and motor coordination, and also logical and strategic thinking.

Negative perceptions mainly focus on addiction and anti-socialization, whereby children, when playing digital games, alienate themselves from family members, not paying attention to them, and these situations are sometimes the subject of family discussions. Parents also have fears, such as children having access to inappropriate content (e.g. violent and explicit language videos on YouTube) and contact with strangers.

However, most parents see digital as an intrinsic and inevitable feature of contemporaneity and believe in a balance of all activities—watching TV, playing digital games, running outdoors or playing games—as negative outcomes may result from excesses.

These mixed feelings are somewhat reflected in smart toys, although most parents admit to not being very well informed, not finding them appealing and not being inclined to buy them for their children.

> *Daniel (F7, father)*: I don't know such toys, and very proudly!
> *Soraia (F12, mother)*: I am not very familiar with such toys…
> *César (F12, father)*: I didn't even know those interactive stuffed animals existed!

Most families identify as smart toys technological devices such as tablets, consoles, watches, cameras and even smartphones that are marketed to children or belong to children. Tablets and consoles existed in most homes, the other devices were less frequently found: we found Toys-to-Life (Invizimals and Super Mario) in the homes of families F1 and F2, we found a drone, a smartwatch and Emilio with family F4, we found a Hatchimal with family F13 and we found a drone with family F19. Other parents justified this absence by arguing that children already use technology for long enough and do not intend to further stimulate such use.

> *I*: Do you ever think of offering him something like this?
> *Camila (F20, mother)*: No, let her be happy and ignorant about it.
> *I*: In the near future do you think you will invest in this type of toy?
> *Sónia (F6, mother)*: Only if he asks because we strongly encourage physical contact, the reality and not so much the virtual world. In fact, this Christmas he asked for a Playstation 3 but we still gave him Monopoly because in the previous year he had asked for PlayStation vita, then PlayStation 3 and I started to think I should take it easy. I opted for a game where everyone could play, more didactic.

Parents are curious about the educational potential of smart toys, mentioning interest in complex and stimulating play for their children, which scaffolds the development of different skills, such as problem-solving or coding.

> *Nádia (F9, mother)*: I think it is very interesting. The idea, the concept, it might develop other skills in them. Anyway, these toys are part of the development of our society, and there is no use in rowing against the tide. We had better find the advantages.

However, parents are also nostalgic about non-digital play and fear that children might become isolated or underdevelop their social skills and creativity, consistent with the notion of adults idealising their childhood, as presented in Media Panics literature (Drotner, 1999).

> *Camila (F20, mother)*: I think that the most technologically advanced toys deprive children of their creativity and of contact with other children. Back in our day, we played outdoors with our neighbours, and we had to be creative!
> *Luciana (F21, mother)*: These smart toys can be a bit restrictive for their imagination and fantasy.

Also, they are reluctant to invest in expensive toys, as they describe children as avid consumers, devoting little time to toys and promptly asking them for the "next big thing", as reported by Mitskavets (2015). Parents did not mention fearing (or being aware of) risks such as privacy invasion and commercial exploitation (Mascheroni & Holloway, 2017).

On the other hand, children are very informed about the newest toys on the market and the most popular toys in their peer groups, but they are not particularly captivated by the features of smart toys such as Internet connectedness, coding or self-learning. The preferences of children mostly depended on gender, on the fictional universes that they enjoy (e.g. princesses or superheroes) and on the individual features of the child. The only exception was robotic pets, which were much desired by the children, particularly by those who were not allowed to have pets. Thus, human-like interaction, or at least pet-like interaction, is the feature of smart toys that children value the most.

So, the children's positive and enthusiastic view contrasts with the parents' more expectant and sceptical perspective.

The Appropriation of Smart Toys

Appropriation refers to the purchase and adoption of technology, and it includes becoming aware of a technological product, developing perceptions and attitudes about it, desiring it, imagining owning it and pondering on a purchase decision (Silverstone & Haddon, 1996; Silverstone & Hirsch, 1992).

Parents report that their children have already asked for smart toys, but claim to be the ones to make the final decision about buying them, thus confirming the traditional roles of children as influencers and parents as decision-makers (Kotler et al., 2017). They complain that children can at times ask insistently for a certain toy, thus acknowledging their "pester power" (Mitskavets, 2015), and they identify TV advertising and peer influence as the main drivers of such insistence.

I: Do you think you will offer her a smart toy in a near future?
Isabel (F5, mother): I guess so ... I can't escape her pressure ... and globalization... [laughter].

However, parents are sceptical about the quality-price ratio, as they consider smart toys excessively expensive and are not sure if children will really make the best use of them or if they will be truly beneficial for them. Some elaborate that they need to consider if the child is going to play with the toy for a long time, if the toy is going to bring the child satisfaction and entertainment, and also if the toy is educational, or if they are going to spend a lot of money on a toy that the child will be bored with after a short time.

> *Cristina (F3, mother)*: They had a smart toy, that was not cheap at all, and it also wasn't as amazing as was expected, and they didn't pay much attention to it...
>
> *Luciana (F21, mother)*: Lara has asked for a smart watch. This type of toy is very expensive and I am not very sure about how useful they are. So I will wait to see if she asks for it for a long time, or if it is just on the spur of the moment. The other day, she played with a smart watch at a friend's house, and after two hours she was tired of it. I am not going to spend that much for her to play for just two hours.

All of the children we interviewed recognized several smart toys depicted in our activity and expressed the desire to have them or at least try them.

> *I*: Do you know any of these? [interviewer shows toys as cardboard images]
>
> *André (F10, age 8)*: This connects to the tablet, doesn't it?
>
> *I*: Yes, do you know it?
>
> *André (F10, age 8)*: I know it but I have never played with it.
>
> [The child recognizes all the smart toys presented on cardboard]
>
> *I*: Ah! You know them all. And do you have any of these?
>
> *Fátima (F15, age 8)*: No, no, no, no, no and no.
>
> *I*: Would you like to?
>
> *Fatima (F15, age 8)*: I would love to have one.

Some parents acknowledged the educational potential of smart toys as a relevant driver for adoption. Most parents stressed the importance of their children's preferences and tastes, and admitted to the possibility of buying a smart toy, even if it was expensive and if they were doubtful about its pedagogical potential, as long as they really believed it would make their child happy.

We found some early adopters of smart toys, but they were scarce (5 in 21 homes), even in homes with high penetration of digital devices and in families with a high income. In these homes, the parents agreed that they decided to acquire them after requests from their children, rather insistent in the case of family F13.

> *Lara (F13, mother)*: She [Alice, F13, age 6] wouldn't shut up about it [asking for a Hatchimal]. Wasn't it? We didn't want to buy it, we found it too expensive, and we were afraid that she would break it.
> *Guilherme (F13, father)*: But then she said that if we gave her a Hatchimal she wouldn't ask us for a cat or a dog anymore…
> *Lara (F13, mother)*: Or a sister… [laughter]
> *Guilherme (F13, father)*: So we bought it. So far, it's working…

The Objectification of Smart Toys

Objectification occurs when new technology is brought into the home, and location, aesthetics, display, use and meaning are negotiated by family members (Silverstone & Haddon, 1996; Silverstone & Hirsch, 1992).

In the case of Toys-to-Life, these are accessories to consoles, so they are usually stored or displayed nearby. We found consoles in 16 of the 21 homes we visited, all displayed in the living room. We only found Toys-to-Life in two of these homes. In family F1, Invizimals toys were stored in a small basket kept on the TV table, next to the console. In family F2, Super Mario characters were stored in a drawer of the TV table, along with console games and remote controls. All the family members associated Toys-to-Life with games and entertainment. In family F1, António (F1, father) played on a console with the older son, Edgar (F1, age 8), namely Grand Theft Auto (GTA) and Call of Duty. But neither of the parents participated in play with the Toys-to-Life. Edgar (F1, age 8) told us that he often played with the Toys-to-Life without using the console, just as regular toys, especially with his sister Maria (F1, age 6), thus revealing the attribution of meaning and the emergence of practices that go beyond the primary affordances of the toy.

Concerning drones, in both families they were adopted with enthusiasm and left abandoned. In family F4, it was stored in the garage, while in family F19 it was kept above the wardrobe, in Vicente's (F19, age 7) room. The children describe their experiences:

> *Armanda (F4, age 8)*: I was excited to try it. I tried to pilot it in the garden, but it was harder than I thought ... I can't control it to take photos or film where I want. Then, I had a hard time transferring the photos and films to my computer. I asked mum for help and she didn't have time. So I got tired of it!
>
> *Vicente (F19, age 7)*: I tried it as soon as I got it, in the living room. It hit the ceiling and it broke, and it also broke my mother's lamp. She was furious! So now I am not allowed to use it inside.

In both cases, children report a lack of intuitiveness in using the toy, which ultimately resulted in negative user experiences and abandonment of the toy.

In the case of toys that afford human-like interaction, we were able to observe incorporation practices.

The Incorporation of Smart Toys

Incorporation is the seamless integration of technological artefacts into the daily routines of the home (Silverstone & Haddon, 1996; Silverstone & Hirsch, 1992).

This is the case of Armanda's (F4, age 8) smartwatch, which she wears every day. She uses it as an alarm clock in the morning, for listening to music; she syncs it with her iPhone in order to get texts, IM messages and calls from her parents and closest friends. She particularly enjoys health and exercise monitoring apps, as she practises acrobatic gymnastics, and she likes to monitor her exercise and health.

In the case of Emilio and the Hatchimal, the children were very familiar with them and were able to show us diverse uses, which they claimed to have learned by exploring on their own. We observed that these toys were integrated into the play practices of the children, although retaining the *status* of "novelty", which is more consistent with objectification than integration (Berker et al., 2006). Nonetheless, we observed that smart toys that afford human-like interaction were able to maintain children's interest for long periods of time, as they committed to nurturing and taking care of such smart toys, creating consistent play routines.

> *Alice (F13, age 6)*: When I get up, I wake up my Hatchimal and I feed her. I take her with me to the bathroom when I am getting ready for school and I talk to her. Now she repeats what I say. I am teaching her, and then she will talk to me. When I get home, she is hungry, so I feed her again. I can only play with Mimi after finishing my homework. Sometimes she gets bored of waiting and falls asleep and then I have to wake her up to play.

Also, children do not express a clear distinction between digital and analogue, or online and offline, as Marsh (2017) describes.

> *Armanda (F4, age 8)*: I use Emilio to record my favourite video clips, I play them on YouTube on my tablet. Then, I carry Emilio around and I can play the songs that I like, and dance.
>
> *Alice (F13, age 6)*: I used my Barbie's bed for Mimi [the Hatchimal], and she sleeps right next to me.

Another interesting observation is that smart toys promote co-use and co-play more than traditional toys. Because they are more complex, children ask their parents for help more often, and parents also become involved in play practices such as taking care of smart pets.

> *Lara (F13, mother)*: Sometimes she asks for my help, to decode the instructions, or when the Hatchimal isn't reacting as she would like. I try to help her, but that toy is new to me too. It's almost as much work as a pet!

Guilherme (F13, father): No, it isn't. You don't have to clean after it and it has an off button. Much better! [laughter]

The Conversion of Smart Toys

In conversion, the technologies become part of the home's routines, they are used to build and express the identity of individuals and influence family dynamics. Also, at this stage, it is possible to identify emergent patterns and trends of domestication, which later influence the subsequent development of the technology (Haddon, 2011; Holloway & Green, 2017).

We only observed some practices related to conversion in family F13. Alice (F13, age 6) perceived her Hatchimal as her pet, and she developed routines for feeding it, grooming it and playing with it. The Hatchimal became part of her identity and is included in family dynamics. Both the parents addressed it as if it was a living being, it has its own improvised bed in the child's room, and it has its place at the family table.

Concerning trends and patterns, the domestication of smart toys is still at a very early stage within our sample, but we observed that, unlike consoles, tablets and smartphones that both children and parents regard as "toys" (Chaudron et al., 2015) or sources of "endless entertainment" (Ofcom, 2017), smart toys are being ascribed meanings that go beyond these categories: taking into account the high price, parents expect an "educational toy" that affords not only entertainment but also learning; for children, the affordances of smart toys appeal to affective meanings, and they describe them as "friend" (Paulo, F12, age 4), "pet" (Alice, F13, age 6), "best friend" (Teresa, F9, age 6) and "buddy" (Bernardo, F7, age 5), and they expect active play from smart toys.

Maria (F1, age 6): I really, really wanted a Furby, but mum says it's too expensive.
I: Why would you like to have a Furby?
Maria (F1, age 6): I wanted a pink Furby and I would name her Mimi. I could teach her to speak, feed her, put her to sleep, and she would play with me.

Conclusion

Our study revealed some interesting insights into how smart toys are being domesticated and showed that this is only happening in a small number of privileged families. Smart toys are being mass-marketed but they are still out of reach, mostly because of the price. Young children are aware of their existence, eager to try them out, and expressed interest in owning them. They perceive them as appealing, mainly because of the human-like interaction that they afford. However, parents do not share this enthusiasm. They mentioned two main barriers to adoption: (a) their perception of the presence of digital media in the lives of their children as already excessive, addictive and harmful to other aspects such as social skills and physical activity and (b) not seeing worth in investment in high-priced toys without being sure that children would play with them for a long time, and benefit from developmental and educational stimulation from them.

As a consequence, smart toys are still at an early stage of the domestication process. In the few homes where we found them, they were regarded as a novelty, although the children revealed expertise in their use. Those early adopter families were not aware of the dangers and risks associated with smart toys, and therefore, they were not taking any care or measures about issues such as privacy or commercial exploitation. This insight points to the importance of promoting the adoption of ethical guidelines by the expanding IoToys industry in order to ensure the protection of children's rights (Livingstone & Third, 2017).

Note

1. We decided to include in our activity pictures of the toys that were featured in all of the Christmas catalogues of the main toy and technology sellers in Portugal: the hypermarkets Continente and Jumbo, ToysRUs and Fnac.

References

Berker, T., Hartmann, M., Punie, Y., & Ward, K. (2006). *Domestication of media and technology*. London: Open University Press.

Boyatzis, R. E. (1998). *Transforming qualitative information: Thematic analysis and code development*. Thousand Oaks, London, and New Delhi: Sage.

Brito, R., Francisco, R., Dias, P., & Chaudron, S. (2017). Family dynamics in digital homes: The role played by parental mediation in young children's digital practices around 14 European countries. *Contemporary Family Therapy, 39*(4), 271–280.

Chambers, D. (2016). *Changing media, homes and households: Cultures, technologies and meanings*. London: Routledge.

Charmaz, K. (2004). Grounded theory. In S. N. Hesse-Biber & P. Leavy (Eds.), *Approaches to qualitative research* (pp. 496–521). New York: Oxford University Press.

Chaudron, S., Beutel, M. E., Černikova, M., Donoso, V., Dreier, M., ... & Wölfling, K. (2015). *Young children (0–8) and digital technology: A qualitative exploratory study across seven countries*. JRC 93239/EUR 27052.

Chaudron, S., Di Gioia, R., Gemo, M., Holloway, D., Marsh, J., Mascheroni, G., ... Yamada-Rice, D. (2017). *Kaleidoscope on the internet of toys—Safety, security, privacy and societal insights*. Retrieved from https://goo.gl/TtuntC.

Chen, Z. H., Liao, C., Chien, T. C., & Chan, T. W. (2011). Animal companions: Fostering children's effort-making by nurturing virtual pets. *British Journal of Educational Technology, 42*(1), 166–180.

Connell, S. L., Lauricella, A. R., & Wartella, E. (2015). Parental co-use of media technology with their young children in the USA. *Journal of Children and Media, 9*, 5–21.

Denscombe, M. (2007). *The good research guide: For small-scale social research projects*. Maidenhead, England and New York: Open University Press.

Dias, P., & Brito, R. (2016). *Crianças (0 a 8 anos) e Tecnologias Digitais*. Lisboa: Universidade Católica Portuguesa. Retrieved from http://hdl.handle.net/10400.14/19160.

Dias, P., & Brito, R. (2017). *Crianças (0 a 8 anos) e Tecnologias Digitais: Que mudanças num ano?* Lisboa: Universidade Católica Portuguesa. Retrieved from http://hdl.handle.net/10400.14/22498.

Dias, P., Brito, R., Ribbens, W., Daniela, L., Rubene, Z., Dreier, M., ... Chaudron, S. (2016). The role of parents in the engagement of young children with digital technologies: Exploring tensions between rights of access and protection, from 'gatekeepers' to 'scaffolders'. *Global Studies of Childhood, 6*(4), 414–427.

Drotner, K. (1999). Dangerous media? Panic discourses and dilemmas of Modernity. *International Journal of the History of Education, 35*(3), 593–619.

Haddon, L. (2006). The contribution of domestication research to in-home computing and media consumption. *The Information Society, 22,* 195–203.

Haddon, L. (2011). Domestication analysis, objects of study, and the centrality of technologies in everyday life. *Canadian Journal of Communication, 36*(2), 311–313.

Hepp, A., & Krotz, F. (Eds.). (2014). *Mediatized worlds: Culture and society in a media age.* London: Palgrave Macmillan.

Holloway, D., & Green, L. (2016). The internet of toys. *Communication Research and Practice, 2*(4), 506–519.

Holloway, D., & Green, L. (2017). Mediated memory making: The virtual family photograph album. *Communications, 44*(3), 351–368.

Holloway, D. J., Green, L., & Stevenson, K. (2015, August). Digitods: Toddlers, touch screens and Australian family life. *M/C Journal, 18*(5). ISSN 14412616. (Special Issue). Available at http://www.journal.media-culture.org.au/index.php/mcjournal/article/viewArticle/1024. Accessed 21 December 2018.

Katz, J., & Aakhus, M. (2002). *Perpetual contact: Mobile communication, private talk, public performance.* Cambridge: Cambridge University Press.

Kotler, P., Kartajaya, H., & Setiawan, I. (2017). *Marketing 4.0: Moving from traditional to digital.* London: Wiley.

Kucirnova, N., & Sakr, M. (2015). Child-father creative text-making at home with crayons, iPad collage and PC. *Thinking Skills and Creativity, 17,* 59–63.

Lawlor, M. A., & Prothero, A. (2011). Pester power: A battle of wills between children and their parents. *Journal of Marketing Management, 27*(5), 551–561.

Ling, R. (2004). *The mobile connection: The cell phone's impact on society.* New York: Morgan Kaufmann.

Livingstone, S., Mascheroni, G., Dreier, M., Chaudron, S., & Lagae, K. (2015). *How parents of young children manage digital devices at home: The role of income, education and parental style.* EU Kids online. Retrieved from https://goo.gl/6rvdhe.

Livingstone, S., Ólafsson, K., Helsper, E., Lupiáñez-Villanueva, F., Veltri, G., & Folkvord, F. (2017). Maximizing opportunities and minimizing risks for children online: The role of digital skills in emerging strategies of parental mediation. *Journal of Communication, 67*(1), 82–105.

Livingstone, S., & Third, A. (2017). Children and young people's rights in the digital age: An emerging agenda. *New Media & Society, 19*(5), 657–670.

Llorente & Cuenca. (2017). *Consumer engagement trends for 2017: The phygital era*. Retrieved from http://www.desarrollando-ideas.com.

Marsh, J. (Ed.). (2005). *Popular culture, new media and digital literacy in early childhood*. London: Psychology Press.

Marsh, J. (2017). The internet of toys: A posthuman and multimodal analysis of connected play. *Teachers College Record, 119*. Retrieved from http://eprints.whiterose.ac.uk/113557/14/38_22073.pdf.

Mascheroni, G., & Holloway, D. (Eds.). (2017). *The internet of toys: A report on media and social discourses around young children and IoToys*. DigiLitEY. Retrieved from https://goo.gl/2C1VsR.

Mitskavets, I. (2015). *Children and teens as influencers*. London: Mintel. Retrieved from https://goo.gl/C9Mkcf.

Mukherji, P., & Albon, D. (2010). *Research methods in early childhood: An introductory guide*. Thousand Oaks, CA: Sage.

Nikken, P., & Jansz, J. (2014). Developing scales to measure parental mediation of young children's internet use. *Learning, Media and Technology, 39*(2), 250–266.

Ofcom. (2017). *Children and parents: Media use and attitudes report*. Retrieved from https://goo.gl/BrmPF2.

Plowman, L., McPake, J., & Stephen, C. (2008). Just picking it up? Young children learning with technology at home. *Cambridge Journal of Education, 38*, 303–319.

Ray, A. (2012). *The methodology of sampling and purposive sampling*. Berlin: Grin Publishing.

Reuver, M., Nikou, S., & Bouwman, H. (2016). Domestication of smartphones and mobile applications: A quantitative mixed-method study. *Mobile Media & Communication, 4*(3), 347–370.

Rosin, H. (2013). The touch-screen generation. *The Atlantic, 20*.

Silverstone, R., & Haddon, L. (1996). Design and the domestication of information and communication technologies: Technical change in everyday life. In R. Silverstone & R. Mansell (Eds.), *Communication by design: The politics of information and communication technologies* (pp. 44–74). Oxford: Oxford University Press.

Silverstone, R., & Hirsch, E. (Eds.). (1992). *Consuming technologies: Media and information in domestic spaces*. London: Routledge.

Valcke, M., Bonte, S., Wener, B., & Rots, I. (2010). Internet parenting styles and the impact on internet use of primary school children. *Computers & Education, 55*(2), 454–464.

Valkenburg, P. (2002). *Beeldschermkinderen: Theorieën over kind en media* [Screen-kids: Theories about children and media]. Amsterdam: Boom.

Vincent, J. (2006). Emotional attachment and mobile phones. *Knowledge, Technology & Policy, 19*(1), 39–44.

Wang, W., Kuo, V., King, C., & Chang, C. (2010). Internet of toys: An e-Pet overview and proposed innovative social toy service platform. *Computer Symposium (ICS)*. Tainan, 16–18 December. Retrieved from https://goo.gl/aR4b89.

7

An Ecological Exploration of the Internet of Toys in Early Childhood Everyday Life

Lorna Arnott, Ioanna Palaiologou and Colette Gray

Introduction

The Internet of Toys (IoToys) are the latest in a long line of technological developments that have permeated children's lives (Mascheroni & Holloway, 2017). Computers and screen-based media no longer monopolise young children's engagement with the Internet; rather, children's tactile toys and artefacts are connecting children to the virtual world. These advances continue to raise questions about the role

L. Arnott (✉)
University of Strathclyde, Glasgow, Scotland, UK
e-mail: lorna.arnott@strath.ac.uk

I. Palaiologou
University College London, Institute of Education, London, UK
e-mail: i.palaiologou@ucl.ac.uk

C. Gray
Stranmillis University College, Queen's University Belfast, Belfast, Northern Ireland, UK
e-mail: c.gray@stran.ac.uk

© The Author(s) 2019
G. Mascheroni and D. Holloway (eds.), *The Internet of Toys*,
Studies in Childhood and Youth, https://doi.org/10.1007/978-3-030-10898-4_7

of technologies in children's lives, reinvigorating the relevance of Craft's (2013) discussion of childhood in a digital age as either passive/at risk or empowered. Similar to James and Prout's (2015) theory, her focus is on how childhood as a construct is changing rather than on examining how play/learning are changing with the introduction of technology (Marsh et al., 2015; Stephen & Edwards, 2017; Yelland, 2015). It provides a broad, holistic analysis of the notion of child and childhood to underpin this chapter. Thus, here, we seek to understand this image of the child in the broader, socio-ecologically mediated digital world.

Throughout this chapter, the focus is on the importance of children's agency in their use of the IoToys. We think about children's capabilities as part of digitally mediated social worlds. Informed by a socio-ecological model, children's, practitioners' and parents' dispositions help to contextualise the factors that shape children's use of IoToys.

We provide the following key messages throughout the chapter:

1. A discussion of passivity or empowerment as part of children's digital lives with IoToys, in line with Craft's (2013) work.
2. A reanalysis of perceptions of childhood in the digital age, linking to the sociological models of childhood and the role of children as competent and agentic.
3. An account of socio-ecological influences on digital lives, likened to Rogoff's (2008) three planes relating to individual, interpersonal and community, alongside a discussion of how the interpersonal plane can be reimagined to include interactions between child and machine.
4. A note of caution against a passive child agenda and recurrent moral panic.

While previous research has acknowledged that children are part of complex socio-economic and technological systems informed by political factors (e.g. Stephen & Edwards, 2017), few attempts capture the holistic, and often messy or complicated, ecological discussions of childhood. The ecological discussions presented thus far offer Bronfenbrennian-style discussions of children in the virtual world (e.g. Johnson & Puplampu, 2008; Wang, Berson, Jaruszewicz, Hartle, & Rosen, 2010), where clear boundaries of separation are presented between systems. They are useful in helping to identify the main influences driving children's play in the era of IoToys, but we suggest that the child's digital life is not so neatly confined and so evidence of childhood needs to document its messiness. Particularly with the introduction of IoToys—which connect children via the Internet to multiple realms and contexts—children's digital lives cannot be compartmentalised or separated into various systems. Instead, children's digital worlds need to be viewed more holistically, in an inter-connected and inseparable manner, similar to Rogoff's (2008) discussion of inseparable mutually constituting planes in children's learning experiences that correspond to personal, interpersonal and community. Within this messiness, we also need to understand the extent to which children's digital lives are empowered or passive (Craft, 2013).

This chapter addresses this complexity by analysing children's everyday digital lives in connected contexts. We utilise three case studies of children's lived experience with IoToys to provide examples of the child's digitally mediated social worlds. In the case of IoToys, we present some specific contributory factors that help to shape the child's sense of empowerment as well as the ways in which the child is capable of directing and leading their own learning experiences through realising their own power to shape experience. Understanding the dispositions of practitioners, parents and children towards how these artefacts form part of the cultural and agentic context offers a route towards understanding the view of the child as either passive or empowered.

The Study: IoToys, Methodology and Ethics

The project employed 12 empirical case studies of children's digital (and Internet-connected) lives across four countries (England, Scotland, Northern Ireland (NI) and Greece) to investigate:

- Parents' and practitioners' dispositions, attitudes and aptitudes towards children (ages 0–8) engaging with IoToys.
- Ecological factors shaping young children's (ages 0–8) experiences with IoToys.

Across the four data collection countries, IoToys were integrated into varying degrees. Households in England were already equipped with IoToys, but in Scotland, Greece and NI families had few artefacts for observation. As such, a range of IoToys (two hybrid learning games which marry the virtual and physical world, Bluetooth-enabled programmable floor robots and a wireless digital microscope, as well as learning robots) were included in the study. The learning robots were purchased as part of the project and loaned to early childhood settings and families.

Data were collected via a case study, across 25 children at home and their early childhood settings with data spanning five months of a continuing study. While the starting point for data collection was early childhood education settings (ages 3–5) siblings were included in home data (our oldest sibling was 6.5 years old). Data collection included:

- Interviews with parents.
- Interviews with key workers.
- Participant observation of children's play with IoToys in early childhood education (3–5 years).
- Multimedia messages (pictures, videos, short written reflections from parents in consultation with children) of children's play in the home, submitted by parents (extending Plowman and Stevenson's [2012] methodology).
- Photo Voice conversations with children, whereby the multimedia data presented by parents and observation photos were used to stimulate conversations with children.

Our project was guided by key characteristics of participatory research (Groundwater-Smith, Dockett, & Bottrell, 2014). Parents were asked to use technologies in a way that fits with their lifestyle. Children's participation was voluntary; parents were advised that children's lack of engagement was a reasonable finding and not to force participation.

The EECERA Ethical Code of Practice (2015) was followed, approval was granted by the University Ethics Committees and relevant local authorities. The standard consents were sought, including parental, key workers' and managers' written informed consent. The research team were also concerned with nuanced ethical considerations for this project, including:

1. The children's own perceptions of the uses of data from this project, the permanency of data collected and their associated consent.
2. The role of Internet safety in children's play.

Our belief that young children are 'reliable, voluntary' participants in research (Farrell, 2016, p. 226) gave grounds for negotiating consent directly with children. To the best of our ability, we sought to inform children about the project and ensure their awareness of the consequences of their participation. Furthermore, the researchers worked in partnership with parents and key workers to encourage discussion and learning experiences, designed around safe Internet use in order to raise awareness. The preschool safe Internet use policy was employed at all times.

Inductive reasoning was employed and emerging codes were grounded in the data. Although specific a priori codes were not employed in the analysis for this chapter, the researchers' thinking was underpinned by Craft's (2013) conceptualisation of childhood in a digital age; sociological interpretations and constructions of child and childhood (James & Prout, 2015); Rogoff's (2008) three planes of participation, alongside our socio-ecological lens (presented next).

Children as Empowered Agentic Digital Creators in Digitally Mediated Social Worlds

Craft (2013) suggests that in response to questions and concerns about digital childhoods, one of two perspectives can be adopted: the view of children as *passive* or *empowered*. The former suggests that they are at risk from the dangers associated with technologies and that it is the role of adults to protect children from associated harm. Alternatively, the view that children are empowered by increased easy access to technologies suggests that new devices, such as IoToys, are giving them increased opportunities for creative expression.

In essence, Craft detailed the evolution of the Sociology of Childhood in a digital age, yet her conceptualisation has not translated into empirical research approaches for understanding children and technology in education. Two decades ago James, Jenks, and Prout (1998) provided an overview of The Sociological Child, which contributed to a significant shift in research, policy and practice regarding children's agency and competence (Ärlemalm-Hagsér, 2014; Esser, Baader, Betz, & Hungerland, 2016; I'Anson, 2013). Yet, while perceptions of 'child' have moved on considerably over this time, the focus on the agentic child around technology still lacks a research base. Digital childhoods may be the focus of tabloid media—predominantly to wallow over lost childhoods and to 'romanticise the past', as described in Plowman, Stephen, and McPake (2010)—but in research the child as a subset of education or households, and in relation to technology, is presented. We see explorations of how technologies can support children's play (Aldhafeeri, Palaiologou, & Folorunsho, 2016; Edwards & Bird, 2015; Marsh et al., 2015), how children interact in the presence of technologies (Arnott, 2013, 2016) and how technologies are transforming or shaping play (Danby, Davidson, Theobald, Houen, & Thorpe, 2017). With the exception of Craft's (2013) theorisation, however, we know very little about the extent to which digital childhoods are characteristically passive or empowered. Furthermore, in the context of IoToys, we do not know what socio-ecological factors are contributing to children's sense of passivity or empowerment and the impact this has on their identity as a digital child.

This disconnect still occurs because there is still a need to understand children's lives as part of digital social worlds. We build on Arnott's (2016) digital play context and Arnott, Palaiologou, and Gray's (under review) recent work on social ecologies in digital childhoods. We present evidence of children living and learning as part of digitally mediated social worlds, which involve an entanglement of play across digital and non-digital resources. We take the position that IoToys are the latest technological development that encompasses this entanglement of digital and non-digital. Similar to Rogoff's (2008) planes of apprenticeship, guided participation and participatory appropriation, our conceptualisation considers the individual (in the ecology of self), the interpersonal (ecology of exosphere—including interactions with IoToys) and the community (social ecology). We propose that this socio-ecological paradigm is seeking to develop an understanding of empowerment in the context of the entanglement of the digital and the non-digital across social worlds. While we collected data across home and education, we do not present these as separated bounded cases, instead we aim to break down barriers and create synergistic relationships between home and early childhood education that synchronise children's play with the digital social worlds in which we now live. This conceptualisation is visualised in Fig. 7.1.

The premise that underpins this conceptualisation is children's own agentic involvement in their digital lives, what Craft (2013) describes as the empowered child. We know from research that children are capable of such an empowered response to technologies when afforded the opportunities to develop their own agency as part of their play. Arnott's (2016) empirical work provided the grounding for the conceptualisation of nano-systems, whereby the empowered agentic child engages

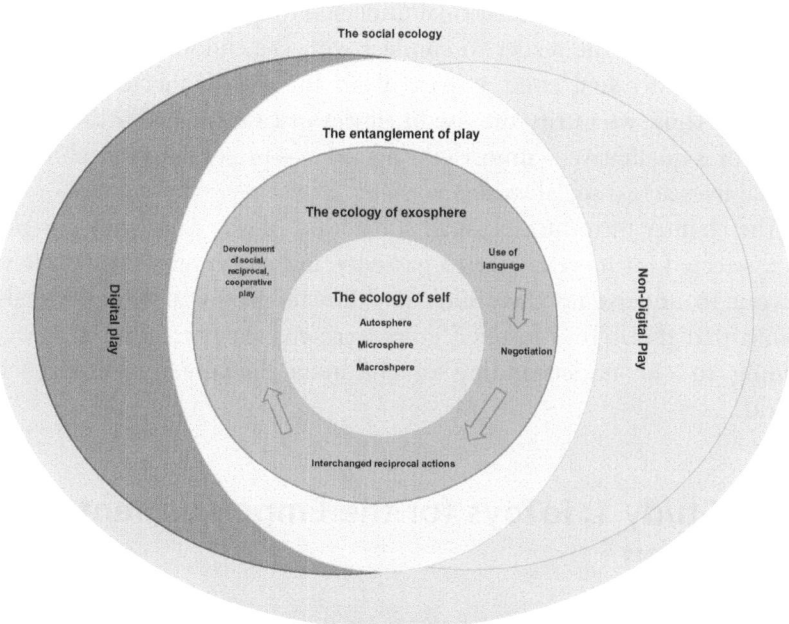

Fig. 7.1 The social ecologies of play in digital lives

in a negotiation process, manoeuvring peers and technologies to direct their own digital play. This process is embedded in an ecological system consisting of agents, cultural contexts and artefacts, which intertwine to contribute to children's digital experiences. Yet, crucially, it suggests that as children engage with their own status as part of the group, position themselves in relation to technology and exhibit tactical behaviours and interactions, they own their digital play (Arnott, 2016).

In the next section, we use the conceptualisation of childhood as either passive or empowered as part of their digitally mediated social world, involving the individual, the interpersonal and the community, to present our empirical data of children's lived experiences with IoToys.

The Lived Experience of Children and IoToys

We present our findings as case studies of children's lived experiences with IoToys to portray a relational understanding of individual children. That is, we want the reader to connect with the children and to understand the individual child as part of an Internet-connected world, in context. Thus, we justify the use of stories or case studies in the importance of a qualitative—almost ethnographic—presentation of children's digital lives across social worlds.

The chapter introduces a small subsection of our data from this project, selected for its relevance to passivity and empowerment. While we set out to understand the child's position in the social world, we also found that the IoToys fostered empowerment for practitioners as well, adding to our understanding of children's digitally mediated social world.

Case Study 1: IoToys for the Empowerment of Children

Case Study 1 demonstrated how technologies may empower children when supportively integrated into the child's world. For example, the case below details how a child who is supported with IoToys is able to overcome a degree of shyness. We see the parent as *facilitator* (Rose & Rogers, 2012) in this learning experience, and she affords him the opportunity to take ownership of the play. Across the child's digitally mediated social world, we then see this ownership transcend into a different physical setting and cultural group (the early childhood setting) in an empowered way.

Case Study 1: Larry Brown and the learning robot

Larry is aged 4. He lives in a relatively affluent area in Central Scotland with his younger brother, Henry (aged 2), his mother Jennifer and his father Peter. We describe the home as a moderately technological household. They have a tablet and a few remote-controlled toys. The parents did not mention any games consoles or more advanced IoToy resources but indicated that Larry loves to operate mechanical or technological household resources (e.g. TV remote control, operating a microwave and unlocking screen-based locks with passwords).

He attends a local childcare setting and has deferred his start at Primary School (an option available to all families in Scotland, when the child's birthday falls in January or February), making him one of the oldest in his setting. The childcare setting describes his family as very engaged with preschool life, with Jennifer regularly attending stay-and-play sessions or engagement events. Despite Larry's mother's active engagement, the staff indicated that prior to the IoToys Project, Larry remained quiet and more reserved in preschool.

Larry's family were loaned a learning robot as their first IoToy for the project. In addition to Larry's interest, Jennifer talked about Henry, saying: 'He loves the learning robot too!' Jennifer took the time to learn how to use the resource in order to support her children's play, as she said: '*I now know how to feed him etc. We couldn't get it to work earlier. Amazing piece of technology. He's currently snoring in his charger!*' The learning robot quickly became a favourite resource. The delight on Larry's face when the learning robot says his name is quite striking (see left side of Fig. 7.2).

Across a 2.5-week period, Jennifer spent a significant amount of time supporting Larry using the learning robot. She sent 24 separate videos of her talking Larry through the process of controlling and operating the learning robot. She facilitated Larry's physical control of the resource, rather than operating the toy for him.

The *progression* in Larry's play with the learning robot became significant. Initially Larry's fascination revolved around observing the tangible learning robot and what he was capable of doing with various blocks. Yet, as the videos progressed, Larry appeared to move on from interacting

Fig. 7.2 Larry and the learning robot

with the learning robot's robotic form, to developing a fascination with manipulating the learning robot's movements using the App on the tablet. For example, Jennifer sent 18 videos of Larry using the App to control the learning robot and 'teach' him to verbally say the names of his family; not just Jennifer, Peter and Henry, but also several cousins and two best friends at preschool. In other videos, Larry is shown practising 'fast' typing and finding this fascinating (see right side of Fig. 7.2).

Over this phase of the project, Larry's confidence and interest in the learning robot grew. This confidence transferred into his life in preschool. The staff talked about their amazement at how Larry appeared to have 'come out of his shell' since beginning the project. After Larry had been loaned the learning robot, the staff facilitated an adult-supported activity with the learning robot involving a small group of children. When reflecting on this task, they talked about Larry's resounding confidence in leading other children in the group, demonstrating to them how the learning robot should be operated, a confidence that was lacking prior to the IoToys project. The staff suggested that the *'responsibility'* of being involved with the project gave Larry this increased confidence. When Jennifer was asked about increased confidence, her response was: *'Definitely! I would agree'*.

As it was time to rotate the IoToy resources that were loaned to the families, Larry was firm and steadfast in indicating his desire to take home the programmable floor robot next...

Larry's empowerment is fostered through relatively informal learning as part of a family or community (Rogoff, 2014), with Larry and Jennifer learning together about the learning robot, alleviating the didactic tendencies of formal teaching. As was the case with earlier Internet technologies, Larry and Jennifer engaged in a trial-and-error approach to understanding the potential of the toy (Plowman, McPake, & Stephen, 2008). What is unique with IoToys is that they are new, not only to children but also to adults, thus creating a sense of learning within digitally mediated social worlds. The power dynamic typically present between adult and child (Laupa, 1994) is somewhat reduced by Jennifer's lack of knowledge about IoToys. In some cases, Larry's expertise outweighed Jennifer's as she described instances where Larry had to teach her what to do with the IoToy. This sense of expertise appeared *empowering* to Larry, shown through his eagerness to direct and teach other children in preschool. Jennifer's willingness to relinquish control and trust her child in his use of the resource supported this empowering movement.

Case Study 2: IoToys for Empowerment of Changes to Practice

In relation to technologies and digital devices, discontinuities between home and education contexts are well established. Plowman et al. (2010) alluded to this several years ago when they talked about how different terminology was used to describe technologies at home and in education, using 'technologies' with parents but 'ICT' with practitioners in the education context (so as to marry up with policy terminology). This divide has only widened since 2010 and now encompasses differences in how technologies are perceived and how uses of technologies are scaffolded and supported.

Research has shown that teachers' uses of digital devices are static and controlling and fail to align with playful pedagogies (Palaiologou, 2016). Thus, we see the fluid integration of technologies in home lives, alongside more static and bureaucratic incorporation of digital technologies in children's early childhood educational ecologies. Edwards, Henderson, Gronn, Scott, and Mirkhil (2017) suggest that the disparities between home and preschool, in terms of technology, are more to do with the differences in purposes behind technology use. With IoToys, however, we begin to see divergence due to infrastructure and practitioner passivity.

In households, fluid integration relates to a lack of restriction and, potentially, looser Internet safety protocols, in comparison with more monitored and governed Internet use in education. These restrictions posed challenges for the integration of technologies; practitioners in this study spoke of slow Wi-Fi and dated hardware, resulting in children getting bored and leaving the activity.

With the introduction of IoToys, this anxiety over integrating technology is compounded because practitioners and parents do not feel knowledgeable about how these resources can be used safely. Two of the four settings in this project refused to use one of the hybrid toys and one preschool refused all the IoToys offered because they did not see what more IoToys could offer compared to traditional toys. For example, one of the teachers said: '*They are glued on screens all day, let them play when they come to preschool and have some free time from screens*'. And another one said: '*I cannot see what these toys add to the real toys we have in the class*'.

From the interviews with the practitioners from these nurseries, it became evident that there was scepticism to include IoToys in their daily activities, and the main concern was that IoToys would not support children's imagination and creativity. They also had concerns about safety; as one teacher said: '*The parents want to know that their children are safe here, so we do not have Internet and no phones are allowed by staff during the day ... we are free of Internet preschool*'. This anxiety not only recreates a passive child agenda but also results in passivity in terms of the adult role in integrating technologies into practice. It widens the divide between children and adults and creates a sense of disconnect within a digitally mediated social world.

In other cases, the tactile adaptive properties of IoToys appeared to alleviate many of these concerns. In one centre, the practitioners' enthusiasm to integrate IoToys into preschool practice paved the way to present a more interconnected digitally mediated social world for children across both home and education. The following case study presents an example of how the integration of IoToys empowered staff's own self-confidence in integrating technologies into their practice.

Case Study 2: Empowering Changes to Practice

Momentum preschool is a small early childhood centre in a relatively affluent area of Central Scotland; they cater for a maximum of 60 children at
any one time. While this may seem like a lot of children, it is relatively
small in comparison with new purpose-built Early Learning and Family
Centres that are emerging across Scotland that cater for around 90 children, expanding to 180 after the early childhood expansion in 2020.
Momentum preschool consists of three smallish rooms, creating a cosy
environment.

The staff were enthusiastic about opportunities for new ways of working and were open to the integration of IoToys into their practice. We
describe the preschool as *typical* in terms of technology use in practice.
They own a small number of tablets for staff and children's use and they
have an interactive whiteboard, but technological artefacts did not form
a significant part of their play-based pedagogy. They did not have any
IoToys prior to the project. When loaned IoToys for this project, they were
delayed in their integration because the toys needed to be verified and
approved by the Local Authority and the setting's IT department. The IT
department also had to install all Apps associated with the IoToy artefacts
due to firewalls and restrictions.

Staff's reaction to the IoToys was energetic and enthusiastic. They
seemed invigorated by the integration of the resources and the possibilities they offered to engage children. Due to concerns about the possibility of damage to the resources, they did not allow children to use the
resources in child-led free play; instead, all IoToys were used during structured activities with practitioners. This also satisfied their Safe Internet
Protocols. The staff used the resources with small groups and two boys,
Iain and Mark, opted to play with them in every session. On one occasion,
the practitioner was observed facilitating the activity for well over an
hour, and the activity only ended because it was time for the whole preschool session to end.

Despite one practitioner being a self-confessed novice with technology, a hybrid game caught her attention and she became emphatic about
using it in practice. She was animated in her expressions during the game,
becoming very excited, which created a 'draw' for other children. The children themselves became similarly animated and enthusiastic about the
play experience (shown in Fig. 7.3).

As they played, the practitioner asked prompting questions for the
children to help them progress with the game and children engaged in
mathematical discussions. When making decisions about how best to balance the animals, they talked, successfully, about the size of the various
objects and whether smaller uneven objects would be able to balance a
larger object on top. They talked about environmental terminology, such

Fig. 7.3 Engagement with a hybrid toy

as endangerment, as they tried to keep their beast creations alive and discussed physical elements as they talked about land versus sea animals.

When interviewed about the resource, the practitioner spoke about children's engagement with both physical tactile resources alongside the virtual world, and the ability to consider numeracy and literacy throughout as they created hybrid animals on the platform and followed their scores. She spoke of a route to engage boys, specifically, with mathematical concepts, as she said, 'The thing I'm finding, you are engaging boys more, because it's appealing to the boys. The boys don't want to sit at a table and do maths activity with sorting activities, but they don't realise how much maths activities they're actually getting out of that [hybrid game]'.

What was striking about this episode was not only children's active engagement and fascination with the resource, but the practitioner's interest in it, too. For a practitioner who previously avoided technologies, this hybrid game empowered her to embrace children's digital lives and transcend the fluid digital learning across the child's social world. She spoke about how the tactile pieces, and not just the screen-based media, were appealing to children of this age group and supported more traditional forms of play. In a sense, the tactile nature of the resource provided a foundation to justify children's play with technologies.

She went on to speak about the interaction involved with IoToys both between practitioners and children—describing how she was able to ask children questions throughout, which prompted their scientific thinking—but also between child and technology. The children were simultaneously engaged with a virtual world and became immersed, so much so that two children chose not to play the game because the animals died if the children failed to stack the pieces quickly enough. Here we begin to see an extension of Rogoff's (2008) interpersonal plane and evidence of the ecology of the exosphere and the ecology of the social world, i.e. the child's interactions and relationships with others *and* with IoToys.

The practitioners used these resources on the same day that children's parents were invited to the preschool for Stay and Play sessions. Children eagerly dragged their parents over to the play area to show them the game. Similarly, because the resources had been sent home with children and subsequently utilised in practice, the parents were becoming increasingly aware of the type of technologies used in the preschool and, vice versa, the practitioners were beginning to understand digital lives at home. The gap across contexts in this social world was narrowing through an empowered practitioner's enthusiastic integration of IoToys.

Creating Empowering Digital Spaces Across Social Worlds

One of the defining characteristics of IoToys is their complexity. They are built around complex software and hardware, without which their interactivity and multidimensional nature would not exist. It is this complex system of interaction packaged in tactile machines, which separates IoToys from traditional analogue learning resources, and to a large extent from screen-based media, which has dominated the children and technology market for decades. This complexity requires adults to support children with the devices and for children to support each other. In a study about construction technologies versus traditional Froebelian construction toys, Arnott and Duncan (under review) detail the need for children's familiarity with technologies in order for children to embrace the potentiality of these resources. The same is true for children and adults with IoToys. Adults spoke of both the need to invest time in learning to use IoToys and how play progressed along with their familiarity. The practitioners and children learned together as equals in the process.

What we saw across the study settings was both Craft's (2013) discussion of passivity (in centres that did not want to integrate some of the IoToys) and empowerment as Scottish children, parents and practitioners embraced the opportunities that IoToys offered. In the Scottish examples, adult involvement was not aimed at *protecting* children from the suggested dangers of IoToys; rather, adults appeared to be learning alongside children about how best to use these complex devices. This sense of the unknown for practitioners and the realisation that IoToys were about exploration, discovery, tinkering and 'learning by doing' provided the foundation to justify children's own exploration with technologies. When the confidence in the child's capabilities is there, we can see children's attempts to support each other, as can be seen by Emily and Aaron in an English home context (Fig. 7.4).

Case Study 3: Scaffolding

Aaron (6 years) approaches Emily (3 years and 5 months) who is playing with a hybrid learning game, using the tactile pieces without using the App (at this stage, Emily has not made the connection that the pieces can be linked with the APP) and asks her if he can join her. They start playing together. Aaron sets the tablet in position and chooses the App by explaining to Emily how it is played. Then together they choose which puzzle they will make and they play.

Aaron: Let's start! Ok, you start first.

Emily: [Takes the pieces and starts while Aaron points to the tablet image. She places the first three pieces of the puzzle and starts looking at the tablet, but she struggles with the smaller one and she cannot find how to fit it.]

Aaron: The other way, yes! The other way! Pick up the purple one first … no the purple one, this is the orange one, look [pointing to the tablet]. Emily still struggles to find out how the piece will fit so the puzzle will be complete and Aaron is asking her whether he can help her. Takes the piece and completes the puzzle. Looks at Emily and applauds her with his hands.

Aaron: You did it! Well done!

Fig. 7.4   Scaffolding with a hybrid toy

In this instance, Aaron is empowered by scaffolding Emily's confidence to extend her play with the pieces of the hybrid game from the non-digital space (Emily was playing without the App) to a digital space (Emily plays with Aaron scaffolding her with the App).

In further episodes (not presented here) Emily starts playing on her own with the same hybrid game, using it as an IoToy. From within a socio-ecological paradigm (Fig. 7.1), we can see that Aaron (exo-sphere in Emily's play) supported her to understand the digital space (social world) and when Emily played alone later (ecology of self) her play with the hybrid game pieces was entangled between digital and non-digital. Compared to a more traditional technology which is screen-based, IoToys, because of their interactive nature, facilitate the entanglement of digital and non-digital and children utilise them as part of their play repertoire, as we have shown in all three cases.

When technologies are embraced and accepted as part of children's everyday lives, we begin to see empowered digital spaces, where the whole social world learns together. The children's and adults' understandings are treated equally, as they bring together their varied expertise. When Larry began using the programmable floor robot, his mother explained:

> I was working it manually and he told me we had to download an APP to work it from the tablet. I thought he was confused with the learning robot but he was right! [emoji of monkey covering eyes] (Practitioner Interview, Momentum Preschool)

The power divide between adult and child is narrowed because the adults are no more expert than the children in using the device. By accepting the notion of learning together, parents and practitioners can create empowering digital spaces across social worlds.

Concluding Thoughts: The Internet of Toys; Changing Childhood and Cautioning Against the Recurrent Moral Panic

Over the last few decades, deficit style debates about the role of technologies in early childhood (e.g. Palmer, 2015) had somewhat appeared to have plateaued. While concerns about digital childhoods were still evident in the popular press and in the media, in research spheres, the discussion had moved beyond *whether* children should engage with technologies to *how best we can support children* to engage with technologies. The realisation that technological developments are inevitable and going to feature in children's lives and futures has driven forward pedagogical discussions about how technologies feature in early childhood practice; for example, discussions of Guided Interaction (Plowman & Stephen, 2007), A Digital Play Framework (Edwards & Bird, 2015) and Digital Pedagogy (Fleer, 2017) emerged. We even reached a point where technologies were not as often held accountable for children's social development (or lack thereof) and, instead, appropriate reflection and consideration were given to supporting the framing of children's technological experiences (Arnott, 2017). In essence, we were entering a period of *acceptance* of technologies as supportive of multi-modal practices (Yelland & Gilbert, 2017), affording opportunities for new forms of symbolic play and engagement with STEM at young ages.

In the last 3–5 years, however, the increased production of IoToys, that are now part of children's everyday experiences (Mascheroni & Holloway, 2017), has (re)aroused new/recurrent concerns about digital childhoods. The intermittent moral panic that has been voiced around Radio, Television, ICT and Screen-Based Media has now been somewhat resurrected for IoToys. While concerns over screen-based media in the late 2000s focused on the potential reduction in children's 'real' play, the concern for IoToys is to do with online safety and the datafication of childhood. In essence, we have arrived back at the deficit model of digital childhoods and debates about the appropriateness of technologies (specifically IoToys) are at the forefront of research and practice.

In this chapter, our empirical evidence, in combination with our theoretical frame, suggests that digital childhoods are messy, multifaceted, multi-modal and ultimately complex. With the onset of IoToys, the digital lives of young children cannot be compartmentalised across various bounded systems. As our data show, IoToys (as new technology still developing) are creating a synergy between the digital and the non-digital (entanglement, as in Fig. 7.1). Similarly, children's interactions *with* IoToys and with other children *around* IoToys are inseparably linked across the individual, the interpersonal and the community (Rogoff, 2008) in digital and non-digital spaces. For practice, this means that a complex approach to supporting and framing children's digital lives is necessary, one which has a balanced and nuanced interpretation of the agency of IoToys in children's lives. If we are to stay true to now long-established sociological perspectives on childhood, which see children as capable and competent, then this agenda needs to transcend the digital realm. A moral panic and deficit model around IoToys, as described above, will ultimately be unhelpful in a rapidly changing child-consumer market. A passive child approach (Craft, 2013) will only hinder the child in learning to safely navigate this unfaltering progression in contemporary life.

We must facilitate children's empowerment with IoToys, by respecting children's own agency and trusting that, with the right framing and guidance, children have the competence to drive forward their digital lives in a responsible, safe and creative manner. This cannot be achieved in isolation and children cannot be expected to shoulder the burden of this learning journey alone. *Framing and guidance* to support children as part of their digital lives are the crucial factors on this journey. Such framing need not be didactic but can take the form of informal learning where children learn by *observing and pitching in* (Rogoff, 2014). Framing and guidance must be foregrounded as we learn, *together*, about how best to integrate IoToys into our social worlds. However, in order to achieve that, we need to move away from the tyranny of 'anxieties' and the 'panic' over divisive ideologies around technology in early childhood education and embrace them critically as offering another resource empowering potentialities in children's lives.

References

Aldhafeeri, F., Palaiologou, I., & Folorunsho, A. (2016). Integration of digital technologies into play-based pedagogy in Kuwaiti early childhood education: Teachers' views, attitudes and aptitudes. *International Journal of Early Years Education, 24*(3), 342–360. https://doi.org/10.1080/09669760.2016. 1172477.

Ärlemalm-Hagsér, E. (2014). Participation as 'taking part in': Education for sustainability in Swedish preschools. *Global Studies of Childhood, 4*(2), 101–114.

Arnott, L., Palaiologou, I., & Gray, C. (under review—minor revisions). Internet of toys across home and early childhood settings: Understanding the ecology of the child's social world. *Technology, Pedagogy and Education*.

Arnott, L. (2013). Are we allowed to blink? Young children's leadership and ownership while mediating interactions around technologies. *International Journal of Early Years Education, 21*(1), 97–115. https://doi.org/10.1080/09 669760.2013.772049.

Arnott, L. (2016). An ecological exploration of young children's digital play: Framing children's social experiences with technologies in early childhood. *Early Years, 36*(3), 271–288. https://doi.org/10.1080/09575146.2016.1181049.

Arnott, L. (2017). Framing technological experiences in the early years. In L. Arnott (Ed.), *Digital technologies and learning in the early years*. London: Sage.

Arnott, L., & Duncan, P. (under review). Exploring the pedagogic culture of creative play early childhood education. Submitted to *Journal of Early Childhood Research*.

Craft, A. (2013). Childhood, possibility thinking and wise, humanising educational futures. *International Journal of Educational Research, 61,* 126–134. https://doi.org/10.1016/j.ijer.2013.02.005.

Danby, S., Davidson, C., Theobald, M., Houen, S., & Thorpe, K. (2017). Pretend play and technology: Young children making sense of their everyday social worlds. In D. Pike, S. Lynch, & C. A. Beckette (Eds.), *Multidisciplinary perspectives on play: From birth to beyond* (pp. 231–245). Singapore: Springer.

Edwards, S., & Bird, J. (2015). Observing and assessing young children's digital play in the early years: Using the digital play framework. *Journal of Early Childhood Research*. https://doi.org/10.1177/1476718x15579746.

Edwards, S., Henderson, M., Gronn, D., Scott, A., & Mirkhil, M. (2017). Digital disconnect or digital difference? A socio-ecological perspective on young children's technology use in the home and the early childhood centre. *Technology, Pedagogy and Education, 26*(1), 1–17. https://doi.org/10.10 80/1475939X.2016.1152291.

Esser, F., Baader, M. S., Betz, T., & Hungerland, B. (2016). *Reconceptualising agency and childhood: New perspectives in childhood studies*. New York: Routledge.

Farrell, A. (2016). Ethical responsibilities in early childhood education and care. In J. Ailwood, W. Boyd, & M. Theobald (Eds.), *Understanding early childhood education and care in Australia: Practices and perspectives* (pp. 187–207). Sydney: Allen & Unwin.

Fleer, M. (2017). Digital pedagogy: How teachers support digital play in the early years. In L. Arnott (Ed.), *Digital technologies and learning in the early years* (pp. 114–126). London: Sage.

Groundwater-Smith, S., Dockett, S., & Bottrell, D. (2014). *Participatory research with children and young people*. London: Sage.

I'Anson, J. (2013). Beyond the child's voice: Towards an ethics for children's participation rights. *Global Issues of Childhood, 3*(2), 104–114.

James, A., & Prout, A. (2015). *Constructing and reconstructing childhood: Contemporary issues in the sociological study of childhood*. London: Routledge.

James, A., Jenks, C., & Prout, A. (1998). *Theorizing childhood*. Cambridge: Polity Press.

Johnson, G. M., & Puplampu, K. P. (2008). Internet use during childhood and the ecological techno-subsystem. *Canadian Journal of Learning and Technology* [La revue canadienne de l'apprentissage et de la technologie], *34*(1), 19–28.

Laupa, M. (1994). "Who's in charge?" Preschool children's concept of authority. *Early Childhood Research Quarterly, 9*(1), 1–17.

Marsh, J., Plowman, L., Yamada-Rice, D., Bishop, J. C., Lahmar, J., Scott, F., … Winter, P. (2015). *Exploring play and creativity in preschoolers' use of apps: Final project report.* Retrieved from www.techandplay.org.

Mascheroni, G., & Holloway, D. (2017). *The Internet of Toys: A report on media and social discourses around young children and IoToys.* Retrieved from http://digilitey.eu/wp-content/uploads/2017/01/IoToys-June-2017-reduced.pdf.

Palaiologou, I. (2016). Children under five and digital technologies: Implications for early years pedagogy. *European Early Childhood Education Research Journal, 24*(1), 5–24. https://doi.org/10.1080/1350293X.2014.929876.

Palmer, S. (2015). *Toxic childhood: How the modern world is damaging our children and what we can do about it.* London: Orion.

Plowman, L., McPake, J., & Stephen, C. (2008). Just picking it up? Young children learning with technology at home. *Cambridge Journal of Education, 38*(3), 303–319. https://doi.org/10.1080/03057640802287564.

Plowman, L., & Stephen, C. (2007). Guided interaction in preschool settings. *Journal of Computer Assisted Learning, 23*(1), 14–26. https://doi.org/10.1111/j.1365-2729.2007.00194.x.

Plowman, L., Stephen, C., & McPake, J. (2010). *Growing up with technology: Young children learning in a digital world.* London: Routledge.

Plowman, L., & Stevenson, O. (2012). Using mobile phone diaries to explore children's everyday lives. *Childhood, 19*(4), 539–553. https://doi.org/10.1177/0907568212440014.

Rogoff, B. (2008). Observing sociocultural activity on three planes: Participatory appropriation, guided participation, and apprenticeship. In *Pedagogy and practice: Culture and identities* (pp. 58–74). London: Sage.

Rogoff, B. (2014). Learning by observing and pitching into family and community endeavors: An orientation. *Human Development, 57*(2–3), 69–81.

Rose, J., & Rogers, S. (2012). *The role of the adult in early years settings.* Maidenhead: Open University Press.

Stephen, C., & Edwards, S. (2017). *Young children playing and learning in a digital age: A cultural and critical perspective.* London: Routledge.

Wang, X. C., Berson, I., Jaruszewicz, C., Hartle, L., & Rosen, D. (2010). Young children's technology experiences in multiple contexts: Bronfenbrenner's ecological theory reconsidered. In I. Berson & M. Berson (Eds.), *High-tech tots: Childhood in a digital world.* Charlotte: Information Age Publishing.

Yelland, N. (2015). iPlay, iLearn, iGrow: Tablet technologies, curriculum, pedagogies and learning in the twenty-first century. In S. Garvis & N. Lemon (Eds.), *Understanding digital technologies and young children: An international perspective* (pp. 122–138). London: Taylor & Francis (Routledge).

Yelland, N., & Gilbert, C. (2017). Re-imagining play with new technologies. In L. Arnott (Ed.), *Digital technologies and learning in the early years.* London: Sage.

8

Persuasive Toy Friends and Preschoolers: Playtesting IoToys

Katriina Heljakka and Pirita Ihamäki

Introduction

Toys are an expressive medium. In today's world, they are more persuasive than ever in the way they invite players to engage in interaction, caretaking and communication. Children learn and entertain themselves by exploring and interacting with playthings, such as the Internet of Toys (or IoToys), in both domestic and educational contexts. These contemporary smart toys have embedded modules that provide processing and wireless communication. With both computing and communication capabilities, their connectivity is so well integrated with the plaything that it becomes a 'technology that disappears' (Satyanarayanan, 2001). For example, IoToys-related playthings may

K. Heljakka (✉)
University of Turku, Pori, Finland
e-mail: Katriina.heljakka@utu.fi

P. Ihamäki
Prizztech Ltd., Pori, Finland

© The Author(s) 2019
G. Mascheroni and D. Holloway (eds.), *The Internet of Toys*,
Studies in Childhood and Youth, https://doi.org/10.1007/978-3-030-10898-4_8

provide aural, visual, motion, tactile and other feedback, and be able to sense speech, physical manipulation and absolute and relative location.

Through technological connectivity, these hybrid toys, most often representing anthropomorphized characters, allow players to connect to online environments in order to get involved in digitally enhanced and socially mediated play. In this way, current character toys, such as technologically enhanced dolls, soft toys and action figures, function as both portals to digital play worlds and *extensions* of their players (Heljakka, 2013, 2016; McLuhan, 1987; Ruckenstein, 2010). Simultaneously, they function as 'toy friends' or companions.

By the late twentieth century, new electronic toys had fundamentally changed *how* we play, but not *why* we play (Eberle, 2015). Our study is interested in the various dimensions of 'connected play' (Marsh, 2017), which emerge through interaction with smart, hybrid and connected playthings, such as IoToys. We approach play from a perspective similar to that of Deterding (2016), who suggests that play is an 'enjoyable, intrinsically motivated activity, associated with a wide range of positive effects on motivation, social interaction, learning, and other experiences' (Deterding, 2016, pp. 101–102).

Following Marsh, connected play represents movements between different domains 'online and offline, digital and non-digital, material and immaterial, but also the public and private, global, and local domains' (Marsh, 2017, p. 2). This type of play can also be understood as *hybrid play*, by which we mean that play encompasses the realms of the physical and the digital. Hybrid play with toys like the emerging category of IoToys challenges the strict dichotomy between physical and digital, non-mediated and mediated play by resting on the intersection of the material and the digital (Tyni, Kultima, & Mäyrä, 2013)—between the physicality of the traditional toy and the connectivity of IoToys. Moreover, hybridity in relation to IoToys means that toys connected to digital worlds provide potential added play value within physical and material experiences.

As suggested by Holloway and Green (2016), the emerging category of IoToys will require critical inspection and evaluation of how these new playthings are integrated into children's culture and how connected toys may change play practices. This question can be further divided into more detailed enquiries into play, for example, whether the play patterns associated with the IoToys align more closely to physical or digital play, to structured or open-ended play, and whether playing with IoToys is more akin to entertaining or educational play.

This chapter draws from a systematic review and analysis of hybrid and so-called connected toys launched in recent years. In our analysis, we focus on the persuasion strategies used in four contemporary character toys (which are hybrid fantasy figures, most often cutified dolls, robot-like toys or plush animals with embedded technologies). Namely, we focus on: first, these toys' ways of inviting their players to connect to digital realms of play; second, their ways of enticing their players to nurture toy characters by fulfilling their special requests for play; and third, their tendency to offer opportunities to their users to become engaged with others in the name of social play.

The chapter describes a study conducted with preschool-aged children in a Finnish kindergarten. It represents part of a larger body of research regarding IoToys from multiple perspectives. For example, in the earlier stages of research we investigated IoToys from the perspectives of education, toy literacy and transmedia play (Heljakka & Ihamäki, 2018; Ihamäki & Heljakka, 2018).

This part of the study highlights the persuasion strategies of IoToys to signify them as 'toy friends' and children's interaction with them. It provides an overview of preschool-aged children's first responses to IoToys in a playtest and group interview situation, and it suggests how connected toys may engage children in both solitary and social play.

We begin by providing an overview of the most popular, mass-marketed, physical and connected toys of recent years (launched in 2014–2016) targeting preschoolers, and we present the toymakers' strategies of persuasion. Firstly, we explore how these toys present *possibilities to connect with digital technologies* (i.e. through the use of built-in computers, mobile devices and apps). Secondly, our interest turns to solitary play, or *intrapersonal interaction between toy and player*, mainly from the viewpoint of 'nurturing' these toys through requests to be cared for. Thirdly, we explore how a connected toy friend suggests that the player participates in interpersonal interaction, meaning social play with others. In the next part of the chapter, our attention turns to playtests and group interviews conducted with preschool children. We conclude the chapter with a discussion of the reviewed persuasion strategies of connectivity, nurturing and social play and suggest their importance as values in design and play with IoToys.

Preschoolers and Their Hybrid Playworlds

Currently, the technological aspect of contemporary toy characters is becoming a more normalized part of the toy-design process as toy companies try to reach out to preschoolers, toddlers and even infants. Therefore, it is of crucial importance to investigate the interaction between children and connected toys in order to understand how they respond to character toys as players and what kind of play experiences IoToys facilitate through their various affordances—physical, digital and hybrid.

Play materials, again, may motivate, stimulate and promote play in different ways (Mayfield, 2007, p. 252). Today, technology-based toys, which we refer to here as hybrid toys, are increasingly popular with children (Cagiltay, Kara, & Aydin, 2014). Hybrid toys, or dimensions of hybridity in playthings as defined by Tyni et al. (2013), include games and toys that utilize digital environments to give added value to tactile, physical or material experiences. Hybridity in the use of playthings, as previously mentioned, refers to transitions between physical and digital play patterns or play environments (Heljakka, 2012).

In most cases, the IoToys in the current marketplace represents *hybrid characters* that offer hybrid play value to their users. Important affordances of these playthings include their ability to persuade children to play, which we divide into technological, solitary (child-to-toy) and social (child-to-toy-to-child) connectivity. Connectivity refers to the toys' ability to access content that is mediated by digital communication technology, as well as both their demands for attention and nurturing from their players in the name of solitary play, and their ability to encourage their players to seek social interaction with others.

Earlier Studies on Play with Toy Friends

In their study, Bleumers et al. (2015) found that playful technologies that promote social interaction and cooperation among children, like a toy that a child can cherish and care for, benefit social and emotional development. Previous research on technologically enhanced character toys that demand nurturing is represented by examples such as Tamagotchi (1996), Furby (1998) and My Real Baby (2000). For example, Ruckenstein (2010) writes about virtual pets such as Tamagotchi inviting children to nurture them. Turkle, Breazeal, Dasté, and Scassellati (2006) write about the child's point of view in accepting a caretaker role, which the researchers see as a crucial step in creating a bond with an inanimate object. A central aspect of the formation of this bond is the child's immersion in the belief about the character's 'inner state', that is, its desire to interact with its player and learn from this interaction.

In their study from 2001, Smart Toy Lab developers D'Hooge and Goldstein listed the 'ground rules' for interactive play products to be developed collaboratively by Mattel and Intel, which included the following criteria for what they consider 'technology toys'. Here, we interpret the listed criteria as a set of envisioned *design values*: the toy should (1) be fun, (2) open-ended, (3) enable the child to be in control, (4) offer a challenging and creative experience, (5) be educational, (6) grow with the child, (7) involve a personal computer, (8) be considered as high technology, (9) represent innovation and (10) include at least one truly magical feature (D'Hooge & Goldstein, 2001, pp. 1–2).

How the developers define their criteria is clarified in the following. First, they claim fun to be synonymous with toys. Although fun is a much-contested term in the design of play products (Koster, 2013), the developers suggest that focus-testing gives a good indication of whether a toy is fun. Second, the toy needs to promote open-endedness; there is no fixed set of rules for the use of a toy. Third, the toy should put the child in control, ensuring that it functions as a tool in the hands of a child. Fourth, the toy must be creative and offer enough challenge in order to have re-playability value. Fifth, learning comes for 'free' with a toy that is educational. Sixth, the toy should grow with the child. In other words, it should facilitate play of different kinds and, in this way, support the child's development. Seventh, in order for an IoToy to be designed according to the listed criteria or design values, it should involve a technological device, usually a built-in computer that extends the toy. Eighth, the toy should be considered 'high technology', which we interpret within the framework of our chapter to mean that the smart toy is a connected one. Ninth, the toy should be 'first-of-its-kind', conveying a truly innovative take on toys. Tenth, and finally, the toy should encompass a 'magical feature', meaning that it 'has to have that one special feature that makes a kid go "wow"' (D'Hooge & Goldstein, 2001, p. 2).

Our Study

In this study, four IoToys were chosen, based on their gender neutrality, as character types of toys and their awarded innovativeness, popularity and availability on Amazon USA (in August 2017): (1) CogniToys Dino (2015), (2) Wonder Workshop's Dash Robot (2014), (3) Fisher-Price Smart Toy Bear (2015) and (4) Hatchimals (2016). These toys satisfy the criteria of IoToys: they are 'smart' and their connectivity usually occurs through mobile devices (smartphones and tablets). Researchers Holloway and Green identify IoToys as screen-less platforms that allow online experiences related to playing and socializing (2016, p. 11). In some cases, smart toys also have their own computer inside it (e.g. the CogniToys Dino and the Fisher-Price Smart Toy Bear), and the interaction happens mainly through playful dialogue, rather than the manipulation of a screen. Connected toys are sometimes used with remote-control systems to interact with children. Furthermore, they often use sophisticated, sensor-based technologies to collect information from their players and cloud-based platforms to process this information through real-time interactions. This means that IoToys offer new opportunities for personalized content to be used in play. In terms of play, IoToys represent a shift from playing with physical objects such as historical mechanical toys to interacting with seemingly unlimited, pre-programmed content; furthermore, they include the possibility to connect to similar devices.

According to their marketed play affordances, these toys have the potential to invite their players to engage in both imaginative and creative play and learning experiences. What is of particular interest to us is to explore the question of how connected toys are used in the play of preschool-aged children, and thus, how they are evaluated in terms of their play value, both educational and entertainment. The reason for our selection of IoToys was also based on our interest in mapping out their various features and, through this, their capacity to invite their users to try different play patterns. In particular, what guided our interest was our curiosity about toymakers' persuasion strategies in terms of the toys' connectivity, demands for nurturing and their capacity to promote social play. Another criterion for the toys was that they are not only operated through a screen but represent a multidimensional experience. Moreover, the selected character toys represent 'toy friends', which invite friendly interaction through voice recognition and sensors, even if not all are huggable. In this way, the toys encourage the child as a player to interact.

Method

In order to be able to understand the potentialities of IoToys, empirical engagement with their primary users is crucial. In this study, research materials were gathered from two Finnish preschool groups (September–October 2017), with 20 preschoolers between the ages of 5 and 6 years. The preschool setting was chosen for its practicality. By conducting the study in a preschool environment, a group of 5–6-year-old children could be recruited and involved in a playtesting session and group interview. Furthermore, the researchers could evaluate the suitability of those toys in the chosen environment of the preschool.

We address the following research question (targeting the children, who were asked about each of the IoToys): What could this toy teach you, and how would you play with it (a) alone with the toy and (b) with other children?

We conducted two group interviews and interactive playtests with 20 preschool-aged children. The interviews and playtests were conducted in October 2017 in cooperation with two Finnish preschool groups. The empirical enquiry includes questions concerning the toys' educational potential and possibilities for play. This is because the study was conducted in a preschool setting where play is considered an important avenue to learning, or instrumentally, but also valued for its own sake, or intrinsically, as a natural part of children's everyday activities and orientation to the world.

Our methods include participatory observation, playtests, written and visual types of documentation through photographing and videotaping the test groups while playing, learning and interacting with our IoToys. This included the children drawing their chosen IoToys after the playtests.

Results

In the two group interview sessions, the researchers introduced all four IoToys to the children one by one, first by showing the toy and then allowing each child to interact with it. Each of the IoToys was presented in three stages: a general introduction to the toy, demonstrating its key features; a one-on-one session for play with the toy; and a group interview. Finally, we showed the children a short video of the toys' functions based on non-commercial material found on YouTube. In general, each of the IoToys was given approximately 20 minutes' time in the playtest and group interview situations.

Our main goal was to explore the children's toy engagements, which for most of the selected toys meant their first encounters and interactions with IoToys. Our approach was to interfere as little as possible in these engagements. However, during the child-toy interactions, the group was asked the following three questions: (1) What the toy could teach him or her, (2) how the child would play with the toy alone, and (3) how the child would play with the toy in the company of other children.

CogniToys Dino

The connectedness of this IoToy results from syncing with a smartphone. The Dino's mouth lights up when it speaks, and it indicates different states of being. CogniToys Dino's speech-enabled technology allows players to speak directly to the toy and, for example, to ask questions to receive age-appropriate answers. In our playtest situation, the toy lit up and started to play music, to which the preschoolers reacted with physical movement and perceived educational play patterns related to singing and music-making. The light sparked ideas about using the toy for other purposes, for example, in solitary play, such as a lamp when tenting outside.

Fisher-Price Smart Toy Bear

The Fisher-Price Smart Toy Bear is, according to its maker, an interactive learning friend with all the brains of a computer, but without the screen. Social and emotional growth of the player is made possible through updated content, an app and voice recognition. The connectedness via the app offers access to games, stories and interactive activities. The preschoolers in our study detected the educational play pattern of language-learning with the Smart Toy Bear. A solitary play pattern associated with the Smart Toy Bear was nursing it, and a social play pattern detected was to play school with it.

Wonder Workshop's Dash

Wonder Workshop Dash acts as if it is 'alive' in the way it moves and talks. According to its makers, the toy supports open-ended play using a remote-control app to make the toy move around and play various sound effects. The connectedness of the toy, which allows the use of applications, enables players to code movements for the toy. In our playtest, the preschoolers reacted particularly to the sounds created by the toy by associating educational play patterns with it, such as learning the English language and reacted to its movement by perceiving physical play patterns, such as playing tag and learning to make different sounds. In terms of solitary play patterns, the children said it could be used to play hide-and-seek and house with. Socially, Dash could be used, according to the preschoolers, to play football and do disco dancing with.

Hatchimals

Hatchimals peck their way out of a plastic egg. After this, when appropriately 'nursed', the toy goes through three stages of development, from baby to toddler to kid, and the players are able to teach it to walk, dance and play games. In our playtesting session, the preschoolers witnessed the hatching of the toy and were able to play with it in its first stage of development. The playtesters associated educational play patterns with it, although the toy represents a non-educational toy. The Hatchimal was said to be able to teach preschoolers singing, reading and flying. Of the four playtested IoToys, this toy sparked the most ideas of nursing the toy through solitary play patterns, for example, 'petting' the toy friend, taking it for a walk or using it as a bedtime companion. In terms of social play, the preschoolers said the Hatchimal invited them to take care of the toy with others and to watch it play by itself.

Summary

According to our study, some of the playtested IoToys are more educational (CogniToys Dino and Wonder Workshop's Dash) and some are more entertaining (Hatchimals). However, the preschoolers who participated in our study associated educational play patterns with all four IoToys featured in the study. What these toys were believed to teach the children included the cognitive skills of how to make sounds and sing, how to learn the English language and how to read. On the other hand, the preschoolers also believed the Hatchimal was able to teach the imaginative skill of how to fly. In this way, the educational potentiality of the toys was verified in the children's interactions. At the same time, the IoToys were also considered to be 'fun'.

To give examples, the CogniToys Dino successfully fulfilled other values apart from fun, such as open-endedness, child-in-control, challenging and creative experiences, room to grow with the child, and it includes at least one truly magical feature, which we interpret as a wow feature: CogniToys Dino knows the player's name, learns their likes and dislikes, and is able to entertain through storytelling. Wonder Workshop's Dash Robot educates by enabling creatively and collaboratively challenging coding projects. Moreover, it is able to teach language skills and other school subjects. Apart from its educational affordances, the Fisher-Price Smart Toy Bear invites 'magical' interaction through Smart Cards. The Hatchimal 'wows' through its 'hatching', by literally unboxing itself when pecking itself out.

According to a common belief, technologically enhanced toys may lead to more solitary play. But in contrast, following Sutton-Smith's idea, 'Toys decrease the sociability of play. We hasten to add, however, that new toys also, in time, make a contribution to social play' (Sutton-Smith, 1986, p. 38). Our group interviews and playtests supported Sutton-Smith's claim, in that these new toys were capable of inviting their players to engage in social play: three of the four IoToys afforded possibilities of both solitary and social play. The IoToys' sound, light and movement-based features allowed the preschoolers to envision various *solitary play patterns* for toy friends, such as music-related play (e.g. singing and dancing), physical play (e.g. playing tag and hide-and-seek) and *nurturing the toy* (e.g. playing house, using it as a bedtime companion and pet). Moreover, the *social play patterns* associated with IoToys were also mentioned by the preschoolers, for example, taking care of Hatchimals with other children, playing school with the Fisher-Price Smart Toy Bear and playing football with Wonder Workshop's Dash. In this way, the strategies that contemporary character toys employ to persuade their players to nurture, connect and take part in social play were found in all the IoToys, except for social play patterns that the children did not report for the CogniToys Dino.

Table 8.1 Play affordances, children's perceptions of play patterns and design values for IoToys

Playtested IoToys	CogniToys Dino	Wonder Workshop's Dash Robot	Fisher-Price Smart Toy Bear	Hatchimals
Marketed play affordances (Communicated by companies and marketers)	• Connects through computer/Wi-Fi and app • Tells stories • Play of games • Makes jokes • Communicates fun facts • Offers interactive dialogue • Teaches educational subjects including vocabulary, math, geography and science	• Connects through computer/Wi-Fi and app • Tells stories • Play of games • Dances • Records player made choices • Sings • Navigates objects • Responds to voice • Offers puzzles • Functions as a coding canvas	• Connects through computer/Wi-Fi and app • Recognizes voice • Talks, listens and remembers what the player says • Tells stories • Playing of games • Makes jokes • Knows the time of day, weather and world events	• Connects through an app • Toy walks • Toy talks • Toy dances • Play of games • Goes through 3 stages of development
Perceived play patterns (Communicated by preschoolers as play testers): a. educational b. solitary play c. social play	Educational play patterns: • How to make different sounds • How to sing music Solitary play patterns: • Dancing • Singing with the toy • Playing disco with it • Using it in play in which you need music • Using the toy as a lamp • Taking videos with it • Nurturing it Social play patterns: • No answer (N/A)	Educational play patterns: • How to make different sounds (e.g. farm animals) Solitary play patterns: • Playing tag • Playing hide-and-seek • Playing house Social play patterns: • Playing disco dancing • Playing football • Making arts & crafts	Educational play patterns: • Teaches English language • Tells stories • Plays tag Solitary play patterns: • Nursing the toy • Playing hide-and-seek Social play patterns: • Playing school with the toy • Sharing the toy • Playing house	Educational play patterns: • How to sing • How to fly • How to read Solitary play patterns: • Taking a walk with it • Using it as a bed-time companion • Playing it with it as a pet • Swinging with it Social play patterns: • Taking care of it with others • Watching it play

(continued)

Table 8.1 (continued)

Playtested IoToys	CogniToys Dino	Wonder Workshop's Dash Robot	Fisher-Price Smart Toy Bear	Hatchimals
Detected design values for all IoToys based on the 'ground rules' for technology toys by D'Hooge and Goldstein (2001): • Fun (Entertaining) • Open-ended play patterns (Imaginative play) • Child is in control of play • Challenging and creative • Involves a computer • Educational value • Grows with the child • Perceived to be high technology • Innovative • Magical feature/Wow	New design values for IoToys developed by the authors: • Involves hidden technology: language-based interaction through technology • Structured game play patterns (Rule-bound): mini-games such as quizzes • Caretaker is in control of content: Parents Panel app • Connectivity and content updates: Wi-Fi, app (updates physical toy) • Nurture/Emotional engagement: personal play experience through player recognition • Invites to social play: N/A	New design values for IoToys developed by the authors: • Involves hidden technology: movement through sensor-based technology • Structured game play patterns/Rule-bound: coding games and challenges • Caretaker is in control of content: N/A • Connectivity and content updates: Wi-Fi, app (updates physical toy) • Nurture/Emotional engagement: personal play experience through physical interaction • Invites to social play: engages in physical play socially (e.g. dancing, playing tag, hide-and-seek)	New design values for IoToys developed by the authors: • Involves hidden technology: aural and visual recognition of player through technology • Structured game play patterns/Rule-bound: mini-games through Smart Cards • Caretaker is in control of content: the Smart Toy Parent App • Connectivity and content updates: Wi-Fi, app (updates physical toy) • Nurture/Emotional engagement: personal play experience through player recognition • Invites to social play: listening to the toy's stories together (e.g. playing school through Smart Card use)	New design values for IoToys developed by the authors: • Involves hidden technology: physical and mechanical 'hatching' through technology • Structured game play patterns/Rule-bound: mini-games through the ColIEGGtibles app • Caretaker is in control of content: N/A • Connectivity and content updates: app (updates app only) • Nurture/Emotional engagement: personal play experience through physical interaction • Invites to social play: spectating and participating socially in the toys developmental stages (e.g. hatching)

The criterion of 'perceived to be high technology' suggested by D'Hooge and Goldstein (2001) applies to all the IoToys examined in our research. In order to update the list of criteria, we replaced this with the design value of 'hidden technology'. The remaining criteria set out for early toys, envisioned before the birth of IoToys as a category, offered us a useful resource and possibility to consider the four IoToys in our study. They also offered us the opportunity to reflect upon the play patterns communicated by the preschoolers in order to verify whether or not the toys studied fulfilled these different qualities considered important by Mattel and Intel in their collaborative design work at the Smart Toy Lab. The marketed play affordances as well as the children's answers to our questions collected from the group interviews are shown in Table 8.1. Based on our findings gathered and analyzed in our playtests, the list of design values needed to be complemented with the concepts of connectivity, nurturing and social play in order to set up a new set of design values for IoToys, which are also collected in Table 8.1.

Discussion

This study has focused on preschool children and their responses to four IoToys. Four contemporary toys were selected by the authors based on their availability, recognizability and popularity in the toy markets of the Western world: CogniToys' Dino, Wonder Workshop's Dash, Fisher-Price's Smart Toy Bear and one non-educational toy, Hatchimals. We playtested these toys in a case study with preschool-aged children in Finland. The purpose of the study was to investigate how children respond to IoToys and their capacity to function as persuasive toy friends that can be both enjoyed solitarily and shared in social play as companions needing attention and nurturing.

Our primary goal was to focus on discovering the strategies of persuasion that the chosen toys employed from three perspectives: connectivity, tendency to persuade their players to nurture them and, finally, their capacity to invite players to engage in social play. Additionally, what was important for our study was the fact that interaction with the selected IoToys mainly happens through other forms of playful dialogue, rather than the manipulation of a screen. Nevertheless, some of the toys featured in our study included possibilities to interact with a mobile device either though coding operations (Wonder Workshop's Dash Robot) and/or playing with an app (Hatchimals). The IoToys offered various hybrid functions to children, both in terms of their physicality as manipulable and poseable characters and also because of their digitally mediated content. The results show that the key affordances of the current IoToys investigated in our study may be categorized into physical affordances, technological affordances (sound, light, movement, interaction, and connectivity to able content) and, finally, educational affordances that, once used in play, transform into various play patterns as described in the following.

Physical Play Affordances

Despite a relatively large body of research devoted to the inspection of the digital dimension of current IoToys, the physical aspect of these toys is not to be neglected. Holloway and Green (2016) have, for example, noted how these toys should also be considered from the perspective of potential changes in children's material culture. Therefore, it is also important to consider the physical properties of these toys. In contrast to, for example, digital games or apps operated with mobile devices, the IoToys employed in our study represent character toys that, in addition to possibilities to connect online, also need physical space around them in order to take full advantage of their playability and affordances. That is to say that physical patterns of traditional play, such as displaying, posing and making the toys move, require room for play.

Pre-programmed (Technological) Play Affordances

Some of the features of the toys explored in this chapter offer limitless possibilities in terms of pre-programmed content due to their connectivity. Our discoveries regarding preschool-aged children's use of the IoToys are that young children are enthusiastic about digital features accessed through physical play objects such as interaction and narrative content, but they undertake a range of activities with these toys that foster play, creativity and learning, not only by turning to the digital features but also to the capacity of these toy friends to invite multifaceted play.

Pretend Play and Personal Meaning-Making

The connected toys under scrutiny seem to present suggestions for play beyond their digital features, connectivity and even educational potential. As character toys representing anthropomorphized creatures, the toys' promotion of educational features over their play affordances, in some cases, becomes irrelevant for preschool-aged children, as illustrated in our study. In fact, the IoToys playtested by the preschoolers in our study also invited emotional engagement with them.

As Sutton-Smith (1986) reminds us, toys are an agency for the imagination. As our results show, preschoolers seem to associate traditional play patterns with toys such as CogniToys' Dino, Wonder Workshop's Dash and Fisher-Price's Smart Toy Bear. The children in our study informed us that these toys can be nurtured, used to play hide-and-seek, as bedtime companions, to play house with etc. The toys that included sound and movement inspired the children to envision play patterns such as disco dancing and playing tag. The toys that included lights were observed to be useful in practical situations as well, such as using those toys as lamps.

Implications

One gap in the existing literature regarding play guided by IoToys is that previous research does not provide a clear description of how children learn to use these toys in play. Without a basis for understanding how children interact with the 'hidden technologies' of the toy friends that IoToys represent in play, it is difficult for parents, caretakers and teachers to understand the manifold potentialities of these connected toys.

In a study on hybrid play by Bleumers et al. (2015), it was noted that adults needed to assist children with hybrid play products by, for example, downloading an app, setting up an account and connecting toys and devices. Therefore, we assume that young children are not necessarily able to employ all the play affordances of IoToys without some help from adults. Furthermore, adults' roles as parents, educators and caretakers are important in initiating and facilitating play with IoToys for two reasons: first, in order to be able to guide play with them in open-ended ways; and second, when used in an educational context, to guide structured play that has educational goals.

Based on our findings on preschoolers' perceptions of play affordances and associated play patterns, we have built on the work of D'Hooge and Goldstein (2001) to establish a revised set of design values for IoToys (Table 8.1), including connectivity, nurturing and social play. We consider these to be valuable aspects of potentiality to consider for researchers, designers of new IoToys and the adults who supervise, guide and control their use both in the home environment and in the educational contexts.

Conclusions

The main goal of the study was to consider the strategies that makers of IoToys use to persuade preschoolers to play with them. What guided our interest, was to study how these toys could be used in an early education context. We asked how playing with IoToys can be considered a form of hybrid play between physical and digital play, whether the play is structured or open-ended play, and whether playing with IoToys is more akin to entertaining or educational play. Our study demonstrates that IoToys allow possibilities for rich and multifaceted play, including ludic engagement with character toys aimed at both open-ended, leisurely play and structured play with educational outcomes. The IoToys featured in this study mainly represented content-driven toy characters whose (play) value may be derived not only from their aesthetics, which are akin to traditionally recognized character toy forms, or mechanics, as toys with lights, sound and movement, but also from the play material they offer their users via their digitally mediated content, including the narratives, tasks and mini-games they offer.

At the same time, we found out that the imaginative component in play with IoToys is not diminished. Jeffrey Goldstein has noted how digitally enhanced toys may also be played with in more traditional ways (Goldstein, 2012, p. 3). As our research illustrates, future studies on IoToys could benefit from not only exploring their digital connectivity but also their capacity to understand these play objects more comprehensively as physical playthings with possibilities for play beyond their technologically mediated features. As we found in our own study on a preschool context with 5–6-year-old children, the persuasive play ideas of IoToys do not necessarily relate to the toys' 'smart' features but instead to the aesthetics and personalities of toys and their open-endedness in terms of play patterns. Therefore, we confirm that connected toy friends are multidimensional playthings that afford connections between the player and the toy beyond digitality.

According to the organizers of the Spielwarenmesse International Toy Fair, Nuremberg, digital media appear set to assume a lasting place in the toy industry. A publication from 2013 states that: 'iToys do not pose a threat but should instead be seen as a complement to classical toys' (*Play It! The Global Toy Magazine*, 2013). In order to evaluate their full potentiality as devices that afford rich play patterns, further agency needs to be given to educators and parents as well as to preschoolers themselves. As demonstrated in our study, an important part of this process is to ask the players of IoToys: How would you play with this hybrid toy (friend)?

Acknowledgements We wish to express our gratitude to the preschool children and their teachers for participating in and facilitating our group interviews and playtests. This study was partly funded by the Centre of Excellence in Game Culture Studies (decision #312396) research project.

References

Bleumers, L., Mouws, K., Huyghe, J., van Mechelen, M., Mariën, I., & Zaman, B. (2015). Sensitivity to parental play beliefs and mediation in young children's hybrid play activities. In *Proceedings of IDC* (pp. 170–177). Boston, MA: ACM Press.

Cagiltay, K., Kara, N., & Aydin, C. C. (2014). Smart toy based learning. In J. Spector, M. Merrill, J. Elen, & M. Bishop (Eds.), *Handbook of research on educational communications and technology* (pp. 703–711). New York, NY: Springer.

Deterding, C. S. (2016). Make-believe in gameful and playful design. In P. Turner & J. T. Harviainen (Eds.), *Digital make-believe* (pp. 101–124). Basel: Springer.

D'Hooge, H., & Goldstein, M. (2001). History of the Smart Toy Lab and Intel® Play™ Toys. *Intel Technology Journal, Q4,* 1–6. Retrieved from http://www.ericpaulrose.com/wp-content/uploads/2015/04/History_of_the_Smart_Toy_Lab_and_Intel_Play_Toys.pdf.

Eberle, S. G. (2015). Epilogue: What's not play? A meditation. In J. E. Johnson, S. G. Eberle, T. S. Henricks, & D. Kuschner (Eds.), *The handbook of the study of play* (Vol. I, pp. 489–501). Rochester, NY: Co-published with The Strong.

Goldstein, J. (2012, February). *Play in children's development, health and well-being.* Brussels: Toy Industries of Europe Publication (TIE).

Heljakka, K. (2012). Hybridisyys ja pelillistyminen leikkituotteissa De-materiaalisen ja re-materiaalisen rajankäyntiä [Hybridity and gamification in playthings—At the crossroads of de-materialisation and re-materialisation]. In J. Suominen, R. Koskimaa, F. Mäyrä, & R. Turtiainen (Eds.), *Pelitutkimuksen vuosikirja* (pp. 82–91). Tampere: Tampereen Yliopisto.

Heljakka, K. (2013). *Principles of adult play(fulness) in contemporary toy cultures. From wow to flow to glow.* Doctoral dissertation. Aalto University publication series, 72/2013.

Heljakka, K. (2016). Strategies of social screen play(ers) across the ecosystem of play: Toys, games and hybrid social play in technologically mediated playscapes. *Wider Screen, 1*(2). Turku. Retrieved from http://widerscreen.fi/numerot/2016-1-2/strategies-social-screen-players-across-ecosystem-play-toys-games-hybrid-social-play-technologically-mediated-playscapes/.

Heljakka, K., & Ihamäki, P. (2018). Preschoolers learning with the Internet of Toys: From toy-based edutainment to transmedia literacy. *Seminar.net, 14*(1), 85–102.

Holloway, D., & Green, L. (2016). The Internet of Toys. *Communication Research and Practice, 2*(4), 506–519. https://doi.org/10.1080/22041451.2016.1266124.

Ihamäki, P. & Heljakka, K. (2018, January 3–6). *Smart, skilled and connected in the 21st century: Educational promises of the Internet of Toys (IoToys).* In Proceedings of Arts, Humanities, Social Science Education Conference, Prince Waikiki Hotel, Honolulu, Hawaii.

Koster, R. (2013). *Theory of fun for game design.* Sebastopol: O'Reilly Media.

Marsh, J. (2017). The Internet of Toys: A posthuman and multimodal analysis of connected play. *Teachers College Record, 119*(15), 1–32.

Mayfield, M. I. (2007). Toy libraries, play, and play materials. In D. J. Sluss & O. S. Jarrett (Eds.), *Investigating play in the 21st century* (pp. 249–258). Lanham, MD: University Press of America.

McLuhan, M. (1987). *Understanding media: The extensions of man*. London: Routledge.

Play It! The Global Toy Magazine. (2013). Evolution, not revolution. Spielwarenmesse International Toy Fair Nürnberg publication 30.1.–4.2.2013.

Ruckenstein, M. (2010). Toying with the world: Children, virtual pets and the value of mobility. *Childhood, 17*(4), 500–513.

Satyanarayanan, M. (2001). Pervasive computing: Vision and challenges. *IEEE Personal Communications*. Retrieved from http://www.cs.cmu.edu/~./aura/docdir/pcs01.pdf.

Sutton-Smith, B. (1986). *Toys as culture*. New York, NY: Gardner Press.

Turkle, S., Breazeal, C., Dasté, O., & Scassellati, B. (2006). Encounters with kismet and cog: Children respond to relational artifacts. *Digital Media: Transformations in Human Communication*, 120.

Tyni, H., Kultima, A., & Mäyrä, F. (2013). Dimensions of hybrid in playful products. In A. Lugmayar, H. Franssila, J. Paavilainen, & H. Kärkkäinen (Eds.), *Proceedings of 17th International Academic MindTrek Conference: Making Sense of Converging Media* (pp. 237–244). New York: ACM.

Part III

Design and Research Methodologies

9

Designing the Internet of Toys *for* and *with* Children: A Participatory Design Case Study

Maarten Van Mechelen, Bieke Zaman, Lizzy Bleumers and Ilse Mariën

Introduction

The phenomenon of the Internet of Toys presents media scholars with both theoretical and methodological challenges. On a theoretical level, it taps into recent discussions calling for a better understanding of how children's online and offline experiences blend into one. The Internet of Toys embodies hybrid experiences where the digital and physical

M. Van Mechelen (✉)
Delft University of Technology, Delft, The Netherlands

M. Van Mechelen · B. Zaman
KU Leuven, Leuven, Belgium
e-mail: bieke.zaman@kuleuven.be

L. Bleumers · I. Mariën
Vrije Universiteit Brussel, Brussels, Belgium
e-mail: Lizzy.Bleumers@vub.ac.be

I. Mariën
e-mail: ilse.marien@vub.ac.be

© The Author(s) 2019   181
G. Mascheroni and D. Holloway (eds.), *The Internet of Toys*,
Studies in Childhood and Youth, https://doi.org/10.1007/978-3-030-10898-4_9

coincide on a technological level (Zaman, Van Mechelen, & Bleumers, 2018). To date, however, previous literature has mainly focused on how to study existing Internet of Toys applications, but few studies have focused on how to design new connected toys (e.g. McReynolds et al., 2017), let alone how to design them for and with children. Maintaining a multi-perspective lens throughout the design process, while reconciling technological and social demands, necessitates several stakeholders collaborating (Donoso, Verdoodt, Van Mechelen, & Jasmontaite, 2016). When envisioning children as end-users and considering them as people who have the right to be heard about matters affecting their lives (Livingstone & Third, 2017), the question then arises of how to give children *a say* in the design of Internet of Toys applications.

The aim of this chapter is to discuss participatory design (PD) strategies that can be used in interdisciplinary design projects for new Internet of Toys applications. From its origins, PD was driven by democratic and emancipatory values to empower envisioned users of the technology, including children, as legitimate participants in the design process. Similar values are expressed in the Convention on the Rights of the Child (United Nations, 1989). More particularly, the chapter presents the WOOPI project as a case study to ground methodological reflections. The overall aim of the chapter is to shed light on how participation in the design process can empower children, and what kind of knowledge is generated and validated in this context.

Participatory Design

PD is an '*approach towards computer system design in which the people destined to use the system play a critical role in designing it*' (Schuler & Namioka, 1993, p. xi). It is a diverse field, with by a rich history and drawing on different disciplines including the social sciences, software engineering and design.

A Brief History

PD originated in Scandinavia in the 1970s and 1980s out of a democratic commitment to empower workers in an increasingly computerized work environment. The idea was that those who would use or be impacted by technology in the workplace should have a critical role in its design (Robertson & Simonsen, 2013). This premise to give workers a voice had its roots in society at large. Since the early '60s, various social, political and civil rights movements had been striving for more decision-making power for those affected by these decisions. Motivated by the values of democracy, action researchers partnered with labour unions to enable workers to co-determine the shape and scope of the technology in their workplace (Spinuzzi, 2005). These early PD practitioners saw themselves as facilitators who attempted to empower workers to make their own decisions, which they considered a basic human right (Clement, 1994). The ultimate goal was to develop inclusive and democratic design solutions (Robertson & Simonsen, 2013). This ethical stance, that still underlies PD today, stems from a responsibility to consider the impact of design on people's lives and environments. Often cited in this context are Winograd and Flores (1986, p. xi): '*We encounter the deep question of design when we recognize that in designing tools we are designing ways of being*'.

The political and emancipatory rationales of PD went alongside more pragmatic ones; users[1] and designers[2] had to learn from each other in order to develop suitable technological solutions. Users were seen as experts in their work domain, and designers as experts in the design process and technology in general (Robertson & Simonsen, 2013). However, in the early years of PD, most technology was custom-made for the workplace and PD typically addressed small-scale systems. Corporations nowadays are increasingly buying generic software, and, at the same time, technology use has expanded into our homes and leisure time. This proliferation of new technologies and domains has widened the scope of PD, making it increasingly difficult to anticipate all different use practices, both desirable and undesirable ones.

In addition to this widened scope, PD has achieved the status of a useful commercial approach to developing better consumer products. Involving users is believed to give better insights, which could not have surfaced otherwise. In this discourse, PD is often framed as simply a design method to optimize outcomes, i.e. a user-friendly and desirable solution. In this pragmatic view of PD, decision-making power is more likely to remain in the hands of the designers, whereas sharing decision-making power used to be an explicit goal of PD (Frauenberger, Good, Fitzpatrick, & Iversen, 2015). Although this mainstreaming of PD has not been greeted by all with enthusiasm, PD has had a profound influence on the recognition of the value of user participation in design (Muller, 2002).

Core Principles

Reflecting on PD's rich heritage, three core principles can be distinguished that form the backbone of PD: (1) *having a say* or the sharing of decision-making power between designers and users; (2) the continual process of *mutual learning* between these participants; and (3) and the iterative, collaborative development or *co-realization* of future technologies and practices (Bratteig, Bodker, Dittrich, Holst, & Simonsen, 2013).

Having a Say

The first principle, *having a say*, refers to users having influence on the actual outcome of the design process, and it relates to participation and decision-making power in design (Bratteig et al., 2013). Having a say means going beyond a one-directional information flow whereby users voice their opinions, but designers make the final decisions. For designers, it is often difficult to share their decision-making power with users, because it may infringe on their autonomy and design expertise, or at least they may view it in that way. At the same time, having decision-making power may also be difficult for users who are not used to having such power, because it implies shared responsibility for the direction and outcome of the design process. In addition, designers tend to define design problems in a top–down fashion based on their expertise (e.g. technical knowledge), which makes it difficult for those without this knowledge to genuinely participate in the design process. This phenomenon, whereby designers have symbolic power over users in the design process, is referred to as *model monopoly* (Braten, 1973).

To address model monopoly, PD takes actual use practices as the basis for design instead of designers' preconceived ideas about users, and a broad variety of stakeholders are invited to join the design process to expand the universe of discourse (Bratteteig et al., 2013). In addition, a problem statement rather than a fixed goal or research question is used as a starting point for design to further increase users' influence. Relying on Schön (1983), problem-setting and problem-solving are thereby regarded as intertwined and inseparable. This means that users co-determine the agenda (what is being discussed) and the scope of the design process (which problems are defined and judged relevant), and they envision and concretize ideas together. This process requires continual participation, revisiting earlier steps and sustained reflection (Spinuzzi, 2005).

Mutual Learning

The second principle, *mutual learning*, refers to the learning process between users and designers. This is a two-way process, in that designers learn about the use context from the users, and, in turn, users learn about the design process and technical possibilities from the designers. The basic idea is that no participant knows everything and a process of mutual learning is necessary in order for participants to respect and recognize each other's expertise. This mutual learning process develops when users and designers jointly and creatively explore the design space (Bratteteig et al., 2013).

Users' knowledge, however, is often difficult to tease out because of its tacit nature. Tacit knowledge refers to the kind of knowledge that cannot readily be expressed in words (Polanyi, 1983), but requires sustained and iterative reflection on the user's current practices and/or use of a designed artefact (Spinuzzi, 2005). Ehn (1993) has referred to this process as *collective reflection-in-action*, meaning that mutual learning does not develop as detached reflection but through practice, which simultaneously encompasses action and reflection. Users and designers work directly together in order to find common ground that encourages and enhances mutual understanding (Kensing & Greenbaum, 2013). Put differently, knowledge and ideas in PD develop continuously as a result of the interaction between users, designers and the particular context in which they engage.

Kensing and Munk-Madsen (1993) have identified three knowledge domains that should be established in PD projects: current practices, technological options and practices with new technology. First, *current practices* constitute the knowledge and experiences that users bring to the design process. Second, *technological options* refer to what designers experiment with and are knowledgeable about. Third, *practices with new technology* are the result of a mutual learning process and refer to ideas for future practices and how technology can support these (Kensing & Munk-Madsen, 1993). This balancing act or tension between current practices (what is) and future practices (what could be) forms the dialectical foundation of design.

Co-realization

The third and last principle, *co-realization*, refers to users taking an active part in visualizing and prototyping ideas and in learning about the qualities of the ideas in use or use-like settings (Bratteteig et al., 2013). This is an iterative process that requires continual participation and reflection on the designed artefact and the design process in general (Spinuzzi, 2005).

To this end, many tools and techniques have been developed, all with the same goal of enabling users to express their needs and visions for the future (Kensing & Greenbaum, 2013). By creating tangible artefacts (e.g. through paper prototyping), it becomes easier to understand the use context and technological possibilities and to imagine the consequences of a design suggestion. This relates to Bratteteig's and Wagner's

(2012) argument that, in order to avoid model monopoly and expand the universe of discourse, users should not be forced to adopt any abstract or formal language in order to participate in the design process (Bratteteig & Wagner, 2012). For instance, if users had to speak a technical programming language to get their voices heard, they would have to adopt the perspective or model within that language. This would limit their ability to express alternative visions and, hence, limit their decision-making power.

Ideally, co-realization takes place in a hybrid, third space that belongs neither to the domain of the users, nor to that of the designers. Muller (2002) describes PD as a border region between these two domains or spaces. This border region is characterized by *hybridity* and contains unpredictable and changing combinations of attributes of both domains. The practices that happen within this third space are uncertain and ambiguous in nature, but they provide fruitful ground for mutual learning between users and designers (Muller, 2002). In sum, co-realization serves a dual purpose: understanding the contextual conditions for design and exploring opportunities for change.

Case Study

WOOPI Project

The WOOPI case study presents an interdisciplinary project in which academia and industry partners collaborated to design a scalable framework for the development of Internet of Toys applications that incorporate physical, tradable, personalized cards and toys in an interactive multi-platform media experience. The academic partners included social scientists and human–computer interaction (HCI) researchers, as well as technical research partners. The industrial partners included a manufacturer of cards and games, a commercial media company, the national public broadcaster and a start-up company specialized in the creation of platforms for 3D printing and the customization tools.

Over the course of the project (ca. 18 months), a PD and research process was followed, including four main stages: (1) exploration of the problem space, (2) generating user insights, (3) concept definition and evaluation, and (4) iterative prototype development. At the end of the first three stages, development weeks were organized in which the project team gathered to share insights, brainstorm ideas, develop prototypes and boost decision-making.

Design and User Research Process

The four stages of the design and research process are discussed from the perspective of the authors (HCI researchers and social scientists), who were responsible for the user research and served as intermediaries for the academic and industry partners involved in the WOOPI project.

Exploring the Problem Space

To explore the problem space, the authors conducted conceptual, empirical and technical investigations (Friedman, Kahn, & Borning, 2008) that focused primarily on adults (i.e. parents, grandparents and teachers) as indirect stakeholders in the design of connected toys for young children.

First, a *conceptual investigation* was conducted by means of a literature study. The aim was to better understand the users and the values they might hold. Research was examined that focused on parents' perceptions of play and parental involvement in shaping young children's (4–6 years) facilitated play. This conceptual investigation resulted in two main research questions that were addressed in the empirical and technical investigations. The first question relates to parents' play beliefs and how connected toys may support or hinder these beliefs. The second question relates to parents' mediation practices regarding play and how connected toys may shape parents' involvement with children during play (Bleumers et al., 2015).

Second, an *empirical investigation* was conducted that served to complement findings from the literature. A survey was conducted that was directed towards parents with one or more children between the ages of four and six. The survey addressed digital media usage, children's play practices and parents' attitudes towards and mediation of those practices. A total of 2177 parents participated in the online survey, which resulted in 1398 completed entries. The survey results provided insights into the sociocultural context of connected toys (Bleumers et al., 2015).

Third, a *technical investigation* was conducted to assess how connected toys could support particular play beliefs and forms of parental involvement. Online customer reviews of connected toys and games for children were analysed. In such reviews, the properties of connected toys are described from the perspective of adults based on their experiences with these products. The reviews were coded bottom-up, resulting in descriptive codes for the actors involved, aspects of children's play and types of intergenerational play. In total, 270 reviews for 27 different products were analysed (for more details, see Bleumers et al., 2015).

The results of the conceptual, empirical and technical investigations were presented to the project partners at the start of the first development week. This was done in an interactive and informal way. For example, a quiz was organized to communicate the survey results, which resulted in lively debates among the project partners. During the second day of the development week, brainstorm sessions with design students, teachers and parents were organized. The leading questions stemmed from the conceptual investigations. For instance, in one such workshop, the participants were asked to brainstorm ideas for connected toys that would facilitate co-play between children, siblings, parents and/or teachers. At the end of the workshops, all participants gathered to present their ideas and paper prototypes to the project consortium. For the remainder of the week, the project partners selected ideas that were considered to be both novel and feasible, and they decided to further explore two use-case scenarios.

The first use-case scenario focused on the home context, proposing a hybrid gaming environment for young children consisting of physical objects (e.g. a card deck) that can communicate with a tablet application. Through a companion app, adults are allowed to play an active role in children's experience. The second use-case scenario focused on the school context. Building on the same platform as the application for the home context, schools can add educational content. A companion app for teachers allows them to modify the content and follow children's progress. The aim of the educational use case is to improve children's technical skills, collaboration and creativity.

Generating Contextual User Insights

After exploring the problem space and defining a point of view in the form of two use-case scenarios, in-depth user research was conducted to gain insights into contexts of use for both scenarios: the home environment and kindergarten. This user research consisted of a brief questionnaire, observations and semi-structured interviews with 8 teachers from 4 schools and 11 parents with preschool-aged children.

Upon arrival in the school, the researcher first informed the teacher about the research and asked for his/her written consent. Then, the teacher filled out a form with questions about children's digital media usage in class, the teacher's attitudes towards digital media and the teacher's digital skills and how they acquired these skills. Afterwards, a two-hour observation was conducted in the classroom. Focus points during the observation were toy preferences, types of play, the role of play in the class activities and the teacher's mediation practices. Next, a semi-structured interview was conducted in which the researcher asked about the meaning and role of play in the classroom, the types of (connected) toys that are used and the teacher's personal preferences, the perceived learning gains of play, the influence of play practices at home on children's behaviour in class, the role of the teacher in play practices (e.g. supervision, co-play, assistance) and the extent to which the personal vision of the teacher aligns with the vision of the school board.

A similar structure was applied for user research in the home environment. First, the parent was informed about the research and gave his/her written consent. Then, they filled out a form with questions about the child's use of digital media, their attitudes towards digital media and their skills. Next, the researcher asked the child to show his/her favourite toys and asked some clarifying questions (e.g. why is this your favourite toy?). Afterwards, a semi-structured interview was conducted with the parent in the presence of the child. The topics were similar to those of the interviews with teachers, focusing on the parent's play beliefs and mediation practices in the home environment.

The qualitative interview data were coded bottom-up and triangulated with the data from the questionnaires and observations. The user research resulted in a profound understanding of both usage contexts and the current role of (connected) toys within these contexts.

During the second development week, the results were presented and discussed with the project partners in a workshop format. Afterwards, a brainstorm session was conducted with the partners resulting in three main ideas for connected toys. Three multidisciplinary teams were composed, with each team focusing on further development of one of the main ideas for the remainder of the week. At the end of the week, each team presented their paper or low-tech prototype to the other teams.

The first concept is a high-tech bracelet for children that connect to an application on smart devices. The bracelet can be personalized by small, tradable and printable 'pins' that have an effect on the game narrative and the (educational or entertainment) content in the application. The bracelet also includes a digital passport that can be linked to other applications and safely stores individual (progress) information.

The second concept presents a collection of connected objects, including a personalized 3D-printed figurine, a themed card deck and a tablet application. In the application, there is a special module that allows children to personalize a figurine or create their own and have it 3D printed and sent to their home. This figurine connects with the application and facilitates 2-way communication between physical cards and the smart device. Depending on the card deck, children can interact with either educational or entertainment content.

The third concept is a robot that interacts with other objects, including physical cards. Children can program the robot's behaviour (e.g. how it moves) via an application on a smart device or by tapping it with physical cards that connect with the robot. When the robot is used to play one of the (entertainment or educational) games initiated with the application, a LED display provides feedback. The robot can also be customized (e.g. with Lego bricks or 3D printed shells).

Concept Definition and Evaluation

After the second development week, the three concepts were further refined and a formative evaluation was conducted with the same kindergarten teachers and parents who were involved in the previous stage. The three concepts were explained by means of storyboards (see Fig. 9.1). After discussing the teacher's or parent's overall impression, the researcher asked them to pick one concept and, by means of open questions, tried to reveal the underlying motives for this choice (cf. laddering interview technique).

First, the parent or teacher was asked to clarify which aspects or properties of the selected concept stood out compared to other concepts. Each property was written on a separate sticky note, and, when a large number of properties emerged, they were prioritized before moving on to the next step. In the second step, the perceived consequences of each property were discussed in detail. The teacher or parent explained why that property is important and how it may contribute to children's play experience. Then, in the third step, the researcher asked why this perceived consequence is considered important for the child, and how it relates to the teacher's or parent's personal values. To wrap up the

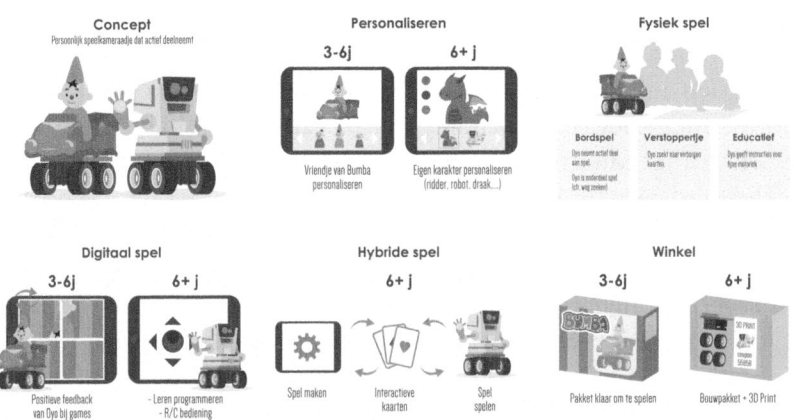

Fig. 9.1 Storyboard visualizing the third concept, a customizable robot that interacts with other objects, including physical cards

evaluation, the researcher asked what, if anything, the teacher or parent would like to change about the selected concept and why.

The feedback from eight teachers and 11 parents on the three concepts was thematically analysed and shared with the project consortium during the third development week. During this week, it was decided to further develop the robot concept and, for now, focus on the school context. The school context was considered most challenging in terms of facilitating co-play, mediation by adults, providing suitable content and durability. During the remainder of the week, the use-case scenario of the robot concept was elaborated based on the feedback from parents and teachers (stage 2), and high-tech prototyping was initiated. Furthermore, decisions were made about what had to be done by which partner in the final months of the project. The ultimate project goal was to deliver a workable demonstrator of a connected toy for the school environment.

Iterative Prototype Development

In stage four of the project, the selected concept was further developed into a high-tech prototype (see Fig. 9.2) consisting of a robot with an LED display and speaker that can move in different directions, a set of physical cards and a tablet application. All these objects can communicate with each other in two directions.

While the high-tech prototype was being developed, four gameplay scenarios for the robot were created: free play, memory, mastermind and storytelling. In the *free play* modus, children tap the robot with one of the cards and the robot immediately executes the behaviour indicated on the card (e.g. turning to the left, playing a tune, showing a smiley on the display). In the *storytelling* modus, children can program the robot's behaviour and save the sequence of steps on an empty card. The tablet application provides a visual overview of the programmed behaviour, which children can edit afterwards. In the *memory* modus, the robot does something (e.g. the LED display turns red, the robot moves one step forward) and children need to pick the corresponding card as quickly as possible and tap it on the robot, which provides feedback

Fig. 9.2 The final prototype that was evaluated by 266 children aged 4–6 years in eight schools

accordingly. In the *mastermind* modus, the robot executes four steps that children have to replicate by tapping the corresponding cards in the right order on the robot. Compared to the memory modus, speed is not a factor and the robot executes a sequence of steps instead of just one at a time.

When the high-tech prototype and game scenarios were finished, they were evaluated by 266 preschool children aged 4–6 years in eight schools. During each playtest, two researchers were present, one facilitator and one observer who did not intervene. Children played with the robot in small groups of 3–4 boys and girls. First, the facilitator explained the purpose of the evaluation and what was expected. Next, children played the different game scenarios, starting with the free play mode. Between modes, the children indicated whether they liked the game and if they wanted to play it again. To this end, a Smileyometer was used that consists of five smileys ranging from very sad through neutral to very happy. Children were asked to choose the smiley that resonated with their experience (see, Read & MacFarlane, 2006). In addition, we asked children to indicate which play modes they found the easiest and hardest and which play modes they found the most and least fun to play. After having evaluated each mode, the facilitator had a short conversation about children's favourite toys and games and wrapped up the session. Before the next group of children entered the room, the observer briefly discussed his/her notes with the facilitator and made adjustments where needed.

The observation notes and children's self-evaluations with the Smileyometer provided valuable insights into children's play experiences, the social interactions with peers and the adult facilitator during play, and the extent to which children created their own stories while interacting with the robot, the cards and the application. The results of the playtests were presented and discussed with the project consortium during a closing event and summarized in a report that describes the demonstrator application and indicates areas for improvement. The commercial partners could use these insights to finalize the prototype, develop other variants and, eventually, bring the connected toy(s) to market.

Discussion

The PD approach allowed the WOOPI project team to iteratively design connected toys in close collaboration with envisioned users (children) and those impacted by its use (parents and teachers), but adhering to PD's core principles proved to be challenging.

Revisiting the Core Principles

Having a Say

All major design decisions in the WOOPI project were informed by parents, teachers and, to a lesser extent, children. The degree to which they informed the decision-making process can be seen as a continuum ranging from *no* through *indirect* to *direct influence*. Taking all four stages of the design and research process into account, parents' and teachers' positions on this continuum are somewhere in the middle between indirect and direct influence, whereas the children's position is closer to indirect influence. Although users, including children, have the right to be heard in matters that affect their lives and environments, it was not always possible to achieve this in a straightforward manner.

Most design decisions were made by the project team during the development weeks, whereby the authors advocated the interests of the users. For instance, in the first development week, the project team decided to focus on two use-case scenarios informed by the conceptual, empirical and technical investigations. A similar rather indirect influence on the decision-making process could be witnessed in the second development week. The project team developed three concepts informed by the results of user research earlier conducted (i.e. observations and interviews), which set the future focus of the project. During the third development week, the project team selected the most promising concept based on feedback from parents and teachers. This concept was further developed into a high-end prototype and different gameplay scenarios that were evaluated on a large scale with children. Although children's play practices had informed the design process, it was not until this stage that they could voice their opinion about the design and exert a more direct influence. This was mainly due to a lack of available methods to design with children aged 6 and younger.

In sum, the ideal of directly involving users in *all* decisions proved difficult to achieve. Children's young ages and the time needed to negotiate differing interests among the project partners were the main reasons to choose more indirect methods to give users a *say*.

Mutual Learning

Mutual learning between designers and users occurred in different stages of the WOOPI project. For instance, during the first development week, brainstorm sessions were conducted with designers, parents and teachers that allowed for an exchange of expertise and ideas. A similar process could be witnessed in the third stage, when parents and teachers evaluated three design concepts. By means of storyboards, the concepts and the technology needed to realize them were explained. Afterwards, parents and teachers elaborated on what features they liked and disliked for their children, and what should be added or changed. Through this dialogue, new insights into the opportunities and risks of connected toys in the home and school context emerged.

Mutual learning also occurred in the fourth stage. Children experienced the possibilities of the high-end prototype first-hand, and, simultaneously, designers gained insights into children's interactions with the prototype and gameplay scenarios. Compared to the concept evaluation in the third stage, the learning did not happen through extensive dialogue. Since children's verbal skills are rather limited at ages 4–6 years, long conversations about the prototype and its potential impact on children's lives were avoided. Instead, careful observations were combined with short clarifying questions.

Mutual learning between designers and users did not happen in all stages. In stages 1 and 2, the learning was mainly one-directional. Designers gathered information about users via secondary research and by studying users' current practices. For instance, observing children in their homes and schools unravelled tacit knowledge about children's play practices and how they interact with peers and adults during play, but children did not yet learn anything from designers.

Finally, mutual learning also occurred between the designers (i.e. project partners), especially during the development weeks. During these week-long meetings, the project partners gathered in a design lab to share and discuss new insights and work on prototypes. This was challenging due to the multidisciplinary nature of the project team and the difficulty of bridging various expertises and conflicting interests. However, by engaging in hands-on activities, the meetings resulted in new insights that were materialized in design concepts, storyboards and high-end prototypes.

Co-realization

Whereas parents, teachers and children informed the design process in all four project stages of the WOOPI project, they hardly participated in visualizing ideas and making prototypes. One exception was the brainstorm activities in the first development week in which designers collaborated with parents and teachers. In most cases, though, conventional user-study methods such as interviews and observations were used. For instance, in stage 3, parents and teachers evaluated three design concepts that were presented as storyboards. Although they were invited to voice their opinions on these early designs, this happened in a verbal manner. No generative or *making* activities were added in which designers and users (in this case parents and teachers) co-realized connected toys.

A similar situation could be witnessed in stage 4 when children evaluated a high-end prototype. Children were observed while playing with the connected toy, but they could not modify or appropriate it to their own preferences. As mentioned earlier, a lack of research on PD with young children was the main rationale for not initiating generative design activities. In future work, it would be worthwhile to see if *making* techniques used for older children are suitable for design projects with 4–6-year-olds (see, e.g., Van Mechelen, 2016).

Co-realization was mainly achieved during the three development weeks in which the project partners, each with their own expertise, engaged in *making* activities. During the week-long meetings, they shared research results in workshop-like settings, brainstormed ideas on sticky notes, sketched storyboards and developed prototypes with low-tech materials that were tested in use-like settings and modified afterwards.

These hands-on activities with easy-to-use materials established a common language that all project partners understood. Muller (2002) has referred to this process as the enactment of a *third space*, i.e. a border region between the knowledge domains of participants with different backgrounds. In the first development week, these activities resulted in two use-case scenarios for connected toys. During the second development week, three design concepts were realized; and in the third week, the most promising concept was developed into a high-tech prototype. In sum, all project partners actively participated in realizing the design.

Guidelines to Increase Participation

Despite the authors' best intentions, adhering to PD's core principles in the design of connected toys was a challenging endeavour. Differing interests among the project partners, the target group's young age (4–6 years) and a tight schedule were among the most important barriers. However, looking at the principles as desired ends on three continuums helped the authors in preparing, conducting and reflecting on the PD activities.

Based on the lessons learned in the WOOPI project, six guidelines were formulated for adhering to PD's core principles and increasing users' participation in the design of connected toys. These guidelines are by no means exhaustive, and, when applying them, the context in which they were developed should be carefully considered. The guidelines are as follows:

- To expand the universe of discourse, involve a broad range of stakeholders in the design process, including those who are indirectly impacted by the use of the technology and the project partners. Think of a strategy for involving users, including children, early on and continuously in the design process.
- Instead of a fixed goal or research question, use an open-ended problem statement grounded in use practices as a starting point for design. Often, the solution that is being developed and the initial problem statement mutually influence each other as the design process unfolds. Allow for such flexibility.
- Establish an atmosphere of trust and openness towards each stakeholder's expertise. Broadly speaking, there are two knowledge domains at the start: (1) the current practices of the user, including tacit knowledge that is often hard to express in words, and (2) knowledge about the design process and technological possibilities.
- Avoid a one-directional learning process when engaging with users. Instead, explore the design space together and co-determine the agenda. This allows for mutual learning and the emergence of a third hybrid knowledge domain that belongs neither to the users, nor to the designers: (3) future practices mediated by technology.

- Engage users in *making* things. Jointly visualizing and prototyping ideas make it easier to understand current practices and technological possibilities. Moreover, it helps to imagine the consequences of the design suggestions and creates a common language that all participants can understand.
- Whenever possible, show users, and in particular children, what decisions go into the development of technology. Make them realize that they do have a choice with regard to the use of new technology and raise critical awareness about how such technology may influence their lives and environments.

Conclusion

This chapter provided methodological insights of how Internet of Toys applications can be designed together with children as well as other relevant stakeholders such as parents and teachers. Richly illustrated by a case study (i.e. the WOOPI project), it was shown how technological and social demands can be reconciled in the design of connected toys. In this process, the team jointly and creatively explored the design space, iteratively developing knowledge about current practices (what is) and ideas for future practices mediated by connected toys (what could be).

In line with PD's core principles (sharing decision-making power, mutual learning and co-realization), continuous reflection and participation of multiple stakeholders, including children, were aimed for. As for the first principle, *having a say*, children's decision-making power was rather limited, because the design problem was defined upfront, and all major design decisions were made by the project team. In terms of *mutual learning*, the second principle, the project team learned about the viewpoints of children, parents and teachers and gained profound insights into two envisioned use contexts: home and school. Children, parents and teachers, in turn, learned about the possibilities of the Internet of Things, and how this technology, in the form of toys, can be implemented in schools and at home. *Co-realization*, the third principle, was achieved via design sprints during three development weeks with the project partners. Children did not participate in these design sprints but evaluated the prototypes and gameplay scenarios afterwards in real-life settings.

Overall, parents and teachers were more systematically involved than children, both through conventional user-study methods (e.g. interviews) and more hands-on methods (e.g. brainstorming sessions). To better adhere to PD's core principles and further strengthen children's participation in the design process, the guidelines presented in the discussion section provide a useful starting point. In line with the Convention on the Rights of the Child (United Nations, 1989), these guidelines are a step forward in giving children *a say* in all matters affecting their lives and environments.

Acknowledgements This study was part of WOOPI (http://bit.ly/1F24wRO), a cooperative-PLUS project facilitated by (former) iMinds Media and funded by the IWT for participating companies. Ethical clearance from the ethics committee (SMEC, KU Leuven) was obtained during the project. The authors are grateful to the project partners and the children, parents and teachers who participated in the research and design activities.

Notes

1. In this chapter, the term 'users' refers to the envisioned end-users of technology, and those who are directly or indirectly impacted by its use.
2. In this chapter, the term 'designers' refers to the whole project team, including designers, researchers, developers and industry partners.

References

Bleumers, L., Mouws, K., Huyghe, J., Van Mechelen, M., Mariën, I., & Zaman, B. (2015). Sensitivity to parental play beliefs and mediation in young children's hybrid play activities. In *Proceedings of the 14th International Conference on Interaction Design and Children* (pp. 170–177). New York: ACM.

Braten, S. (1973). Model monopoly and communication: Systems theoretical notes on democratisation. *Acta Sociologica, 16,* 98–107.

Bratteteig, T., Bodker, K., Dittrich, Y., Holst, P., & Simonsen, J. (2013). Methods: Organising principles and general guidelines for participatory design projects. In *Routledge International Handbook of Participatory Design.* Oxford: Routledge.

Bratteteig, T., & Wagner, I. (2012). Disentangling power and decision-making in participatory design. In *Proceedings of the 12th Participatory Design Conference: Research Papers—Volume 1* (pp. 41–50). New York: ACM.

Clement, A. (1994). Computing at work: Empowering action by "low-level" users. *Communications of the ACM, 37*(1), 52–63.

Donoso, V., Verdoodt, V., Van Mechelen, M., & Jasmontaite, L. (2016). Faraway so close: Why the digital industry needs scholars and the other way around. *Journal of Children and Media, 10*(2), 200–207.

Ehn, P. (1993). Scandinavian design: On participation and skill. In D. Schuler & A. Namioka (Eds.), *Participatory design—Principles and practices* (pp. 41–70). Hillsdale: Lawrence Erlbaum Associates.

Frauenberger, C., Good, J., Fitzpatrick, G., & Iversen, O. S. (2015). In pursuit of rigour and accountability in participatory design. *International Journal of Human-Computer Studies, 74,* 93–106.

Friedman, B., Kahn, P. H., & Borning, A. (2008). Value sensitive design and information systems. In K. E. Himma & H. T. Tavani (Eds.), *The handbook of information and computer ethics* (pp. 69–101). Hoboken: Wiley.

Kensing, F., & Greenbaum, J. (2013). Heritage: Having a say. In J. Simonsen & T. Robertson (Eds.), *Routledge international handbook of participatory design.* Oxford: Routledge.

Kensing, F., & Munk-Madsen, A. (1993). PD: Structure in the toolbox. *Communications ACM, 36*(6), 78–85.

Livingstone, S., & Third, A. (2017). Children and young people's rights in the digital age: An emerging agenda. *New Media & Society, 19*(5), 657–670.

McReynolds, E., Hubbard, S., Lau, T., Saraf, A., Cakmak, M., & Roesner, F. (2017). Toys that listen: A study of parents, children, and internet-connected toys. In *Proceedings of the 2017 CHI Conference on Human Factors in Computing Systems* (pp. 5197–5207). New York: ACM.

Muller, M. J. (2002). Participatory design: The third space in HCI. In J. A. Jacko & A. Sears (Eds.), *The human–computer interaction handbook* (pp. 1051–1068). Hillsdale: L. Erlbaum Associates.

Polanyi, M. (1983). *The tacit dimension.* Gloucester: Peter Smith.

Read, J. C., & MacFarlane, S. (2006). Using the fun toolkit and other survey methods to gather opinions in child computer interaction. In *Proceedings of the 2006 Conference on Interaction Design and Children* (pp. 81–88). New York: ACM.

Robertson, T., & Simonsen, J. (2013). Participatory design: An introduction. In J. Simonsen & T. Robertson (Eds.), *Routledge international handbook of participatory design*. Oxford: Routledge.

Schön, D. A. (1983). *The reflective practitioner: How professionals think in action* (1st ed.). New York: Basic Books.

Schuler, D., & Namioka, A. (Eds.). (1993). *Participatory design: Principles and practices*. Hillsdale, NY: L. Erlbaum Associates.

Spinuzzi, C. (2005). The methodology of participatory design. *Technical Communication, 52*(2), 163–174.

United Nations. (1989). *Convention on the rights of the child*. United Nations. Retrieved from http://www2.ohchr.org/english/law/crc.htm.

Van Mechelen, M. (2016). *Designing technologies for and with children: Theoretical reflections and a practical inquiry towards a co-design toolkit*. Doctoral thesis defended in June 2016, UHasselt—KU Leuven. Retrieved from https://bit.ly/2tDS0te.

Winograd, T., & Flores, F. (1986). *Understanding computers and cognition*. New York: Addison-Wesley.

Zaman, B., Van Mechelen, M., & Bleumers, L. (2018). When toys come to life: Considering the internet of toys from an animistic design perspective. In *Proceedings of the 17th ACM Conference on Interaction Design and Children* (pp. 170–180). New York: ACM.

10

Including Children in the Design of the Internet of Toys

Dylan Yamada-Rice

Introduction

Like previous work in the field of co-design with children (Bruckman & Bandlow, 2003; Jones, McIver, Gibson, & Gregor, 2003; Williamson, 2003), this chapter seeks to ask: 'How can the ideology and practice of participation improve design practices?' (Lee, 2008, p. 34) and thus produce better products. In the case of the specific focus here, this is in relation to improving the quality of digital and connected toys by better matching design to children's play patterns and interests. To make this point the chapter draws on three different collaborative research projects in which I have considered children in relation to the design of digital play.

Through the sharing of specific insights from the findings of these three projects, I advocate that there are benefits in considering toy design and play in relation to one another (Nesset & Large, 2004). Further, this is better done by positioning the child as a knowledgeable

D. Yamada-Rice (✉)
Royal College of Art, London, UK
e-mail: dylan.yamada-rice@dubitlimited.com

© The Author(s) 2019
G. Mascheroni and D. Holloway (eds.), *The Internet of Toys*,
Studies in Childhood and Youth, https://doi.org/10.1007/978-3-030-10898-4_10

and able partner in this process (Carsaro & Molinari, 2017; Roberts, 2017). In order to achieve this, the chapter is structured first to review past literature about designing digital play and second in the area of co-design and participatory research with children.

Following the literature review, the remainder of the chapter is divided into sections that outline one key design-related finding from each of the three separate research projects. These are projects that considered (1) the extent to which children's use of a connected toy matched the designers' intentions, (2) how children can be included in the early stages of digital games design, and (3) children's making in the context of Virtual Reality (VR), a rapidly emerging form of digital play. These three studies are used to show how children's play and design should be mapped more carefully to one another. Specifically, that there are differences between designers' intentions and children's use. Second, children are experts in play and can therefore make a very valuable contribution to design. Third, adults' and children's use of cutting edge play technology (in this case VR) are different from one another. This is particularly important because technology is usually developed for adults first and then this is used as a benchmark for younger users. Collectively, these findings are used to emphasise the value of including children in the design process of connected toys.

Designing Digital Play

In an earlier publication (Yamada-Rice, 2018), I drew on theories of object-orientedness (Kaptelinin, Nardi, & Macaulay, 1999), object ethnographies (Carrington, 2012), artefactual literacies (Pahl & Rowsell, 2010) and material stuff (Miller, 2008, 2009; Shove, Watson, & Hand, 2007) to show how the design of digital toys and content, and the materials used, can be framed as having equal agency in play to the child. In other words, digital play is the product of two agency-bearing halves, that of product/content and that of the player.

'Knowing', in this case understanding children's use of digital toys and play, necessitates looking beyond the child and his/her use to that of the 'matter' of the play as well. We must do this, Barad (2003) says, because 'practices of knowing cannot be fully claimed as human practices, not simply because we use non-human elements in our practices but because knowing is a matter of part of the world making itself intelligible to another part' (p. 829). With regard to digital play specifically, Giddings and Kennedy (2008) also support Barad's ideas:

> ...that the distinct nature of video game play is generated in the intimate and cybernetic circuit between the human and the nonhuman.
>
> (Giddings & Kennedy, 2008, p. 15)

Applying this theory to gaming practice, Giddings and Kennedy (2008) describe how accomplished gamers should not be solely defined as highly skilled. Instead, the authors ask the reader to consider a perspective in which decentring the human can show how highly skilled gamers are not necessarily gaming geniuses but rather the:

> ...game has thoroughly and completely mastered him [the player], it had taught his fingers the precise micro-movements needed to fulfil its intentions (continued play), and had imprinted on his brain cognitive analogues of its virtually mapped game world. The player is mastered by the machine. We would argue that this mechanic language should not only be read metaphorically. Gameplay is an intense event, a set of intimate circuits between human bodies and minds, computer hardware and the algorithms and affordances of the virtual worlds of videogames.
>
> (Giddings & Kennedy, 2008, p. 15)

These ideas are also shared by others, such as Pérez Ferrer et al. (2016). Thus if children are as much being 'played with' by the game, i.e. by the 'affordances', those are the properties of the game (Norman, 2013); as they are playing with the game then it seems logical that there would be benefits to including children in the design of digital play in order to enable the production of connected toys that better suit child-users. The next section outlines previous literature on children in the co-design process in order to set the context for including them specifically in play design.

Co-design with Children

Continuing to draw on the perspective that digital play is as much a combination of tools as it is of humans, Pérez Ferrer et al. (2016) show how we are currently in an era where 'recent technological advances have enabled large numbers of people to express themselves creatively, who perhaps would not have been able to do so previously' (p. 19), and as a result there have been a number of software applications written that have allowed non-specialists to partake in creating simple video games, such as *Scratch* for children of school age. This, Pérez Ferrer et al. (2016) state, is the 'democratisation of Game Design, i.e. bringing the ability to create digital games to a much broader section of society' (ibid.).

Within the context of design in general, there have been attempts to include users in the design process ever since 'an international conference entitled 'Design Participation' in 1971' encouraged and popularised the process (Lee, 2008, p. 31). Williamson (2003) states that, initially, children were included in the design of technologies as 'testers' of prototypes and end products. In more recent years, there has been an increasing interest in including children in the earlier processes of design. For example, Van Mechelen (2016) produced a tool kit for 'designing technologies with and for children'.

Different methods have been suggested as to the best means to include users in the design process. Lee (2008) states this can vary from the designer having full power through to every part of the process being undertaken collaboratively by both designer and user. With regard to children specifically, Love, Gkatzidou, and Conti (2016) suggest the use of three particular methods: a co-design workshop that draws on principles from participatory design, future workshop techniques and rich pictures with regard to the co-design of technology. Specifically, Nesset and Large (2004) outline four roles children can have in the design process: user, tester, informant and/or design partner. Van Mechelen (2016), on the other hand, writes that children are 'especially useful to generate ideas and co-construct knowledge at the early, fuzzy stages of the design process where the design problem is still being defined' (p. 4).

Following on from the work of these researchers, the rest of this chapter presents findings from three different studies. These findings illustrate what I have learnt from including children in the design of digital play in a variety of roles. These are (1) as testers of a connected toy with the findings being considered in relation to the designers' intentions for their toys, (2) as co-designers in the early stages of game development similar to that used by Van Mechelen (2016), and (3) as informants to the design of play for emerging technologies. Findings and discussion from the three sections show how design and children's role in it should be considered an integral part of academic studies on connected toys and digital play, as well as form part of commercial processes in the production of these toys.

Children as Expert Testers of Digital Play Design

This section discusses a study undertaken during a short-term scientific mission as part of the COST Action DigiLitEY, which is a European network researching young children's digital literacy practices. The project considered the extent to which the design intentions of Justyna Zubrycka and Matas Petrikas for a digitally connected wooden doll known as Avakai (Fig. 10.1) were taken up during play by a group of young children.

Data for the study were collected through a series of interviews and conversations with the two designers and then comparing their answers with observations of 4–6-year-olds playing with the Avakai in an after-school setting in a Northern city of the UK. As discussed in more detail in Yamada-Rice (2018), the findings of the study showed that children's use of the toy coincided with the designers' intentions at some points, but in others, children used the Avakai in ways that had not been considered by the adult-makers. This section focuses on two ways in which the toy was used that had not been accounted for by the designers. These examples illustrate that children have expertise and imagination

Fig. 10.1 Avakai

beyond that of adult-designers and toy manufacturers, which if listened to could be fed into the design process in order to produce products that better match children's play practices.

Justyna and Matas designed and built a heart into each Avakai. When the doll is picked up, the heart can be felt beating through its wooden body. Further, when two Avakai come into contact their hearts beat faster, simulating an emotional response to their connection. While watching the children play it became obvious that the design of the heart intrigued them as much as the designers had hoped. However, not in the exact way they intended. The children anticipated the heart's function in relation to their own. One boy picked up the Avakai and started to run with it, doing laps of the room and trying to raise its heartbeat. As the boy became more and more out of breath he checked the heartbeat to see if its rate had increased, but the speed at which it beat remained constant. In the end, the boy declared the Avakai strong, like an athlete, who was unaffected by racing around the room. The fact that the heart rate did not change did not seem to affect this child's play. However, this observation opens up questions about whether if the Avakai's heart had responded in the way the boy anticipated the product might have produced an entirely different type of play—perhaps one better connected to children's practices. In other words, if we take the ideas of Giddings and Kennedy (2008), that digital play is a unique connection between technology and humans, then we must also consider that adult-designers and child-users might make these connections in different ways from one another. This is an idea that is also supported by Mazzone, Read, and Beale (2011):

> A User-Centred approach is recommended in the design of novel technology for children in order to reduce the discrepancy between the system conceptual model, defined by adult designers, and the mental model of children users.
>
> (Mazzone et al., 2011, p. 1)

Another example is the way in which the designers embedded speakers into the Avakai doll in a place that made them seem to the children as though they represented ears. The speakers disseminate sounds based on emotional responses to movements made with the doll. For example, if an Avakai is shaken it makes a noise representing annoyance.

One girl in the study became very attached to the Avakai. At the end of the first day, she whispered 'I love you' into one ear (speaker) of the Avakai she had been playing with. On consecutive days, I saw her whispering into the doll's speakers in an inaudible hushed voice. This example illustrates how for this one child, at least, the placement of the speakers in the location of the ears meant she perceived them like her own, in that they were for receiving sounds rather than outputting them. When I reported this finding back to one of the designers, Justyna, she immediately saw ways in which the finding could be incorporated into the doll's design, such as by creating a means of recording sound to allow the doll to be played with in a way that fitted with how this one child had used the doll.

The two examples shared in this section show how, as Barad (2003) proposes, it is important to consider the 'matter' of children's play in order to fully understand a child's use. In this project, the design intentions were known first-hand and so this made it easy to compare them to the children's uptake. The practice of user-testing in commercial play development is not uncommon, but it tends to be undertaken rapidly by market researchers who fund research differently from academia. What this section shows is that academic experts in play have knowledge and resources to map children's use and design together in other ways. Thus, if detailed observations of children's play with objects of the Internet of Things are undertaken, they can allow the design of toys to potentially better reflect the play practices of the children they are aimed at. The next section goes a step further to suggest that not only is the 'matter' of digital play important but that children could be involved in designing it.

Children as Co-designers in the Early Stages of Game Development

The study discussed in this section was funded by the Higher Education Funding Council for England, and it took the form of an industry sabbatical to explore the possibility of including children in the design of video games. At the time of the study, I was a full-time academic lecturing in Early Childhood Education. My research to this point had primarily been concerned with how children use digital tools for play. In other words, I was a researcher working at the end of the design process looking at children's use of products already on the market. During these earlier studies, I often had questions about why certain design decisions were made. For example, if I found a design feature that children didn't like or couldn't use, I wondered how it had materialised. Was it because of limitations in the technology? A financial decision? Or a lack of understanding of young children on the part of the developers?

Just before the start of the project I met Peter Robinson, Head of Global Research at Dubit, a company specialising in research on and development of digital play for children. Peter talked to me about the different research processes Dubit used at the time to ensure the best possible products were being made for children. We had different ideas about the possible usefulness or limitations of regularly including young children in the design of digital products being made for them. To this end we undertook a very small-scale project working with three children aged 5–6 years old to explore what would happen if we included them in the initial design process.

In creating the project methodology, Peter and I positioned the children in the study as experts in their play lives, as many researchers before us had done (e.g. Corsaro & Molinari, 2017; Roberts, 2017). We started by explaining to the child-participants that Peter worked for a digital games company and that we were exploring ways in which children could help make the design of digital play better. All three children were very excited to meet someone who worked for a digital games company and positioned him as an expert in an industry that they held in high esteem. On the days Peter was unable to join the research sessions the child-participants expressed disappointment and sought reassurance that they would meet him again. I took this interest as an early indication that, because digital play is an integral part of most children's lives, they were interested in how the products they use were made and were excited to be included in the process.

Each child was lent a tablet for the duration of the project and we started by asking them to take photographs/videos of the kinds of digital and non-digital play they enjoyed outside school. We then interviewed each participant separately about their physical and digital play using photographs they had recorded as prompts. After this they were asked to choose a collection of themed apps to test until we met again when they were asked what they liked and disliked about the products. The collections offered included groups of apps within the following themes: superheroes; music; food and cooking; art; and animals.

One of the reasons for doing this was to determine if the children would choose a theme that related to their wider play interests and, if they did, whether they could be seen as 'experts' who could bring a highly informed opinion to the design of digital play in that specific area. For example, Peter and I questioned whether or not a child who classified themself as having an interest in animals would also have good insights into how to improve an app with an animal theme. If this proved to be the case, we concluded it would be a straightforward way to work out which children to draw on in relation to the design of specific products. Thus, it would potentially be easier to include children in established commercial digital play development practices. For as Mazzone et al. (2011) and Van Mechelen (2016) state, we also recognised that including children regularly in the design process necessitates the creation of a framework to simplify their involvement and bring about useful results. This should include decisions about the key points in the process for inclusion and a list of best methods for co-designing at specific ages.

The findings which emerged from our thematic analysis (Braun & Clarke, 2006) showed that all three children had threads of interest that linked their physical and digital play. One girl chose the category of apps within the theme 'Art'. Her reasons for doing so related to her interest in drawing. She described how art was part of her home life and that her mum was really good at drawing fonts. She gave specific examples, such as asking me if I knew the Twentieth Century Fox logo and then telling me that her mum can draw it exactly how it looks. The second girl similarly chose art-themed apps. The data about her physical play suggested that, as with the first girl, these matched her other interests. She took many photographs with the tablet and said that ordinarily she liked taking photographs, especially of herself and her family. She also liked to read and write and stated that she loved creating mysteries and had watched and read all the Harry Potter books except the last one, which she did not want to start because it would mean bringing the series to an end. The only boy in the study was very interested in digital gaming and also liked to read comics. He chose to use the superhero-themed apps, which seemed connected to this theme.

Young children having thematic interests that they explore across different domains and platforms of play relates to findings of other research I have undertaken (Yamada-Rice, 2014). As a result, it seems to suggest that children can be seen as experts in relation to specific themes of play in the way Peter and I had anticipated. Thus, unlike the findings of Love et al. (2016), who found that the inclusion of children in the design of new technology can be challenging because they have a more difficult time verbalising their thoughts than adults, the three children in this study were very knowledgeable in seeing links across their physical and digital play and as a result could easily articulate how a game following that particular theme could be made more enjoyable. As a result, children, even those young in age like the ones in this project, could be valuable contributors to the early stages of game design.

The final section discusses children's use of VR and how their understanding of the medium, and how it is different to other media, illustrates that children could be useful partners in the design of emerging technologies and play in its earliest stages of development.

Children as Informants to the Design of Play for Emerging Technologies

This final section focuses on the importance of including children in the earliest stages of emerging forms of digital play, in this case VR. In doing so, I show how children's needs and uses of emerging forms of digital play are likely to be different from adults'. This is important, given that content for new technologies is usually developed for adults first, then this knowledge is applied to products aimed at a child-market.

The findings discussed in this section are drawn from my involvement with Deborah Rodrigues and Justyna Zubrycka on the German part of an EU-funded project called MakEY, about young children and Makerspaces. Deborah runs her own company called Glück which provides tech and play workshops in various locations around the world, where she teaches children how to create with physical and digital materials. Justyna, as outlined in the first case study, is the designer of the connected toy called Avakai. Our ideas for the German part of the MakEY project developed from one of the findings from a study looking at children's engagement with VR (Yamada-Rice et al., 2017), in which children wanted to play across physical and virtual spaces. Thus we sought to explore children's play and making across physical and virtual spaces. Specifically, Deborah produced a virtual world based on Avakai dolls designed by Justyna. We asked children to use physical materials to design something that might be of use to an Akakai in the virtual world. All participants created an object that related directly to the virtual Avakai world and were able to articulate clearly how the object did so. For example, Fig. 10.2 shows the creations of two of the research participants, one created a rocket for the Avakai and the other made a mirror.

Fig. 10.2 Physical making for the Avakai

These examples show how children were able to produce physical objects that directly related to the design of VR content and also imagine how they would play across both domains. Using this finding as a starting point we explored differences and similarities in children's play and making in physical and virtual contexts.

Children were asked to recreate their physical models by using the application *Google Tiltbrush* to create within a virtual world. Children immediately picked up differences in creating with physical and virtual materials. For example, the boy who had created the rocket showed frustration at not being able to make it look as abandoned as the physical rocket he had made when using virtual tools:

Boy trying to create a broken and abandoned looking rocket: "You can't get black on here. It comes out like that [sparks of blue light shoot out everywhere]."
Researcher 1: "Because it [the VR environment] is dark."
Researcher 2: "How about the yellow?"
Boy: "The yellow? This is like an Orange."
Researcher 2: "Oh, OK. How about a green? Remember how sometimes when metal goes rusty it goes green?"
Boy: "Yeah, like coins."
Researcher 2: "Yep."
Boy: [showing frustration]: "You can't see it here."
Researcher 2: "You can walk around, you don't need to stay in the same place always. Walk around."
Boy: "Yeah but how would you make it [the rocket he has drawn] more abandoned?"
Researcher 2: "More abandoned?"
Boy: "Yeah, so it's got like more cracks in it."

In the above example, the child tried to create in the VR world using very similar techniques he had employed with his physical creation. Similarly, another boy tried to recreate a character he had drawn with pen and paper in VR and become frustrated by the three-dimensional space. This is because, unlike drawing on a physical material, there was nothing to resist the pressure of his virtual drawing tool, so when he drew a line in *Tiltbrush* it was impossible for his next line to begin where the last had ended and join it exactly. Therefore, his physical colouring technique could not be employed in VR. The difficulties both children experienced showed how they began to understand and critique the affordances of VR in relation to how they differed from the physical environment and other media they had used. Unlike in the co-design project described in the last section, children found it harder to apply their play skills and expertise across the physical and digital (in this case VR) domains.

An unexpected finding was to discover that including children in the early stages of new technology development allowed them to begin to understand its affordances, how it worked and thus start to critique the content. This is unsurprising given that the anthropologist Tim Ingold (2013) writes that making builds an active connection between thinking and knowing and that we humans have forever learned about the world through our hands. The examples show how including children in the design of digital play with emerging technologies can provide insights into how their use of the medium matches what is known about their play on other platforms, or in this case the physical environment. It also informs design aspects specifically needed for children. For example, each child in this study could have benefitted from better onboarding that allowed them to understand that, unlike other forms of drawing, they could fully immerse themselves in their compositions, such as by walking amongst their virtual brushstrokes. Also, that drawing with light has properties that do not replicate those of physical materials.

Conclusion

The examples given from the three studies included in this chapter show that there is still scope for investigating how best to include children in the design process. In particular, as new forms of digital play emerge, such as VR, existing methods from previous studies (e.g. Van Mechelen, 2016) might need to be adapted or abandoned for new ones. Nonetheless, it seems likely that, in all circumstances, 'due attention will need to be given for how to 'scaffold children's creative abilities' into the [design] process' (Van Mechelen, 2016, p. 16). This scaffolding approach is also shared by Mazzone et al. (2011) who propose a framework for doing so. Once this is established, the examples shared here, along with others that have gone before, such as those from Nesset and Large (2004), suggest there are strong benefits in including children in the design process and that these outweigh any negatives, such as cost. Including children in the design of the Internet of Toys is therefore no exception. For example, in relation to observing them as end-users of designs, such as in the first study with the Avakai doll, it is possible to elicit valuable ideas for the development of digital toys and play. In that particular case, this related to how the doll could include a voice-recording device or making the heart beat differently depending on how the doll is moved. The second study showed how children can be positioned as expert advisers on digital play that relates to their physical interests and thus have ideas which they can clearly articulate on the importance of different game mechanics for the enhancement of the product. Finally, the last case study showed how children explore the affordances of new types of digital play and provided findings that call for adequate on-boarding of children within this process.

There are benefits not only for digital play developers but also for the children included in the design process. First, the empowerment brought about by recognising them as experts in their own play practices builds confidence. Second, by allowing them to gain insights into the processes of the digital games industry, they have an opportunity to decide if they may wish to work in game design when they become adults. Including children also allows them to have digital products that better match their needs. Finally, it allows children to be critical of digital content and toys.

References

Barad, K. (2003). Posthumanist performativity: Toward an understanding of how matter comes to matter. *Journal of Women in Culture and Society, 28*(3), 801–831.

Braun, V., & Clarke, V. (2006). Using thematic analysis in psychology. *Qualitative Research in Psychology, 3*(2), 77–101.

Bruckman, A., & Bandlow, A. (2003). Human-computer interaction for kids. In *The human computer interaction handbook*. Hillsdale, NJ, USA: L. Erlbaum Associates Inc.

Carrington, V. (2012). 'There's no going back': Roxie's IPhone®: An object ethnography. *Language and Literacy, 14*(2), 27–40.

Corsaro, W. A., & Molinari, L. (2017). Entering and observing in children's worlds: A reflection on a longitudinal ethnography of early education in Italy (Chapter 1). In P. Christensen & A. James (Eds.), *Research with children: Perspectives and practices* (3rd ed.). Abingdon: Routledge.

Giddings, S., & Kennedy, H. (2008). Little Jesuses and *@#?-off robots: On cybernetics, aesthetics and not being very good at Lego Star Wars. In M. Swalwell & J. Wilson (Eds.), *The pleasures of computer gaming: Essays on cultural history, theory and aesthetics* (pp. 13–32). Jefferson, NC: McFarland.

Ingold, T. (2013). *Making: Anthropology, archaeology, art and architecture.* London: Routledge.

Jones, C., McIver, L., Gibson, L., & Gregor, P. (2003). Experiences obtained from designing with children. In *Proceedings of the 2003 conference on interaction design and children* (pp. 69–74). Preston, UK.

Kaptelinin, V., Nardi, B. A., & Macaulay, B. C. (1999). Methods & tools: The activity checklist: A tool for representing the 'space' of context. *Interactions, 6,* 27–39.

Lee, Y. (2008). Design participation tactics: The challenges and new roles for designers in the co-design process. *Co-design, 4*(1), 31–50.

Love, S., Gkatzidou. V., & Conti, A. (2016). Using a rich pictures approach for gathering students' and teachers' digital education requirements. In L. Little, D. Fitton, B. Bell, & N. Toth (Eds.), *Perspectives on HCI research with teenagers: Human-computer interaction series.* Cham: Springer.

Mazzone, E., Read J. C., & Beale R. (2011). Towards a framework of Co-design sessions with children. In P. Campos, N. Graham, J. Jorge, N. Nunes, P. Palanque, & M. Winckler (Eds.), Human-computer interaction—*INTERACT 2011.* Lecture Notes in Computer Science (Vol. 6949). Berlin and Heidelberg: Springer.

Miller, D. (2008). *The comfort of things.* London, UK: Polity Press.

Miller, D. (2009). *Stuff.* London, UK: Polity Press.

Nesset, V., & Large, A. (2004). Children in the information technology design process: A review of theories and their applications. *Library & Information Science Research, 26,* 140–161.

Norman, D. A. (2013). *The design of everyday things* (Revised and Expanded Edition). Cambridge: MIT Press.

Pahl, K., & Rowsell, J. (2010). *Artifactual literacies: Every object tells a story.* New York: Teacher's College Press.

Pérez Ferrer, B., Colton, S., Powley, E., Krzywinska, T., Ceelhoed, E., & Cook, M. (2016). *Gamika: Art-based game design.* The MetaMakers Institute, Falmouth University, UK. Available online at http://ccg.doc.gold.ac.uk/ccg_old/papers/perezferrer_artgames2016.pdf. Accessed 1 May 2018.

Roberts, H. (2017). Listening to children: And hearing them (Chapter 8). In P. Christensen & A. James (Eds.), *Research with children: Perspectives and practices* (3rd ed.). Abingdon: Routledge.

Shove, E., Watson, M., Hand, M., & Ingram, J. (2007). *The design of everyday life.* Oxford and New York: Berg.

Van Mechelen, M. (2016). *Designing technologies for and with children, a tool kit to prepare and conduct codesign activities and analyse the outcome.* Mint Lab. Available online at https://soc.kuleuven.be/mintlab/blog/wp-content/uploads/2017/01/CoDesign-Toolkit-Van-Mechelen-2016-highRes-II.pdf. Accessed 1 May 2018.

Williamson, B. (2003). *The participation of children in the design of new technology.* Paper, Nesta Futurelab, Bristol, UK.

Yamada-Rice, D. (2014). The semiotic landscape and three-year-olds' emerging understanding of multimodal communication practices. *Journal of Early Childhood Research, 12*(2), 154–184.

Yamada-Rice, D. (2018). Designing play: Young children's play and communication practices in relation to designers' intentions for their toy. *Global Studies of Childhood, 8*(1), 5–22.

Yamada-Rice, D., Mushtaq, F., Woodgate, A., Bosmans, D., Douthwaite, A., Douthwaite, I., ... Whitley, S. (2017). *Children and virtual reality: Emerging possibilities and challenges.* Available online at http://childrenvr.org. Accessed 1 May 2018.

11

Testing Internet of Toys Designs to Improve Privacy and Security

Stéphane Chaudron, Dimitrios Geneiatakis, Ioannis Kounelis and Rosanna Di Gioia

Introduction

Internet-connected toys (IoToys), like any other Internet of Things (IoT) devices, contain embedded electronic and computing features, such as microphones, cameras, sensors of various kinds, that enable them to interact with users and adapt to their actions. By IoToys, we

S. Chaudron (✉)
European Commission, Joint Research Centre, Ispra, Italy
e-mail: Stephane.CHAUDRON@ec.europa.eu

D. Geneiatakis
European Commission, Joint Research Centre, Ispra, Italy
e-mail: Dimitrios.GENEIATAKIS@ec.europa.eu

I. Kounelis
European Commission, Joint Research Centre, Ispra, Italy
e-mail: Ioannis.KOUNELIS@ec.europa.eu

R. Di Gioia
European Commission, Joint Research Centre, Ispra, Italy
e-mail: Rosanna.DI-GIOIA@ec.europa.eu

© The Author(s) 2019   **223**
G. Mascheroni and D. Holloway (eds.), *The Internet of Toys*,
Studies in Childhood and Youth, https://doi.org/10.1007/978-3-030-10898-4_11

mean not only Internet-connected toys, but any Internet-connected device that interacts with children, such as puericulture and monitoring devices. They can record, store, analyse and share all sorts of data: sounds, images, movements, localities or even body parameters, depending on their configuration. IoToys can offer new, important opportunities to children for play, learning, health and educational support, to mention a few, thanks to their interactive and personalized features. However, they also raise questions about safety, security, privacy, trust and other fundamental rights of children. IoToys, as it is the case with any other connected devices, may gather personal information regarding our children's lives, and then use and share those data.

In fact, IoToys, in contrast to their "traditional" counterparts, are able to communicate with other devices and services, e.g. mobile phones, proxies and entities[1] that collect data for management, data-sharing, data analysis and other activities depending on the service provided. As a consequence, these developments of IoToys not only increase the amount of data available to services and their value to business, but also raise new security and privacy issues, which can affect families' and especially children's privacy when interacting with such devices. Issues that neither users nor manufactures have faced previously.

In addition, an IoToy is a complex environment that unifies digital and physical worlds in a specific context and implies convergence of different types of technologies and services. This increases even more the possible ways that such an environment can be attacked. For example, most of the IoToys on today's market have a corresponding mobile application that acts as a controller. So, the mobile application's execution environment, or other communication services, could be used as an attack vector for an adversary (i.e. an entity that acts maliciously) to gain access to children's private data, as already been demonstrated for a well-known IoToy (Cert.org, 2016).

In recent years, white hat hackers penetrated the data systems and networks of several organizations with the aim of exposing vulnerabilities and remediating them before they "can be taken advantage of by others" (Rouse, 2018), so far, news headlines that have reported security breaches, such as Mattel's Hello Barbie (Gibbs, 2015), Genesis' Cayla Doll (Moye, 2015), VTech Toys (Hunt, 2015; Sullivan, 2016) and

Fisher-Price's Smart Bear (Yadron, 2016), have, fortunately, originated from white hat hackers and found proper solutions or been removed from the market.

Until now, various research has studied security and privacy in the IoT, demonstrating different security and privacy issues (Geneiatakis et al., 2017; Ziegeldorf, Morchon, & Wehrle, 2015), while others (Chaudron et al., 2017) show that Internet-connected devices and objects pose challenges to ensuring the protection of children's identities, rights, data, privacy and security. Nevertheless, to the best of our knowledge, the literature lacks research focusing on testing and challenging technically the designs of IoToys under a security and privacy perspective. To fill this gap, we set up a protocol to perform a security and privacy threat analysis of IoToys.

Our test protocol founds its inspiration in research work that proved to be efficient in testing Internet-connected objects in the context of a smart house scenario using products already available on the market (Geneiatakis et al., 2017). Our work brings together engineers and social scientists who take a closer look at each step of the journey of children's data (recording, storing, analysing and sharing) through the analysis of several cases from technical and user-centred perspectives. The ultimate aim of our work is to identify key elements that need to be taken into account to ensure children's rights, data, privacy and security while designing and using Internet-connected toys, as well as to provide concrete guidelines for protecting children's privacy when using IoToys. Our contribution, in addition to a concrete threat analysis, is a practical feasibility evaluation of identified vulnerabilities showing how they can be exploited in practice.

The remaining of this chapter is structured as follows. After the introduction, in section "IoToys Data Flow" we overview a typical IoToys' architecture with a focus on data flow, and in section "Threat Model" we analyse its threat model. In section "IoToys Security Analysis", we study the realization of the threat model in test-bed architecture and analyse possible consequences to end-users in terms of security and privacy. In section "Discussion and Best Practice", we suggest guidelines and protection measures to improve protection against threats. Finally, in section "Conclusions and Future Work", we conclude this chapter and outline some directions for future work.

IoToys Data Flow

In this new IoToys era, users, especially children, can have (a) a two-way communication and (b) real-time interaction with toys. In such communication and interaction, data are exchanged in a bidirectional way between the user and IoToys, then between IoToys and a remote server. Remote content can be accessed by children while using their toys, which can either be interconnected directly to the Internet, e.g. via built-in Wi-Fi, or by assisting devices, e.g. mobile phones, that play a proxy role.

How are IoToys connected to the Internet? IoToys in order to function need Internet connectivity. Depending on the toy, they do not have to be necessarily always connected, but usually the Internet is essential for their proper functioning, especially during the initialization phase as they need to exchange data with a remote server. Since most IoToys lack a direct user interface, a mobile device, tablet or smartphone is most commonly used for set-up. Using a corresponding mobile app, the mobile phone connects with the toy via a wireless protocol, such as Wi-Fi or Bluetooth; then, the user sends the desired configuration directly to the toy when it is needed. Such configurations can be a password to access the house's Wi-Fi connection, or personal preferences related to the IoToy, such as the child's name, system language, notification settings, etc.

In some cases, the IoToy is not a stand-alone device but is rather accompanied by a hub. The hub acts as an intermediate interface between the IoToy and the Internet to facilitate their interconnection. This usually happens with IoToys, and many IoT devices in general, that have a small computational or network capacity but are unable to perform in a stand-alone mode. In such cases, the hub is the device with which the mobile phone connects to and which then handles communication with the IoToy. For the end-user, the use of a hub is completely "hidden" and makes no difference for controlling IoToys as it is achieved via the use of a mobile device.

Most IoToys, apart from being accessible by a mobile device that shares the same network, e.g. when connected to the same Wi-Fi, can also be accessed from outside their home network via the Internet.

This is achieved through a dedicated server that provides such functionality. The server is connected to the IoToy, and the mobile phone accesses the server in order to get updates and send commands to the toy whenever they are needed. The data flow of IoToys in a typical smart home environment is illustrated in Fig. 11.1 and can be described as follow:

A. The user interacts with the IoToy. He/she provides inputs to the IoToy which transforms them into sharable data.
B. IoToy sends and receives data from a remote server via the Internet. The router is the junction between the household Wi-Fi and the cabled network.
C. IoToy communicates with a smartphone via a wireless protocol. The smartphone acts as an interface/controller for the IoToy.
D. The smartphone connects to the Internet via a router.
E. Data flow between router and remote server.
F. Any device used by a remote user—providing the right credentials, i.e. passwords and user name, e.g. parents—that connects to the server and exchanges data directly, including data originated by IoToys.

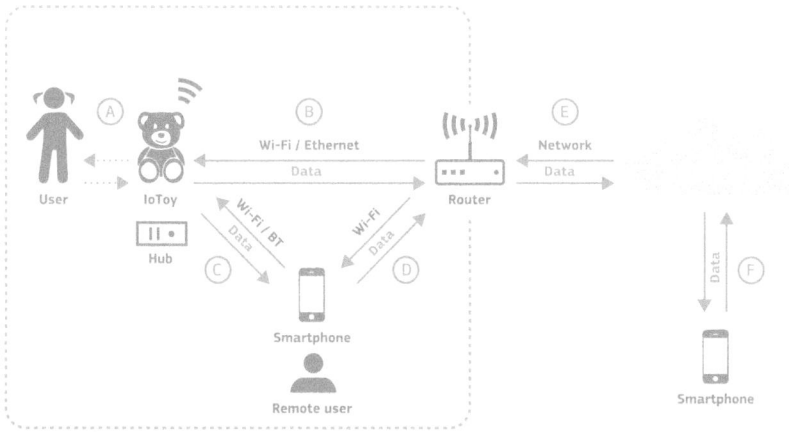

Fig. 11.1 IoToys data flow

During normal IoToys operation, the devices are neither constantly connected to the Internet nor constantly exchanging data. This of course varies from device to device, but the general principle is that communication happens only when needed. For example, a monitoring camera may broadcast live video only when it detects motion in a room, a toy may download new content only when it is not being used. Moreover, it may be the case that communication does not always occur via the Internet, it can also happen locally through a local area network. For example, when the mobile device is in the proximity of home, it can communicate with the IoToy without the need to contact the server.

Threat Model

What types of adversaries can we expect? In general, similar to any other interconnected system, a threat model in the context of IoToys should take into consideration two types of adversaries: *external* and *internal* entities that act maliciously in either a passive or/and an active way. External adversaries are entities located outside the system, meaning that they do not have direct access to IoToys, so they have to find a way to get through to the server. Internal adversaries are entities that may have the same level of access as any other legitimate entity of the system. For instance, consider a user that has an IoToy and would like to identify all other users of the same IoToy. Compared to the external adversary, the internal one has the advantage of already accessing the system, e.g. by having a legitimate account with a username and password, allowing interaction with the services the toy offers.

What types of attacks can we expect? The way adversaries interact with the system *passively* or *actively* depends on their final goal. An adversary who acts passively is able to eavesdrop on underlying communication in order to monitor children's activities or gather information about how the IoToy works, which could be used in a later step, for a more sophisticated and active attack. To do so, an adversary will try to monitor communication at points (B), (C), (D), (E) and (F) of Fig. 11.1, to intercept data collected during interactions between user and IoToy (A).

An adversary is active when instead of passively monitoring the underlying communication, he interacts with the different components of IoToys architecture, i.e. IoToys, mobile devices and supported services (e.g. Web access), in order to gain access to otherwise private information. For instance, an active adversary could try to identify the different components that comprise the IoToys architecture in order to launch an attack at a future time by generating appropriate requests towards different elements.

Furthermore, an active attacker could try to impersonate a user (child) in order to gain access to IoToys-related data. The types of information that can be accessed depend on the types of services provided. For example, the adversary might be capable of understanding the status of the toy, if it is online or not, or from which exact mobile phone the IoToy is accessed. An active adversary is, therefore, not only capable of violating service-data confidentiality but also users' privacy, as well as affecting the integrity of data when a malicious user tries to insert or delete legitimate users' data.

Ultimately, an adversary might try to affect IoToys' availability by causing a denial of service against any of the components of an IoToy's architecture.

IoToys Security Analysis

To study whether the different types of adversary, internal and external ones, described in the previous section can be a real threat to IoToys, we deployed a dedicated test-bed architecture similar to the one illustrated in Fig. 11.1. For our test scenarios, we relied on commercial IoToys. However, as our object is to identify IoToys' robustness against cyber threats and not to criticize specific products and implementations, we do not, therefore, provide here any specific information about the products under test. We have, nonetheless, contacted IoToys companies for which the tests found security-related issues and have informed them of our findings. The contacted companies reacted rapidly, reviewed our findings and quickly implemented measures to overcome the issues raised. The minimization of personal data collection was among our counterstrategies.

In our analysis, we considered scenarios for both types of adversaries, external or internal. We considered external attacks that can only monitor underlying network communication by accessing one of the points (E) and (F) of IoToys architecture. We then considered attacks by an internal adversary who is assumed to be a "powerful" adversary, which not only has in his/her possession a legitimate entity that can interact with the provided service (e.g. by using his/her credentials), but also can monitor the underlying traffic at points (B), (C) and (D). In this way, we are able to simulate how a legitimate entity might try to behave maliciously.

How did we conduct the test? As the details of internal mechanisms and processes for the different IoToys that we used in our test campaign were not known, we deployed different scenarios for the IoToys in order to trigger all the functionalities that they support, and to understand the different protocols they employ for their interactions with Internet-based services. While doing so, our testing adversary was able to capture all underlying communications, clear or encrypted, between the IoToys and the Internet, at points (B), (C), (D), (E) and (F) in Fig. 11.1.

In order to capture the traffic that the tested IoToys generate, we set up our own infrastructure in the following way. We used a computer with a network card that provides hotspot functionalities, i.e. allowing other devices to connect to it over Wi-Fi and gain Internet access. As a result, the computer is able to connect to our router and have Internet access, while at the same time it serves as an access point for other devices. On the computer we ran Wireshark,[2] an open-source tool for capturing network traffic. Once the hotspot was operational, we connected the IoToys to it and started capturing the traffic generated while we were testing the IoToys in different scenarios.

Thanks to this set-up, we could identify if the IoToys exchanged some types of information with a remote service, which was the case for all the IoToys we used. Furthermore, the set-up was able to capture this exchange of information. By analysing the underlying traffic, an adversary can deduce the different types of protocols used by IoToys, as well as whether the IoToys exchange some types of information with their servers. This is an important step for our tests, as we seek to determine if and how IoToys communicate with their servers and what type of data should be analysed. Depending on the provided service, our analysis showed that the following communications ways were used for data exchange:

a. HTTP;
b. HTTPS;
c. WebSockets.

HTTP (Reschke & Fielding, 2014) is a well-known protocol used for data exchange on the World Wide Web (WWW). It exchanges plaintext, while its counterpart HTTPS (Rescorla, 2000) is a similar protocol that functions over a secure connection and exchanges encrypted data. HTTP runs over a TCP connection that is unencrypted, whereas for HTTPS the underlying communication is capable of providing security services such as confidentiality and message integrity through a Secure Socket Layer (SSL) (Freier, Karlton, & Kocher, 2011) or Transport Layer Security (TLS) (Dierks, 2008).

So, an adversary that is capable of capturing HTTP messages can directly read them as real and clear data are provided in HTTP requests and responses. This is why, in most cases of the tested IoToys, HTTPS was used. However, even if the communication is completely secure, IoToys might send personal data without users' consent either to the provided service or to other third-party services. To identify if this was in fact the case, we executed a specific attack on the underlying secure communications, called a Man-in-the-Middle attack (MitM), which enables an intermediate to impersonate a server under specific conditions, and consequently read the encrypted data exchanged between the IoToy and the provided service. A general overview of this type of attack is illustrated in Fig. 11.2. A detailed analysis of the different types of attacks that can be launched against secure connection is beyond the scope of this work but can be found in Benítez-Mejía, Zacatenco-Santos, Toscano-Medina, and Sánchez-Pérez (2017), Zhang et al. (2014), and Onwuzurike and De Cristofaro (2015).

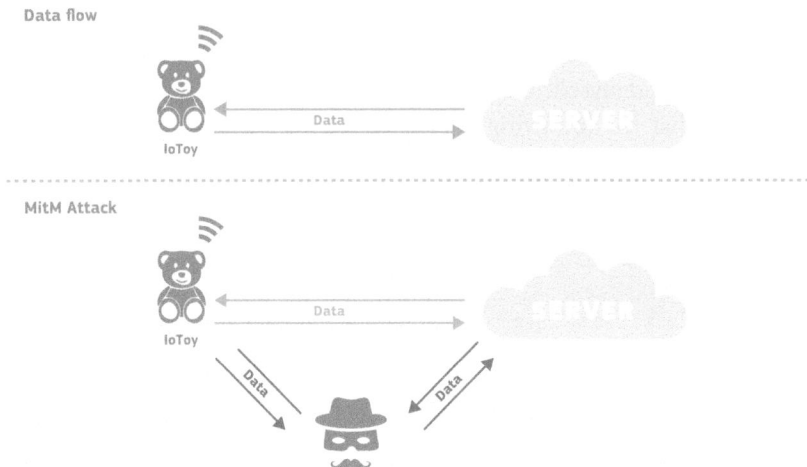

Fig. 11.2 An example of a Man-in-the-Middle attack for capturing/extracting encrypted traffic

To perform the MitM attack, we used the community edition of Burp[3] suite, a free powerful network tool that, among others, can perform a MitM attack. As IoToys are controlled by their corresponding mobile applications, our main target was to capture the traffic that the mobile phone was generating. We thus set up Burp by using the *Proxy* mode it supports. The computer on which Burp was running was connected to the same Wi-Fi network as the targeted mobile device. On the mobile device, we manually changed the Wi-Fi settings and added the computer on which Burp was running as a proxy. In this way, all traffic from the phone was redirected through the computer before reaching the Internet. The final step was to install Burp's certificate on the mobile phone in order to have it recognized as a trusted entity and thus be trusted by any traffic and certificates that were signed by it. What actually happened in the background is that Burp intervened automatically when an encrypted connection was established. It caught all the data transmitted between the IoToy and the IoToy's server without them realizing their traffic had been intercepted. By using Burp and by performing a MitM attack, we were able to read encrypted messages that were exchanged between the IoToys and their servers and thus could see if any personal and sensitive data were exchanged without the user being aware of it, without confronting them with the licence agreement of the product.

What are the key issues? First, in our test-bed architecture, we could get access to data exchanged over both insecure and secure connections. Particularly, we identified that over secure connections IoToys send various personal data to IoToys servers. Some of our most interesting findings include identifying data that were sent to IoToys servers, such as the following:

• Personal information, such as children's dates of birth, names, etc.;
• Unique identifiers, e.g. product hardware address, mobile device model, operating system, time zone of the user, etc., which can be used for distinguishing products and consequently users;
• Users' preferences, e.g. names given to IoToys by end-users;
• Information related to the status of an IoToy, e.g. if it is online or not.

Second, we found out that IoToys do not only send such information to their corresponding servers, as expected, but may also send it to third-party services. Even more, we observed cases where the data are not directly sent to the third party, but instead the third party is given special access to the IoToy's server in order to fetch users' data. This type of data flow is illustrated in Fig. 11.3.

Another important finding is the fact that some IoToys do not only rely on the HTTP Basic Authorization scheme, which is vulnerable to eavesdropping and replay attacks, but they also use the same generic usernames and passwords for all their products. What we found in this case is that the username and password that are needed for user registration are coded in the corresponding mobile application. This means that all users who have downloaded the mobile application are registered on the website with the same credentials. With these credentials, it is possible to query the server and then, depending on which user ID you specify in your request, the server responds with related user information. For example, if we assume that the IoToy was contacting the server https://www.iotoy.com/getIoToy?userID=123456, an adversary could simply

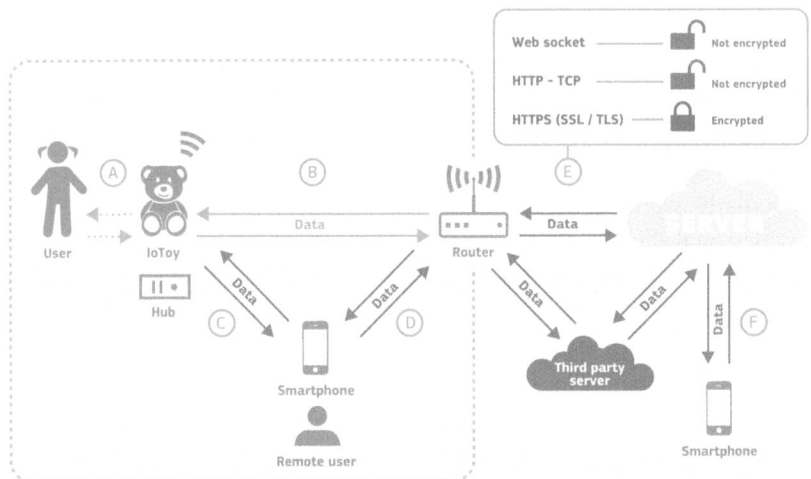

Fig. 11.3 Vulnerable points, in dark grey, of IoToys architecture, as identified by using our test protocol

create a script whereby the user ID changes after every loop in order to gather information about all the users of the same product worldwide. Since the authentication is the same for all users, the adversary would be authorized to send all those requests and receive corresponding responses.

Finally, our last category of findings relates to the use of WebSockets (Fette, 2011). WebSockets is an alternative option for communication that is employed to enable data transfer in cases where a real-time response is required (i.e. video services to mobile devices). The main discovery of our analysis is the fact that IoToys exchange personal data related to the provided service in clear text, i.e. it is not encrypted. This means that any adversary can capture the underlying communication and get access to personal data. For instance, in one of the cases we experimented with, an IoToy captures video and sends it back to a parent's mobile phone. In that case, we were able to demonstrate that any intermediate node between the IoToy and the mobile phone can get access to the broadcast video, without having direct access to the webcam.

Figure 11.3 overviews the different vulnerable points where an attacker could extract information according to our analysis on the basis of our test-bed architecture.

Discussion and Best Practice

IoToys can play an important role in children's development as they provide enhanced interaction and personalized experiences, elements that their predecessors are not able to support. However, their connection to the Internet could make them vulnerable to well-known threats. As IoToys comprise different components, adversaries might try to compromise any or all of them in order to get access to otherwise personal data.

According to our analysis, we identified that IoToys rely on well-known Internet-based protocols, such as HTTP, HTTPS and WebSocket, to provide interaction between a toy and a child. IoToys deploy mainly HTTPS, instead of insecure HTTP, when (personal) data need to be exchanged on the server side, but not always. Some tested devices only use HTTP and therefore exchange clear and readable data and do not offer any additional protection to the data in case of interception. Similarly, when IoToys rely on WebSockets, data can also be sent in clear text, as demonstrated by our analysis. Furthermore, for user authentication, some devices rely on the username and password approach. In some cases, they use schemes such as *basic authentication* in which the username and password are in reality sent in clear text. So an attacker can impersonate a legitimate entity and get access to his/her personal data. Even worse, we identified that there are cases where some elements of IoToys use the exact same username and password for every available product IoToys and rely on unique identifiers to filter the provided data. This means that a malicious internal user can get access to any and all legitimate users' data if he/she generates the appropriate request.

So, an important question that users and IoToys manufacturers should answer is: "What measures can or should be taken in order to enhance data protection for IoToys and eliminate data leakages?"

First of all, IoToy companies should introduce a data minimization approach, meaning that only those data necessary to implement the service should be provided by users. Second, users should be explicitly informed in a transparent way about the types of data that are exchanged between the IoToy and the server, and also if the IoToy server exchanges any of those data with third-party services. In order to enable such data flows, users should give their consent, otherwise the data should not be sent over the network, without affecting IoToys' functionality at all. For instance, users should have the option, if they wish, to share specific data with third parties. Such an option is available through a mobile app that manages the IoToy.

So, in case (personal) data are required for the proper functionality of the IoToy, then the underlying network communication should be sufficiently secured. In this view, a good option is the use of SSL; however, IoToy companies should recognize that SSL can be vulnerable to MitM attacks and thus only specific types of data should be exchanged over it. For instance, it is not advisable to send any authentication data in clear text over SSL. This means that the use of mechanisms like HTTP Basic authentication should be replaced by other more robust solutions. For instance, an alternative more robust solution is the use of HTTP Digest (Fielding & Reschke, 2014) as it relies on a challenge-response protocol in which users' credentials are exchanged in encrypted form.

Finally, IoToys should not use a predefined username and password in order to get access to the provided service. Instead, they should introduce an approach whereby users provide appropriate credentials. This is because, in the recent past, predefined passwords in IoT systems have been exploited by attackers in order to launch distributed attacks (Akamai, 2017) against other resources of the Internet.

Conclusions and Future Work

In the IoToys era, children and/or other actors, e.g. parents, can interact with toys physically or remotely based on their input, thanks to the technological developments of IoT and the enhancements to wireless network communications. Such interactions are technically supported by well-established protocols and mechanisms that have been successfully used on the Internet and rely on heterogeneous network architectures. Besides the advantages that an Internet-based service has, it may also open the door to various vulnerabilities that can be taken advantage of and turned into attacks. Consequently, like any Internet-connected device, IoToys cannot be excluded from this rule. Until now, it is questionable *if IoToys exchange non-authorized personal data with related servers or third-party services.* To answer this question, an IoToy test-bed architecture was deployed and different IoToys were tested in specific-use cases. It is important to highlight that the test bed that was set up did not require any special equipment or expensive software. On the contrary, all the software used was free and easily found on the Internet. Even more, the hardware was normal devices that anyone can find in a retail IT store.

Our analysis identifies that (1) IoToys exchange personal data with related servers and third-party services and (2) they may also provide "opportunities" for malicious actors to gain access to end-users' personal data. The latter is either because IoToys exchange data in clear text or they use a predefined username and password which assumes that the deployment of a secure network connection is sufficient for the provided service. In the current analysis, the focus was mainly on protocols and network interfaces that an attacker might try exploit to gain access to personal data.

However, an important element that has not been considered in this work is the mobile applications used for managing IoToys. Thus, there is a need for further study focusing on the vulnerabilities and threats that mobile applications might introduce to IoToys. Finally, we can also foresee a need to extend our scheme to support a completely automated approach for testing the security of IoToys against well-defined specifications in the form of an IoToys security certification programme. Such complementary studies should be able to build on our analysis and help to identify new threats to data security and privacy and ways to mitigate them.

Notes

1. Entities could be persons, informal groups like hacktivists or formal groups like service providers, institutions, etc.
2. https://www.wireshark.org/.
3. https://portswigger.net/burp.

References

Akamai. (2017, February). *Internet of things and the rise of 300 Gbps DDoS attacks*. Retrieved February 14, 2018, from https://www.akamai.com/us/en/multimedia/documents/social/q4-state-of-the-internet-security-spotlight-iot-rise-of-300-gbp-ddos-attacks.pdf.

Benítez-Mejía, D. G. N., Zacatenco-Santos, A., Toscano-Medina, L. K., & Sánchez-Pérez, G. (2017). HTTPS: A phishing attack in a network. In *Proceedings of the 7th International Conference on Information Communication and Management* (pp. 24–27). New York, NY: Association for Computing Machinery. https://doi.org/10.1145/3134383.3134389.

Cert.org. (2016, February). *Vulnerability note VU#719736—Fisher-price smart toy platform allows some unauthenticated web API commands*. Retrieved February 14, 2018, from http://www.kb.cert.org/vuls/id/719736.

Chaudron, S., Di Gioia, R., Gemo, M., Holloway, D., Marsh, J., Mascheroni, G., ... Yamada-Rice, D. (2017). *Kaleidoscope on the internet of toys—Safety, security, privacy and societal insights* (JRC Technical Report No. EUR 28397). European Union.

Dierks, T. (2008, August). *The Transport Layer Security (TLS) protocol version 1.2*. Retrieved February 14, 2018, from https://tools.ietf.org/html/rfc5246.

Fette, I. (2011, December). *The WebSocket Protocol*. Retrieved February 14, 2018, from https://tools.ietf.org/html/rfc6455.

Fielding, R., & Reschke, J. (2014, June). *Hypertext Transfer Protocol (HTTP/1.1): Authentication*. Retrieved February 14, 2018, from https://tools.ietf.org/html/rfc7235.

Freier, A., Karlton, P., & Kocher, P. (2011, August). *The Secure Sockets Layer (SSL) protocol version 3.0*. Retrieved February 14, 2018, from https://tools.ietf.org/html/rfc6101.

Geneiatakis, D., Kounelis, I., Neisse, R., Nai-Fovino, I., Steri, G., & Baldini, G. (2017). Security and privacy issues for an IoT based smart home. In *2017 40th International Convention on Information and Communication Technology, Electronics and Microelectronics (MIPRO)* (pp. 1292–1297). https://doi.org/10.23919/MIPRO.2017.7973622.

Gibbs, S. (2015, November 26). Hackers can hijack Wi-Fi Hello Barbie to spy on your children. Technology. *The Guardian*. Retrieved February 15, 2018, from https://www.theguardian.com/technology/2015/nov/26/hackers-can-hijack-wi-fi-hello-barbie-to-spy-on-your-children.

Hunt, T. (2015, November 28). *When children are breached—Inside the massive VTech hack*. Retrieved February 15, 2018, from https://www.troyhunt.com/when-children-are-breached-inside/.

Moye, D. (2015, February 9). Talking doll Cayla hacked to spew filthy things (UPDATE). *Huffington Post*. Retrieved from https://www.huffingtonpost.com/2015/02/09/my-friend-cayla-hacked_n_6647046.html.

Onwuzurike, L., & De Cristofaro, E. (2015). Danger is my middle name: Experimenting with SSL vulnerabilities in android apps. In *Proceedings of the 8th ACM Conference on Security & Privacy in Wireless and Mobile Networks* (pp. 15:1–15:6). New York, NY: Association for Computing Machinery. https://doi.org/10.1145/2766498.2766522.

Reschke, J. F., & Fielding, R. T. (2014, June). *Hypertext Transfer Protocol (HTTP/1.1): Message syntax and routing*. Retrieved February 14, 2018, from https://tools.ietf.org/html/rfc7230.

Rescorla, E. (2000, May). *HTTP over TLS*. Retrieved February 14, 2018, from https://tools.ietf.org/html/rfc2818.

Rouse, M. (2018, January). *What is white hat?* Retrieved February 15, 2018, from http://searchsecurity.techtarget.com/definition/white-hat.

Sullivan, B. (2016, December 7). *Your kid's new friend Cayla may not be as innocent as she looks*. Retrieved February 15, 2018, from http://time.com/money/4593703/internet-of-toys-child-safety-spying/.

Yadron, D. (2016, February 2). *Fisher-price smart bear allowed hacking of children's biographical data*. Retrieved February 15, 2018, from http://www.theguardian.com/technology/2016/feb/02/fisher-price-mattel-smart-toy-bear-data-hack-technology.

Zhang, L., Choffnes, D., Levin, D., Dumitras, T., Mislove, A., Schulman, A., & Wilson, C. (2014). Analysis of SSL certificate reissues and revocations in the wake of heartbleed. In *Proceedings of the 2014 Conference on Internet Measurement Conference* (pp. 489–502). New York, NY: Association for Computing Machinery. https://doi.org/10.1145/2663716.2663758.

Ziegeldorf, J. H., Morchon, O. G., & Wehrle, K. (2015). Privacy in the internet of things: Threats and challenges. *CoRR, abs/1505.07683*. Retrieved from http://arxiv.org/abs/1505.07683.

12

Video Methods: Researching Sociomaterial Points-of-View in Children's Play Practices with IoToys

Thomas Enemark Lundtofte and Stine Liv Johansen

Introduction

In this chapter, we will explore how specific video methodologies can be brought into play in studies of young children's engagement with Internet-connected toys (IoToys). We will focus on everyday sociomaterial configurations involving young children and tablet computers, and through empirical observations, we will put forward methodological reflections on how to investigate these situated play practices via observational data using video cameras. The ethnographic methodology presented here will reflect a research interest in young children's everyday play practices with digital toys. We will show how a structured approach to video ethnography can produce highly comparable data and provide

T. E. Lundtofte (✉)
University of Southern Denmark, Odense, Denmark
e-mail: thomas@sdu.dk

S. L. Johansen
Aarhus University, Aarhus, Denmark
e-mail: stineliv@cc.au.dk

© The Author(s) 2019
G. Mascheroni and D. Holloway (eds.), *The Internet of Toys*,
Studies in Childhood and Youth, https://doi.org/10.1007/978-3-030-10898-4_12

insights from both sides of an interaction between a child and a digital toy. Moreover, we will provide reflections on the material complexities in this particular setting and how video equipment and the presence of a researcher add to this complexity. Finally, we will present examples of the levels of analytic sensibility afforded by this method.

Like a tablet computer, IoToys may be able to register a touch, but perhaps not a lingering hand or finger of a child who is about to do something, but then decides not to. An IoToy may also be able to register digital activities pointing to certain play interests, but fail to collect information on how they relate to play activities with multiple digital and non-digital actors and frames of reference. As such, IoToys have the potential to construct vast and complex data sets in relation to user interactions (Holloway & Green, 2016; Mascheroni & Holloway, 2017). Yet, as we know, utilising this aggregated data presupposes knowledge about the complexities and situations of everyday practices—and, of course, access to said aggregated data. After all, 'data' are ideologically angled representations of infinitely complex realities, and so we are always working with considerable blind spots and biases—even when the data sets are big (van Dijck, 2014). Jackie Marsh has described how to play with Internet-connected toys connects 'digital and nondigital components' and takes place 'across physical and digital domains' (2017), pointing also to a complex configured materiality in which data from interactions provide an epistemological basis with important limitations.

These renditions of the complex sociomaterial worlds in which digital toys are domesticated (Lie & Sørensen, 1996) serve to show how we must also look to qualitative observational methods in order to gain multiple perspectives and, concomitantly, the ability to ask relevant questions in relation to children's use of IoToys. This chapter presents a Points-of-View (POV) method that aims to provide empirical insights from both ends of the line of interaction between a child and a tablet computer. Practically, we will present a set-up in which two cameras are mounted on a tablet computer, providing footage of the child as well as of the screen (Fig. 12.1). This ethnographic video method produces comparable data while freeing up the researcher to focus on contextual elements of an informant's environment. As we will argue in the

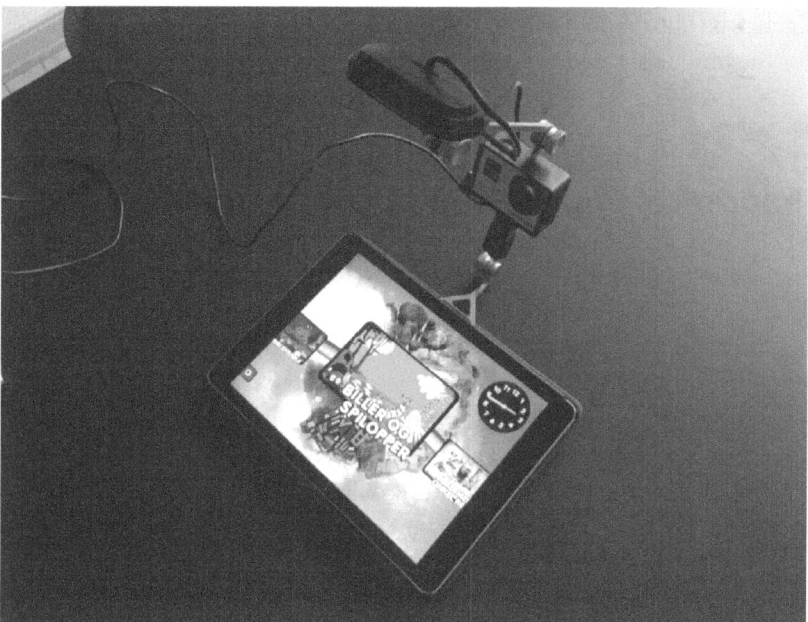

Fig. 12.1   The POV setup

following, this method might prove to be useful in relation to specific studies of children's use of IoToys, but also supplement (and should be supplemented by) other relevant ethnographic methods in the study of children's play practices with digital as well as analogue toys.

The POV method was developed in order to facilitate basic research concerning young Danish children's tablet computer play practices with an emphasis on meaning-making. The empirical study, which forms the basis of a PhD project (Lundtofte, 2017), considering young children's everyday use of the app 'Ramasjang',[1] includes field visits in (so far) seven Danish families with children aged 4–6. The argument, which we will present in the following, will be structured as a continuous zoom focusing on (1) the overall theoretical framework of the study, (2) the home as a site for ethnographic fieldwork with young children, (3) video method in theory and practice and finally, (4) children's play practices with the Ramasjang app. The argument will be connected to examples from empirical fieldwork, which will illustrate analytical and theoretical points. Finally, we will discuss the limitations and make suggestions for further work at the end of the chapter.

Theoretical Foundation

The theoretical framework for this research project draws on practice theory as an umbrella concept along with symbolic interactionism and theories of play. These theories inform an understanding of young children's play practices as teleo-affective (Schatzki, 2001), in the sense that agential actions comprise teleological aspects of means-to-an-end informed by knowledge, and affective aspects in the sense of mood and other types of emotional dispositions on a social level (Reckwitz, 2017). The teleological aspects can be understood using symbolic interactionism. This theoretical framework tells us that human beings are constantly (re)interpreting objects of various kinds in relation to their experiences and the knowledge they share and negotiate amongst themselves (Blumer, 1969). Play practices, however ubiquitous in their nature, are characterised by certain moods, as described by Helle Skovbjerg Karoff (2013). Karoff explains how the main objective in playing is keeping the playful mood going, consequently positioning play as an autotelic concept and practice. In bringing these theoretical perspectives together, we achieve a framework that looks for routines and logic in practices as well as meaning-making from a teleo-affective perspective rooted in play and interpretive knowledge of objects.

We are considering material aspects in social configurations and, thus, viewing objects, such as the tablet computer, as materially defined in relation to other actors. Cathy Burnett has introduced the concept of 'fluid materiality' in regard to tablet computers, which she uses in two respects. She draws on Don Ihde's concept of 'multistability' (1993) in order to speak of ways in which tablet computers '"become" differently as they are constituted differently through different relations' (Burnett, 2017, p. 25). Secondly, the concept of '"fluid materiality"' is intended to evoke how materiality itself is conceived differently through different assemblages' (ibid.). If we think of this definition in reference to symbolic interactionism and practice theory, a tablet computer is, to a large degree, always being defined through teleo-affective practices (Schatzki, 2001), be they playful, educational or something else. These definitions are ever-changing and depend on the human actors in the configuration, and how they structure their notions and desires in relation to the tablet computer and its affordances, as well as to each other. On top of this, a tablet computer is a multimodal tool, consequently expanding its dynamic materiality.

When we collect audio-visual data from both ends of a sociomaterial configuration consisting of a child and a tablet computer, we are able to operationalize these theoretical perspectives and look for instances of sociomaterial meaning-making as well as limitations concerned with affordances for play. We will show how the POV method can reveal what play practices with tablet computers look like on the micro-level, and how we are able to analyse them across a rather consistent and comparable data set. The method does, however, come with some important limitations, and perhaps imperfections, to be improved upon in future research. Even though the cameras were small and the camera rig made it possible to mount them rather easily, there was still an obstructive and somewhat intrusive element to their presence in the field. This method was also not offered to the informants or their parents as a self-reporting technique, hence making it necessary for the researcher to be present when video data were collected. This presence was, however, part of the methodological kinship with ethnography, which will be elaborated in the following section.

Ethnographic Fieldwork with Young Children in the Home

Doing ethnographic fieldwork with very young children in the home-setting seems to be a remarkably undescribed aspect of methodology within media and childhood studies. To some extent, the lack of relevant literature in this field might be caused by the lack of actual empirical studies (with important exceptions found in the work by Plowman et al. [McPake, Plowman, & Stephen, 2013; Plowman, 2016;

Plowman, McPake, & Stephen, 2008], and Marsh et al. [Marsh et al., 2005; Marsh, Hannon, Lewis, & Ritchie, 2017]), and the vast majority of studies on young children's engagement with digital media and technology take place in institutional settings. For some of those studies that actually have the home as the primary field site, there seems to be a lack of consideration regarding the specificities, frames and limitations of this approach. As stated by, for instance, Coad et al. (2015) and Johansen and Karoff (2010), the home as a setting for ethnographic fieldwork is often taken for granted—and therefore not problematised or even discussed as such. Although recognised as a place where children feel safe and comfortable—at home—the home is not necessarily an easy place to do fieldwork. As a researcher, you have to balance being a professional—and turning someone else's home into the site where you perform your professionalism—against being a guest, submitted to the norms and ethics which characterise this particular role.

As we will argue in this chapter, the use of video methods offers a relevant way of overcoming some of the methodological imperfections and limitations when studying young, perhaps not very verbally articulate, children in the home. Still, some basic considerations need to be taken into account in studies like these, regardless of the specific design or use of tools for data collection. These have to do with the way in which researchers negotiate access to the field as well as continuous consent from the children, with the practical and ethical aspects of establishing a rapport with the children, with the physical and structural positioning of the researcher and, last but not least, with the role of the parents as hosts, gatekeepers and interpreters of children's doings and sayings.

Although access to the field (the home) is in most cases permitted by parents, both officially and quite pragmatically (since they open their front door and let the researcher in), and since the negotiation of informed consent will take place between the researcher and the parents, one still has to consider aspects of access and consent in relation to the child. Especially with very young children as objects of study, establishing a rapport and maintaining an accepted and privileged position in the field is a matter of high sensibility towards one's informants. In the empirical work presented in this chapter, the researcher had to balance being on the one hand 'the guy with the camera', who was obviously changing the sociomaterial setting by establishing the video set-up (which we will describe in further detail below), while on the other hand he had to engage with and encourage the child and his or her parents and siblings. This very complex arrangement requires a high degree of flexibility from the researcher, who must be able to switch between several positions, physically as well as relationally, all in one single field visit, rather than sticking to specific and well-defined researcher roles (Fine & Sandstrom, 1988).

It is important to stress that these considerations are important in relation to any kind of fieldwork in which researchers wish to engage actively with children. You always have to consider your physical and relational position and approach, and you have to be considerate of the ethical implications in relation to the power structure between the child and you as an adult, who is welcomed and introduced into the home by the child's parents. You have to broaden your loyalty to the child as well as to the hosting parent(s) during the fieldwork as well as in your analysis and in the following representation of your informants in, for instance, writing. But even more, when introducing a camera set-up like the POV hardware discussed in this chapter, you must be aware of the potential problems, as well as possibilities, it represents. In the empirical examples that we will present below, these will be touched upon. For example, we will discuss how the hardware may in itself function as a sort of communication tool or toy which may strengthen the relation between the researcher and the child when silly play with the cameras is allowed and the child through this gets a sense of the intentions of the researcher.

Recording Fluid Materialities of Play

In the following, we will discuss the use of video in ethnographic fieldwork as such, as well as in relation to the specific empirical work we are building on in this chapter. We sought to understand what was happening between the tablet computer and the child. Researching playful practices with an aspect of meaning-making processes on the micro-level demanded a method that could embrace specificity as well as broader strokes of context. This is underscored by the fluid materiality of tablet computers (Burnett, 2017), as well as the affective aspects of playful practices (Karoff, 2013). The equipment that was brought into the field added to this already complex material configuration in different ways.

To introduce the conditions and dilemmas, we were facing, we will present a field note featuring William, a five-year-old boy who actively and playfully engaged with the recording equipment:

> …I tell William that I've brought something besides the board game we just played, as I'm unpacking the cameras and my laptop. I try to explain to William how I'd like to make recordings of him playing with his iPad, while I show him the video feed from the top-shot camera on my laptop screen. William is eager to experiment with putting his head under the camera and sticking his tongue out. His mum is concerned with the fragility of the equipment and makes attempts to contain his silly play. Field notes, 5 January 2017 (Fig. 12.2)

Instances like the above example were common during the visits with young children in their homes. They were all familiar with video

Fig. 12.2 Interacting with the camera through silly play

cameras and most often they were keen to do something with them. When extra recordings were sometimes made on the fly using a smartphone, the child would usually request to examine the video immediately after the recording had stopped. This acute awareness of the basic affordances of video technologies is part of the everyday lives that so many children are used to. Video cameras are no longer particularly foreign objects in this type of field; however, what we do with and in relation to them must be taken into close consideration.

The physical and financial struggle of using cameras in ethnographic research has improved dramatically over time, as has the body of research utilising audio-visual technologies. Where separate equipment for sound and image operated by several people and powered by cables used to be the norm, the introduction of the 16 mm format 'allowed for the revival of ethnographic film', as put by Jean Rouch in his seminal essay *The Camera and Man* (2003 [1974]). Now, we are able to utilise small, battery-powered, sophisticated recorders of sound and images at a fraction of the previous cost. The ease with which video-assisted research can be performed has resulted in epistemological discussions, since we have become able to generate vast amounts of audio-visual material. How do we determine if the research questions call for video data, and what are the consequences for the field of research?

In her account of visual approaches to ethnography, Sarah Pink notes:

> When researching everyday life as ethnographers, we do this from inside, we become immersed in its flow and, indeed, our own actions and feelings become part of the very context that we are researching. (Pink, 2013, p. 35)

This conceptualisation of visual ethnography underscores how video cameras along with other agents of visual production—however increasingly easy to incorporate—can never provide completely objective records of everyday life. As researchers, we use video cameras to produce knowledge by introducing them in an environment where everyday life occurs (ibid., p. 106); and in doing so, we turn these situations into performances, much like interviews. Calling them performances is not to be understood in a very literal sense, but as a way of grasping the multi-agential production that takes place in the sociomaterial configuration consisting of a researcher, informant(s), artefact(s) and video equipment. When we introduce a video camera into the home of a young child as researchers, this piece of equipment adds to an already challenging and media-saturated field site.

In her recent book *Video as Method*, Anne Harris stresses how a 'strong methods section of any research project will include clear attention to the tools used' (2016, p. 18). Drawing on recent theoretical turns towards practices and sociomaterial versions of actor-network theory (Latour, 2005), the camera and its presence render it an agent in the sociomaterial configuration put together in a research field. Methods are seldom described and categorised on the sole basis of an agent of any kind, but rather on thoughts concerning how agents interact in configurations. An ethnographer, psychologist or sociologist may use paper and pen to note data concerning informants in research, but this is not considered methodologically akin on the basis of using said paper and pen. A video camera and the data it produces mediate something to be decoded, something which has been encoded in the research process in a range of ways. The thoughts and rigour surrounding these encodings and decodings, not to be taken at face value to use Stuart Hall's terminology (2007 [1973]), are part of what makes up a methodology in conjunction with necessary tools, such as video cameras. Conclusively, from a sociomaterial point of view, it is not a matter of 'what video cameras do', but rather of 'what we do with and in relation to video cameras'.

This takes us back to the motivation for using video cameras as research tools in the first place. Using video in research should be tied to the research questions and the identification of video as the most suitable methodological tool for answering said questions. According to Marilyn Fleer, 'Video can capture complexities of dynamics surrounding material conditions and social expectations' (2014, p. 18). Fleer also stresses how video data, in relation to researching young children, allow for iterative layers of analysis (ibid., p. 20). If we are to make distinctions between video data and data such as field notes, photographs and audio, it will be hard to disqualify any of these from affording iterative layers of analysis. However, as video data are audio-visual, they allow us to assess body language along with visible and audible context from different theoretical angles. Even though theory-based choices about framing have been made, the footage that is produced can be analysed from a variety of perspectives.

The theoretical motivation behind the framing choices in the POV method favours approximated actor perspectives. In doing so, the different informants and situations are bridged empirically by similar framing. This method presents a rigidity in camera work that also sets it apart from previous ethnographic video research with young children. Marsh et al. have demonstrated how 'GoPro chestcams' can assist in providing children's perspectives (2015). However, while the child's physical mobility remains relatively unobstructed, a chestcam only captures one side of a given interaction. When doing video observations of young children's tablet computer play, it seems we are faced with choosing between unobtrusiveness and rigidity in perspective(s). Consequently, improvements to the POV method should focus on this particular aspect. In the following, we will describe the practical considerations behind the method in relation to the field of video ethnography.

The POV Model

The method described here is a video-based approach to accessing the sociomaterial configuration of a child and a tablet computer by focusing on audio-visual feedback from both sides of the interaction. However, there is also a wider context than the scope of two cameras. Furthermore, definitions of ethnography often stress the importance of staying within a given field for an extended period of time in order to build a rapport (Hammersley & Atkinson, 2007). This method does not adhere to such firm principles of ethnography and may, consequently, perhaps not be described as such. Rather, the POV model in qualitative research draws on ethnographic principles in building accounts of young children's everyday play practices with technologies.

In order to mount the cameras, a device called *Mr. Tappy*[2] was brought into the field. It comes with a lightweight webcam as well as different pieces of adhesive and magnetic material that allow it to be attached to a mobile device. Onto this device, a second camera, the GoPro Hero 3+ Silver, was attached enabling us to capture a medium shot of the child. If the situation permits, the rig can be attached behind the tablet computer. Otherwise, the rig can be placed on the table next to the device and the cameras turned to capture the desired framings. The set-up comes with some obvious practical limitations, since it is difficult to move it around in a room once it is recording, which is otherwise a rather basic affordance of a mobile device, as well as of most IoToys. A major reason for this obstruction is the webcam which had to be attached via a cable to a laptop in order to record, whereas the GoPro camera uses a flash memory card (microSD). On the other hand, the live feed from the computer proved to be an advantage in showing the children what was going on with the cameras. This was helpful in negotiating informed consent in the sense of being able to assess their reactions to being filmed.

The cameras used to capture audio-visual data function as actors placed in the sociomaterial configuration. They 'had to be there' for this research to be possible but, even so, they affected the situation, as did the researcher, parents, siblings and the materiality of the location and its objects. The video data revealed how the children were reacting to the cameras, usually in a curious fashion, as they were able to see what one of the cameras was capturing directly on a laptop computer screen. This led to some silly experiments where the cameras themselves were being turned into playthings. These instances usually helped relax the situation, as it gave us something to laugh about. It also served as a reminder of the object brought into the field by the researcher and how its role is negotiated, and also materially defined, with the child. Sometimes, the children would ask to view themselves on the computer screen again, leading to shifts in the materiality of the observation.

Video recordings are, as argued by Pink and Rouch, not necessarily a means of conveying informants' experiences, but rather the researcher's experiences regarding informants (2003 [1974], p. 43; 2013). The ongoing research project from which we draw empirical examples for these methodological considerations has important aspects of framing to be considered. Apart from the broader aspects of doing research in the homes of young children that were considered in the section above, the child was asked by the researcher to play with the *DR Ramasjang* app on his or her own tablet computer. The researcher asked the child to show what he or she likes to do when using the app. This would sometimes lead to adult-directed play, in the sense that the children would look for reactions from adults to the different games he or she was playing. At other times, the children would immerse themselves in their playfulness—which was not necessarily a state of excitement—and not be very keen to talk or otherwise seek adult attention. In some cases, a child would run around in the room and play in relation to the tablet computer activities and return again to handle the device.

The POV model in video research with young children and IoToys allows the researcher to see what happens along the eyeline of interaction between a child and an object. It facilitates micro-level analysis and, in relation to practice theory, offers an opportunity to trace shifts and patterns in practices and teleo-affective structures of playful meaning-making. The applied method comes with some physical restraints that limit the tablet computer play to a relatively stationary activity. However, the agency and immersed playfulness demonstrated by the children support the validity of the data. Furthermore, recordings of adult-directed play are not to be deemed 'bad data', since they provide insights into an aspect of children's play culture that also depends on adults and seeks their attention accordingly. Conclusively, the variations in social aspects of play practices, as revealed by the POV method, allow us to perform analyses that can bring play moods together with practices and sociomaterial contexts.

Analysing POV Video Data

The data sets from every visit in the research project drawn upon here consist of dual video recordings, along with audio from a Dictaphone, still images produced when deemed relevant, and field notes produced directly after the visits. The extra audio, the photographs and the field notes were produced in order to provide context and secure a 'thick description' (Geertz, 1973). The video data were edited using Final Cut Pro, in order to represent both video feeds in the same image, favouring the tablet computer in terms of size. The edited video was then exported into a single video file and transcribed into four columns: (1) a time marker and number of sequence, (2) general description of interplay, (3) gestures and (4) facial expressions.

As this research project is in the analytical stage, the transcription and inductive coding of the data are still taking place. However, with this particular strategy in transcription, we seek to transduce the perspectives afforded by the cameras. Furthermore, as these interactions between children and tablet computers fall within the communicative realm of multimodal discourse (Kress & Leeuwen, 2001), we have drawn inspiration from the work of Kate Cowan (2014) as well as from Roberta Taylor (2014) in regard to transcription. The sociomaterial nexus is visible, on the micro-level, in the audio-visual data provided by our method, but is also informed by the contextual data from the audio recordings, field notes and still images. Consequently, the analysis we can perform due to the POV method offers attention to shifts in the fluid materiality (Burnett, 2017), in terms of both the teleo-affective relationships between children and tablet computers, and assemblages of actors and discourses.

Video data are rich data. For the same reason, analysing them can be very time-consuming, especially if strategies for transcribing, coding and otherwise sorting the data are overly ambitious. Christian Heath, Jon Hindmarsh and Paul Luff and Derry et al. describe the benefits of a funnel-shaped taxonomy of analysis when working with a considerable body of video data (2010; 2010). As we have argued, following practice theory and theories on play, the play practices we are researching on the micro-level are entangled in a nexus of practices, some of which we can identify as more or less pertinent towards grasping the horizons of 'shared knowledge' (Reckwitz, 2002). Moving outwards from the micro-level data afforded by the POV method, we see how playful practices are nested and entangled in social situations and, furthermore, shaped and negotiated in relation to public discourse.

Making distinctions between macro- and micro-levels in research may seem intuitive in many ways. However, the connections between macro-level discourses and cultural practices versus everyday practices and the smallest embodiments of practices can render these distinctions somewhat hard to make. Gherardi argues how sociomaterial practices are 'embedded in a wider texture of practices connecting the situated and everyday encounters of embodiments to the macro-institutional context' (2017, p. 44). At the very least, if we are to consider specific micro-level instances of practice through empirical research, we must also consider their place in a wider sociomaterial nexus of practice. This is where the broader level provides an analytical frame of reference. Davide Nicolini argues that analyses drawing on practice theory ought to shift between focusing on macro-, meso- and micro-levels and thus 'zoom in and out' when forming and testing analytical theses (2009).

By looking at a portion of the data from a visit with the four-year-old girl Malou, we can get an idea of what we are able to identify from three levels of analytic context. Malou was playing a game in which she had to match five picture cards to five words. When she matched a card to a word, a sound corresponding to the word was played and the drawing on the card animated briefly. If the match was correct, a star appeared in the bottom right corner of the card. Besides a missing star, sound/image dissonance—for example, a lion making the sound of a trumpet—was a cue to an answer being wrong. Malou's initial strategy was to match all five cards, and if one or more was wrong she would remove all five cards and start again. After eight turns of this strategy, she suddenly realised that she only needed to correct her wrong answers. Upon this realisation, Malou solved the word-to-picture puzzles quickly and efficiently, and she settled into a routine of solving a puzzle, eating a spoonful of muesli, solving another puzzle, eating another spoonful of muesli etc. (Fig. 12.3).

As the camera set-up using the POV method allowed the researcher to attend to different aspects of the field, a conversation with Malou's mother took place during Malou's play. Her mother explained how Malou and her three-year-older brother often played with their iPad together. She also presented her views on tablet computers as well as the specific media environment of DR Ramasjang, which is the focal

Fig. 12.3 Matching picture cards with words

point of this research project. Malou chose to play the game in question shortly after her mother spoke highly of the character the game draws on as its host. The mother's views on technology and media revealed that she liked her children to socialise around their use and that she would sometimes exercise limitations on tablet computer use in favour of the television placed in the living room. These views from the mother relate to a range of discussions in broader society regarding children, media, tablet computers and public service broadcasting, to name a few.

Due to the specific nature of the POV data, we are able to perform several sweeps of analysis, as put forward by Fleer (2014), and thus identify how the sequence with the word-to-image puzzle was part of a recurring pattern in tablet computer play practices across informants, games and settings. This pattern consists of four stages of engagement, where the child progresses his or her playfulness from being (1) tentative to (2) imperfectly rote to (3) efficiently rote upon making a realisation and finally (4) digressive or creative, depending on how the game affords that type of play. These patterns of engagement were susceptible to the current mood of the child. When Malou seemed to feel comfortable and content with being asked to play with the tablet computer, other informants would present different attitudes or play moods. With the method described here, we are able to consider what these different moods look like and engage in analytical discussions informed by the audio-visual data.

Besides the 'analytically satisfying' patterns in play practices that we have been able to identify, the POV method also provides a clear view of responses to comedic elements, interesting digressions and individuality in the meaning-making processes the children were involved in. From the above sequence with Malou, we were able to identify when she thought something was funny, and how her reactions to successful moments or comedic elements would often lead to her reaching out to her mother with an invitation to laugh with her. In another case, a hospital-themed game has a voice-over explaining an image of urinary tracts by saying 'that's where the pee goes through—can you smell it?', leading a five-year-old boy to put his nose down to smell the screen with an unmistakable look of curiosity on his face. Small instances like these, which would hardly show in quantitative data, speak volumes about a young boy's playful attitude. How he, in line with Karoff's points regarding active participation in play (2013, pp. 128–129), goes along with sniffing the tablet computer and how the tablet computer cannot deliver on its promise of conveying the smell of urine (Figs. 12.4 and 12.5).

The video data also enable us to determine shifts and turning points in play practices. These instances were used in transcription to mark the beginnings and ends of sequences, as they usually entailed transitions from one piece of content to another, if not the end of the tablet computer play session altogether. These transitions tell us something about imbalances between the affordances of the digital toy and the potential play mood desired by a child, demonstrated through agentic behaviour. The shifts in practices can be construed as 'breakdowns', in the sense that the materiality of the app, as perceived by the child via meaning-making through symbolic interaction, has been realigned with teleo-affective dispositions (Morley, 2017). In connection with this, digital play media and IoToys demonstrate agency, in spite of being non-human actors, towards affecting the nature of play practices through coercive elements.

Fig. 12.4 Reaching out to share a successful moment with the researcher and mum

Fig. 12.5 Smelling urinary tracts

In summation, when we examine the three different levels of analysis in the sense of (1) a discursively informed backdrop, (2) the identification of practices and (3) the uncovering of micro-instances of meaning-making, we see how these become entangled in the sociomaterial nexus. The POV method allows for comparisons and iterative layers of analysis; however, the researcher plays an important role in the field since he or she provides contextual data through conversations/interviews and observation.

Conclusion and Perspectives

The POV method in qualitative observation of play practices with IoToys encourages the production of audio-visual data from sociomaterial perspectives, proving itself valuable in achieving empirical data that facilitate comparability and iterative layers of analysis (Fleer, 2014), as well as sensitive descriptions of context and views on public discourse. We believe this method may serve as an inspiration for future qualitative studies in the field of IoToys, as it facilitates the importantly nuanced contextual understanding needed to frame and focus large data sets that may or may not be made available for academic research.

Play practices are characterised by teleological and affective aspects. The POV method offers a nuanced qualitative look at the complex and dynamic nature of these across different settings and informants. In this chapter, we have demonstrated how the data sets produced with rigid camera work and a researcher present afford different levels of analysis. These analytical dimensions are valuable to a range of cultural and social research, since they enable us to understand variances in mood and routines, and how online and offline play practices are entangled in sociomaterial configurations. Furthermore, 'the home' as a sociocultural and sociomaterial setting is a rich field site for data, also in terms of understanding values, humour, cultural heritage and numerous other aspects of everyday life.

With the proliferation of IoToys, the importance of this field site to research is only accentuated further. In this chapter, we have only presented a rather narrow picture of children's media use, some concrete interactions between a child and an interactive toy. A broader understanding of the potential meaning and patterns of use should include not only specific IoToys, but also other sorts of digital (and analogue) toys and tools as well as play practices in different contexts (in- and outside the home), with or without peers or siblings, and with children in different age groups and life circumstances. The POV method provides a relevant addition to the methods toolbox regarding children's play practices in relation to digital technologies, which scholars in the field should continue to develop and carefully consider in their research designs.

The fieldwork method presented here can be improved upon—especially in practical terms—in order to achieve higher degrees of object mobility. However, as argued, the ability to provide a live video feed from one or more cameras has proven to be an important aspect in negotiating consent and providing agency for the children. These values should be understood and only sought to be improved upon in future research. Forthcoming research with IoToys will need to address these important practical and methodological issues, as well as issues regarding surveillance and data privacy. Empirical research on play practices with IoToys using the POV method will provide an important context for these issues, as it provides nuanced and situated descriptions of *how* young children are playing. This sort of knowledge enables us to provide research-led guidance on how to implement policies and ensure their alignment with actual practices.

Notes

1. Ramasjang is the name of a television channel, a Web universe and an app for children aged 3–7 years, provided by DR (the National Danish Broadcasting Corporation). The app is amongst the most popular in Denmark and has been downloaded more than one million times since its launch in 2013.
2. https://www.mrtappy.com/.

References

Blumer, H. (1969). *Symbolic interactionism: Perspective and method.* Berkeley: University of California Press.

Burnett, C. (2017). The fluid materiality of tablets: Examining 'the iPad multiple' in a primary classroom. In C. Burnett, G. Merchant, A. Simpson, & M. Walsh (Eds.), *The case of the iPad: Mobile literacies in education* (pp. 15–29). Singapore: Springer.

Coad, J., Gibson, F., Horstman, M., Milnes, L., Randall, D., & Carter, B. (2015). Be my guest! Challenges and practical solutions of undertaking interviews with children in the home setting. *Journal of Child Health Care, 19*(4), 432–443. https://doi.org/10.1177/1367493514527653.

Cowan, K. (2014). Multimodal transcription of video: Examining interaction in early years classrooms. *Classroom Discourse, 5*(1), 6–21. https://doi.org/10.1080/19463014.2013.859846.

Derry, S. J., Pea, R. D., Barron, B., Engle, R. A., Erickson, F., Goldman, R., & Sherin B. L. (2010). Conducting video research in the learning sciences: Guidance on selection, analysis, technology, and ethics. *Journal of the Learning Sciences, 19*(1), 3–53. https://doi.org/10.1080/10508400903452884.

Fine, G. A., & Sandstrom, K. L. (1988). *Knowing children: Participant observation with minors* (Vol. 15). Newbury Park, CA: Sage.

Fleer, M. (2014). Beyond developmental geology: A cultural-historical theorization of digital visual technologies for studying young children's development. In M. Fleer & A. Ridgway (Eds.), *Visual methodologies and digital tools for researching with young children: Transforming visuality* (Vol. 10). Cham: Springer International Publishing.

Geertz, C. (1973). *The interpretation of cultures: Selected essays*. New York: Basic Books.

Gherardi, S. (2017). Sociomateriality in posthuman practice theory. In A. Hui, T. Schatzki, & E. Shove (Eds.), *The nexus of practices* (pp. 38–51). London: Routledge.

Hall, S. (2007 [1973]). Encoding, decoding. In S. During (Ed.), *The cultural studies reader* (Vol. 3., pp. 90–103). London: Routledge.

Hammersley, M., & Atkinson, P. (2007). *Ethnography: Principles in practice* (Vol. 3). London: Routledge.

Harris, A. M. (2016). *Video as method*. New York, NY: Oxford University Press.

Heath, C., Hindmarsh, J., & Luff, P. (2010). *Video in qualitative research: Analysing social interaction in everyday life*. Los Angeles and London: Sage.

Holloway, D., & Green, L. (2016). The internet of toys. *Communication Research and Practice, 2*(4), 506–519. https://doi.org/10.1080/22041451.2016.1266124.

Idhe, D. (1993). *Postphenomenology: Essays in the postmodern context.* Evanston: Northwestern University Print.

Johansen, S. L., & Karoff, H. S. (2010). På besøg som forsker: feltarbejde i private hjem. In T. Bjørner (Ed.), *Den oplevede virkelighed: 11 eksempler på kvalitativ metode i praksis* (pp. 17–35). Aalborg: Aalborg Universitetsforlag.

Karoff, H. S. (2013). *Om leg: legens medier, praktikker og stemninger* (Vol. 1, udgave). Kbh: Akademisk Forlag.

Kress, G., & Leeuwen, T. v. (2001). *Multimodal discourse: The modes and media of contemporary communication.* London: Arnold.

Latour, B. (2005). *Reassembling the social.* Oxford: Oxford University Press.

Lie, M., & Sørensen, K. H. (1996). *Making technology our own? Domesticating technology into everyday life.* Oslo: Scandinavian University Press.

Lundtofte, T. E. (2017). *Young children's media play in an app-based transmedia environment.* Paper presented at Nordmedia 2017, Tampere. http://www.uta.fi/cmt/en/Conferences/NordMedia2017/Downloads/TWG6_Abstracts.pdf.

Marsh, J. (2017). The internet of toys: A posthuman and multimodal analysis of connected play. *Teachers College Record, 119*(15), 1–32.

Marsh, J., Brooks, G., Hughes, J., Ritchie, L., Roberts, S., & Wright, K. (2005). *Digital beginnings: Young children's use of popular culture, media and new technologies.* Retrieved from Sheffield http://www.digitalbeginnings.shef.ac.uk/DigitalBeginningsReport.pdf.

Marsh, J., Hannon, P., Lewis, M., & Ritchie, L. (2017). Young children's initiation into family literacy practices in the digital age. *Journal of Early Childhood Research, 15*(1), 47.

Marsh, J., Plowman, L., Yamada-Rice, D., Bishop, J., Lahmar, J., & Scott, F. (2015). *Exploring play and creativity in pre-schoolers' use of apps: Final project report.* Retrieved from http://www.techandplay.org.

Masheroni, G., & Holloway, D. (2017). *The internet of toys: A report on media and social discourses around young children and IoToys.* Retrieved from: http://digilitey.eu/wp-content/uploads/2017/01/IoToys-June-2017-reduced.pdf.

McPake, J., Plowman, L., & Stephen, C. (2013). Pre-school children creating and communicating with digital technologies in the home. *British Journal of Educational Technology, 44*(3), 421–431. https://doi.org/10.1111/j.1467-8535.2012.01323.x.

Morley, J. (2017). Technologies within and beyond practices. In A. Hui, T. Schatzki, & E. Shove (Eds.), *The nexus of practices* (pp. 81–97). London: Routledge.

Nicolini, D. (2009). Zooming in and out: Studying practices by switching theoretical lenses and trailing connections. *Organization Studies, 30*(12), 1391–1418. https://doi.org/10.1177/0170840609349875.

Pink, S. (2013). *Doing visual ethnography* (Vol. 3). London: Sage.

Plowman, L. (2016). Rethinking context: Digital technologies and children's everyday lives. *Children's Geographies, 14*(2), 190–202. https://doi.org/10.10 80/14733285.2015.1127326.

Plowman, L., McPake, J., & Stephen, C. (2008). Just picking it up? Young children learning with technology at home. *Cambridge Journal of Education, 38*(3), 303–319. https://doi.org/10.1080/03057640802287564.

Reckwitz, A. (2002). Towards a theory of social practices, a development in cultural theorizing. *European Journal of Social Theory, 5*(2), 243–264.

Reckwitz, A. (2017). Practices and their affects. In A. Hui, T. Schatzki, & E. Shove (Eds.), *The nexus of practices* (pp. 114–125). London: Routledge.

Rouch, J. (2003 [1974]). The camera and man. In J. Rouch & S. Feld (Eds.), *Ciné-Ethnography* (New ed., Vol. 13, pp. 29–46). Minneapolis: University of Minnesota Press.

Schatzki, T. R. (2001). Practice mind-ed orders. In T. R. Schatzki, E. V. Savigny, & K. K. Cetina (Eds.), *The practice turn in contemporary theory* (pp. 50–63). London: Routledge.

Taylor, R. (2014). Meaning between, in and around words, gestures and postures—Multimodal meaning-making in children's classroom discourse. *Language and Education, 28*(5), 401–420. https://doi.org/10.1080/095007 82.2014.885038.

van Dijck, J. (2014). Datafication, dataism and dataveillance: Big Data between scientific paradigm and ideology. *Surveillance & Society, 12*(2), 197–208.

13

Hybrid Methods for Hybrid Play: A Research Toolkit

Giovanna Mascheroni and Donell Holloway

Introduction

As proposed in the Introduction to this edited collection, we draw on Lievrouw and Livingstone (2006) and conceptualise the Internet of Toys as articulated in three interrelated dimensions: its materiality as a technological artefact and a physical toy; the set of communicative and/or play practices in which users engage; and the data collected, generated and communicated by the connected toy itself, which feed into dataveillance as the dominant business and social model. As a result of the triple articulation of these new playthings, connected play is

G. Mascheroni (✉)
Department of Communication, Catholic University of the Sacred Heart, Milan, Italy
e-mail: giovanna.mascheroni@unicatt.it

D. Holloway
School of Arts and Humanities, Edith Cowan University, Mt Lawley, WA, Australia
e-mail: donell.holloway@ecu.edu.au

actualised as a complex entanglement of the digital and the material that is always socially situated and contingent. The digital has become part of our material and sensory environments to the point that, as Pink, Ardevol and Lanzeni explain, the digital and the material are no longer separated but, rather, "entangled elements of the same processes, activities and intentionalities" (2016a, p. 1), which emerge from and within everyday practices. From this perspective, digital materialities represent both the conditions and outcomes of social practices.

In this chapter, we argue that one way to approach digital–material configurations as processual and situated, and to account for the complex and varied ways in which the interactions between children and IoToys—as media and material objects—emerge through play practices, is through novel theoretical and methodological approaches to materialities in media studies and media anthropology. On the theoretical level, the understanding of connected play as a digital–material assemblage fits well with the contemporary "non-representational" and material turn in the social sciences (Pink, Ardèvol, & Lanzeni, 2016a), the notion of a materialist phenomenology developed within mediatization research (Couldry & Hepp, 2017) and the notion of affordances in its recent re-conceptualisation (Costa, 2018). On the methodological level, such a conceptual framework suggests the adoption of an ethnographic methodology that would enable researchers to experiment with hybrid research methods that draw on media studies, (media) anthropology, science, technology studies and design. Accordingly, in what follows, we will outline a research toolkit for the study of the processual and situated affordances of robotic Internet-connected toys, which builds on an adapted version of the walkthrough method developed by Light, Burgess, and Duguay (2018) to critically analyse apps and combine it with recent calls in Children and Media studies to overcome discursive reductionism through a focus on practices (Storm-Mathisen, 2016). Before delving deeper into the idea of the walkthrough as a research method within the digital ethnographic toolkit, though, we will define affordances in light of the materialist-phenomenological approach in media studies (Couldry & Hepp, 2017) and "more-than-representational" frameworks in digital ethnographies (Pink et al., 2016b).

Situating the Affordances of the Internet of Toys

What links the current approach to affordances in media studies to the notion of digital materialities and the so-called material turn in the social sciences is the focus on practices as both the object of study and the analytical lens through which the embedding of digital media into the realm of everyday life can be grasped beyond deterministic and essentialist accounts.

Digital materialities, as briefly outlined above, are not conceived as an intrinsic quality of digital media, nor as the end product of users' encounters with digital media. In posing digital materialities as processual and emergent, Pink et al. (2016b) emphasise how digital materialities and social practices are mutually constitutive. In other words, not only are digital materialities an integral part of the mediatized environment that social actors inhabit, they are also enacted and enlivened through the practices of social actors.

A similar emphasis on the heuristic value of practice characterises the strand of mediatization research which theorises a non-media-centric approach to the media, in the belief that it is only through a focus on everyday media practices that the complex interdependence of the social world on mediated process and communication infrastructures can be captured and interpreted (Couldry & Hepp, 2017). The question, pragmatically, becomes what people do, say and think, which is related to the media; and, ultimately, what is the role of media practices in the ordering of social life (Couldry, 2004)? The focus on media practice constitutes the point of departure for the development of a materialist phenomenology that attends to both the material and the symbolic aspects of everyday media use. Such a materialist-phenomenological approach, in other words, situates (a) the materiality of the media as both technological artefacts and infrastructures of communication, (b) their symbolic dimension as sets of shared understandings and norms around ways of doing and (c) social actors' practices of media use and meaning-making as interconnected and interdependent forces in the texture of everyday life.

Both the notion of digital materialities and the materialist-phenomenological approach that de-centres the media and foregrounds practices, then, provide the theoretical coordinates for the rethinking of affordances as a conceptual tool for the study of connected play. Affordances—a term that originated in ecological psychology (Gibson, 1979) and was later popularised in design and HCI studies (Norman, 1988)—have been broadly defined as the possibilities for agency opened up by a material artefact. Hence, theoretically, the notion of affordances suggests that the materiality of the object or technology shapes it, without completely pre-determining its use (Hutchby, 2001); that is, it suggests that technology and society are co-determined and mutually shaped. As the term has become increasingly popular across a range of disciplines, though, it has lost its heuristic value and been used as a synonym for functionalities (Evans, Pearce, Vitak, & Treem, 2017). On this basis, a number of scholars have recently reclaimed the original notion of affordances as both "functional" and "relational" (Hutchby, 2014) and, as such, its ability to provide a middle-ground concept that overcomes the duality between technological determinism versus social constructivism. Against the failure to grasp the encounter between the materiality of an object and the practices of a situated social actor—which characterised the appropriation of the notion of affordances in much work in media studies and beyond (Costa, 2018; Evans et al., 2017)—there is currently an attempt to reframe affordances as processual and culturally situated. The emphasis is now on the repeated interactions between social actors and technologies in a given social and cultural context. In this light, rather than affordances as intrinsic properties of technologies that bear homogenous and generalised effects, "affordances-in-practice" (Costa, 2018) refer to the ongoing and always situated enactments of the properties of technological artefacts through practices of use-in-context. Depending on the context, on the practices through which they are enacted and on the specific digital–material entanglement that is thus configured, affordances variously operate by demanding, requesting, allowing, encouraging or discouraging users' practices (Davis & Chouinard, 2016). Affordances as *demands* constrain use, since they set the specific circumstances that habilitate or hinder certain practices. In contrast, *requests* orient the user towards preferred uses. Whereas demands and requests push users towards particular outcomes of their engagement with the artefact, the mechanisms of *encourage*, *discourage*, *refuse* and *allow* refer to the object's responses to users' negotiations of the possibilities for agency opened up by a particular object. The way affordances operate is relative to the subjects who use the artefact, and to the subjects' position in relation to the artefact, and to other objects and subjects in a given context (Davis & Chouinard, 2016).

Researching the digital materialities of connected play through the lens of affordances, therefore, entails understating how the affordances of Internet-connected robotic toys are situated in specific sociocultural contexts and materially and symbolically enacted through children's play practices. On these grounds, we believe that the affordances of IoToys are better grasped through an ethnographic approach that combines: (a) a walkthrough of the digital materiality of the physical interface (the toy) and the digital interface (the app through which the robot may be remotely controlled and potentially programmed; (b) the discursive methods traditionally employed in children and media research that focus on the symbolic dimension of media practice—that is, on the system of meanings that frames and orients practices (Couldry, 2004); and, (c) novel observational and visual methods designed to capture children's practices also from the viewpoint of haptic and sensory engagement with technologies.

The WalkThrough Method Revisited

The walkthrough method is an empirical and analytical tool designed by Light et al. (2018) for the study of apps, whose strength lies in its approach to social media platforms as both political-economic structures and socio-technical constructs. In other words, it aims to understand how an app shapes its use through both a political-economic analysis of apps' governance, business model and vision, and a technical walkthrough that critically analyses the user interface.

Vision, governance and business model form what Light et al. (2018) call "the environment of expected use", which provides insights into how apps' producers (owners, designers, developers) expect users to appropriate the technology and, therefore, encode the materiality of an app with their expectations and cultural values (du Gay et al., 2013).

More specifically, the vision of an app includes its discursive and symbolic representation as controlled by the producer, and as presented in the app's description on the App Store or Google Play platforms, in marketing materials, on company websites and/or in blogs and press releases. In the case of robotic IoToys, our prior research (Mascheroni & Holloway, 2017) showed the double symbolic representations of IoToys in commercial discourses, where different sets of meanings and anticipated uses are mobilised, often in the same advertisement, to talk to different audiences (whether parents or children).

The second element that defines the "environment of expected use" is the business model and revenue sources. Whereas the operating model of the apps analysed by Light and colleagues (2018) involves payment for an app, in-app purchases or free services in exchange for users' personal data, the revenue generation of IoToys is still based on the actual sale of the physical toy, whose Internet-connected functionalities are, however, activated through the download of an app and the registration of a user profile. In order to fully realise the Internet functionalities of the toy, the user has no choice other than to agree to extensive data collection, which may include the recording of interactions between the child and the robot/doll (Holloway & Green, 2016). This is the "tool reversibility" (Couldry & Hepp, 2017, p. 132) that turns things into media, and consumers into producers (of data). As a consequence, the business strategy combines more traditional monetary exchange with revenue generation strategies based on users' data shared with third parties, which is typical of "surveillance capitalism" (Zuboff, 2015).

Beyond the price of the toy on the market, and the diverse online and offline platforms through which it is distributed, then, an indication of the income generating mechanism of the toy is also provided by the formal Terms of Service (ToS) of the product, which also constitute the third component of the "environment of expected use": governance. In Light et al. conceptualisation, governance refers to both the formal (e.g. ToS) and informal ways (e.g. FAQs) in which "the app provider seeks to manage and regulate user activity to sustain their operating model and fulfil their vision" (2018, p. 890). The ToS of IoToys are generally difficult to locate, lengthy and user-unfriendly (Holloway & Green, 2016), and their data policies are often not transparent. As European consumer associations and various child-protection organisations across Europe and the United States reported in a 2016 campaign, ToS violate existing regulatory frameworks, such as the Children's Online Privacy Protection Act (COPPA) and the General Data Protection Regulation (GDPR), for they often require consent to the ToS being updated and changed without prior notification, and to personal data collected about users being shared with undisclosed third parties (see Mascheroni & Holloway, 2017). The analysis of the polit-ical-economic environment of an Internet-connected toy, as explicitly embedded in the business model and the ToS, and as discursively con-structed in a number of promotional texts, is fundamental if we want to understand how IoToys operate within a regime of "dataveillance" and monetise users' data (Van Dijck, 2014).

However, focusing on the political dimension alone would prevent researchers from fully understanding apps (and technologies more generally) as complex ethnographic environments—as Barassi (2017) argued in her study of pregnancy apps. Along the same lines, Light et al. complement the analysis of the app as a political-economic struc-ture with a step-by-step approach to apps as socio-technical environ-ments. The step-by-step technical walkthrough designed by the authors "requires the researcher [to] assume a user's position" (2018, p. 891) while engaging with the app—in both its symbolic and material dimen-sions—during the three processes of registration/entry, everyday use and suspension/closure/leaving. The digital–material entanglements that emerge through users' interaction with an app at the moments of reg-istration and entry, everyday use and closure or leaving are embedded, according to Light et al. (2018, pp. 891–892), in how the app guides users through activities via (a) compulsory fields, requests and pop-ups (*functions and features*); (b) buttons and menus (*user interface arrange-ment*); (c) the discursive power of text (*textual content and tone*); and (d) the look and feel of the app (*symbolic representation*). This analytical lens—focused on different stages of user engagement, and on the inter-play of material (user interface arrangements, functions and features) and symbolic (textual content and tone, symbolic representation) characteristics of the app that shape its use—can be extended to the study of the affordances of IoToys, though some adaptations are needed. Essentially, IoToys continue to be physical toys: their physicality extends the materiality of the app into a complex digital–material assemblage. While the environment of expected use promotes preferred connected play practices in which the child engages with physical toys via the Internet, in reality connected play is much more complex and less linear (Marsh, 2017). Past research has shown that children can interact with physical toys independently of the app or videogame to which it is connected (Manches, Duncan, Plowman, & Sabeti, 2015).

The introduction of a physical interface (physical toy) adds complexity and hybridity to any digital play assemblage. The toy itself becomes the main interface and any associated apps (virtual interfaces) typically play a supportive role.[1] Thus, everyday interaction (play) with the toy operates through its physical interface, with any app (or digital interface) generally less frequently used. Digital interfaces (apps) can be investigated using the walkthrough method. However, the toy itself, as the primary user interface, also has symbolic and material dimensions.

Accordingly, in order to be adapted to the study of IoToys, a step-by-step walkthrough should analyse both the digital interface (the app interface, with its features and functions, its arrangement, its textual and iconic dimensions) and the physical interface, as well as the relation between the two. A walkthrough of the physical interface (toy) could analyse the tactile qualities of the toy (whether soft, hard, fluffy), its kinetic qualities (static or dynamic, and in what way), its auditory qualities (language, sounds and their content and tone) and the overall visual imagery of the toy (whether anthropomorphic, zoomorphic or machine-like) in order to read the different levels of meaning embedded in it.

The walkthrough could also investigate the level and type of toy/child interactivity and agency that are afforded by the toy; whether the toy and child can raise independent queries or requests and to what level. This could mean a robot dog simply barking for a child's attention or a child asking a geography question to a CogniToys' Dino—a dinosaur toy similar to a virtual assistant. This could also mean one-way interactivity, where only the child instructs the toy, as in remotely controlled toys. The degree of machine learning involved in ongoing interactions with the toy could also be assessed by the researcher as well as the learnings afforded to the child by the toy.

As with an app walkthrough, user interface arrangements of the toy also warrant investigation. Technical mechanisms, such as buttons and sensors, can be analysed to see how they guide the child and shape the play experience. Whether and how interaction with the app software guides interaction with the hardware and vice versa is also important and can initially be grasped by the researcher from a walkthrough of the toy (Table 13.1).

The combined analysis of both the physical and the digital interfaces of IoToys helps us to grasp how the environment of expected use, and its underlying logic of dataveillance, is materialised in the mechanisms through which the toy encourages, discourages, allows, requires or demands certain practices of usage.

Table 13.1 Walkthrough analysis of connected toys. Adapted from Light et al. (2018)

Walkthrough analysis of connected smart toy	
Toy walkthrough	App walkthrough
Symbolic representation: tactile, kinetic, auditory and visual qualities of the toy (their connotations and cultural overtones)	Symbolic representation: logos, colour schemes, images, music (their connotations and cultural associations)
Textual content and tone: voice, sound, text, and movement (content and tone how they shape child's play and communication)	Textual content and tone: drop down menu options, hierarchy of categories etc. (how they shape usage)
User interface arrangement: placement of buttons and sensors (how they encourage/discourage/shape play and interaction)	User interface arrangement: placement of buttons and menus (how they shape usage)
Function and features: required user activity (actions, words etc.) and/or apps that enable toy's digital affordances	Function and features: compulsory fields, pop-ups, linking requests (app arrangements that mandate or enable an activity)
Co-play features: on-board software and cloud computing that enable interactive play and/or learning between child and toy (including AI and machine learning)	

However, in line with our understanding of the affordances of IoToys as situated practices of engagement, we believe that an ethnographic approach to IoToys should combine the political-economic and the step-by-step analysis of the digital–material environment of robotic Internet-connected toys with other methods, such as observation, sensory ethnography and play-based interviews. Indeed, Light et al. (2018) understand the walkthrough not as a standalone method but as a tool that fits within traditional or digital toolkit methods. Moreover, they recognise that users often expand upon and even subvert the possibilities for agency opened up by technology. To overcome the limitations of the walkthrough method, and to grasp the lived experiences of Internet-connected playthings—including children's emotional bonding with toys—through which digital–material affordances are enacted, we discuss how both discursive and non-discursive methods can be used in research around children's (and their families') experiences with IoToys.

Rethinking Discursive Methods in Research with Young Children

The position of children within the research process has varied across time and disciplines—shifting from children as research objects to children as research subjects, to social actors and, more recently, active participants in the research process itself (Christensen & Prout, 2002). However, due to numerous methodological and ethical challenges (Aarsand, 2016), most research in the field of children and media has continued to predominantly rely on discourse-based methods such as interviews and surveys. Such "discursive reductionism" (Storm-Mathisen, 2016) has been criticised for failing to uncover the non-verbal, embodied and sensory dimensions of media practices, thus risking offering a partial account of children's own engagement with digital media. To overcome those biases, ethnographic approaches that focus on media practices in the context of everyday life and employ observational methods are suggested.

While our understanding of the affordances of IoToys as "affor-dances-in-practice" (Costa, 2018) that are embedded in digital–material configurations fits well with recent calls for observational methods, we equally adhere to the notion of a "materialist phenomenology" and agree that "the social world remains something accessible to interpreta-tion and understanding by human actors, indeed a structure built up, in part, *through* those interpretations and understandings" (Couldry & Hepp, 2017, p. 5). Therefore, we still value the use of interviews within an overall ethnographic approach that pays attention to both the sym-bolic and the material, representations and meanings, along with prac-tices and experiences. In our research experience with young children in the home setting, we have favoured non-directive interview styles that mimic everyday life conversations and facilitate the child's "free narra-tive" (Cameron, 2005, p. 601). In order to be more inclusive as regards young children, and facilitate their engagement in research, the inter-view guide can also incorporate non-narrative elements and play-based interview methods (Koller & San Juan, 2015). For example, one of the authors of the present chapter participated in a seven-country study of digital technologies in families with 0–8-year-old children (Chaudron et al., 2018). The interviews were structured into three stages, with a short family introduction that involved both children and parents in a joint ice-breaking activity (filling in with stickers a table of the family's typical day); a central part of the interview, where children and parents were interviewed separately, each by a different researcher; and a final ses-sion in which the family got back together, along with the two research-ers. The child interview relied on the use of age-appropriate incentives, such as a play-tour of the home—with the child showing the researcher around their home, the digital media, traditional toys and internet-connected toys she/he uses, and their material location in the domestic context (see also Plowman & Stevenson, 2012)—and a memory-like card game that helped children rate their favourite toys and digital media.

Similarly, in the Toddlers and Tablet project recently carried out in Australia (Haddon & Holloway, 2018; Green et al., 2017) a play-based approach was used. Children (3–5) were shown cards of play activities (both digital and non-digital) and asked to sort them into three piles (yes, no and maybe). This sorting activity functioned as a springboard or catalyst for play-based chat with the researcher. The cards were similarly used as a springboard for conversations with children under three but without the sorting activity. The researcher then accompanied the older children (3–5) on a digital tour of the home with the child pointing out and discussing various devices, their uses, their users and spatial placement and movement of the devices. The interviewer used child-appropriate language cues, such as "where does it live?" and "where does it go?", to gain an understanding of the domestic placement and mobility of devices within the child's home. Subsequent to this, the child undertook a device tour, where the child took out their favoured device, showed and discussed with the researcher their digital play world—usually favourite apps and photograph and video galleries.

When conducting child-centred research in the domestic context, researchers should account for the triangular power relations involving the researcher, the child and the parent(s) (Noppari, Uusitalo, & Kupiainen, 2017). Provided that researchers avoid the artificial pursuit of a presumed "authentic" children's voice, de-contextualised from the research context where it originated, the presence of parents can actually facilitate children's engagement in the research process. Researchers involved in the Toddlers and Tablet project, for example, developed two interview strategies that turned parents into field collaborators. First, the child's proximity to their parent during the parent interview (held before the child was interviewed) helped both child and researcher to develop a trustful rapport. This proximity allowed the researcher to engage with the child sporadically—and build rapport before the child interview occurred. The child would also watch the casual conversation style between parent and researcher to gradually confirm that the interviewer was safe to engage with. Secondly, the parent's proximity to the child during the subsequent child interview helped to scaffold a mutual understanding between researcher and child. When needed, the parent tended to reinterpret the interviewer's requests and questions for the child, as well as praise and encourage their child's efforts. Parents were also apt to translate (for the interviewer) their child's own responses and communicative efforts with the researcher. In this way, the parent not only scaffolded the child within the interview process, but also the researcher into their own child's discursive world. "These two strategies take advantage of the social and physical world that pre-verbal and early verbal children live in. They utilise the everyday home environment and a supportive framework provided by the parent who acts as field collaborator in the research process" (Holloway & Stevenson, 2017).

Beyond Discursive Methods: Sensory and Visual Ethnography

The new digital–material configurations that emerge within connected play practices fit well with contemporary work in digital ethnography aiming to investigate the affective and haptic dimensions of people's engagement with digital media (Pink et al., 2016b). The increasing focus on embodied and embedded experiences, the senses and the visual in contemporary digital ethnography practices (Hine, 2015; Pink et al., 2016b) emerges in parallel and in dialogue with shifting theoretical and substantive foci of research in media studies—namely, a non-media-centric, socially oriented media theory (Couldry, 2012).

The ethnographic turn to understanding media and digital practices also fits well with child-centred research practices that have experimented with various approaches for involving children in the research and giving them visibility. Ethnographic approaches to children's everyday lives have largely drawn on video-recording techniques (Aarsand, 2016) as a way to incorporate children's own perspectives into the research process. It is within a child-centred and ethnographic approach that children have been asked to record and narrate a variety of experiences, practices and contexts with which they engage through pictures, videos and drawings or maps. In addition, methods relying on a variety of communication modalities, while sometimes difficult to set up, are more likely to fully capture children's lifeworlds. For instance, drawing activities are often carried out in tandem with conversations (with the researcher) around and about the topic of the drawing. These elements (voice and drawing) combine to make a multimodal text that needs to be reflected upon as a holistic text—as the act of drawing shapes the conversation with the interviewer and vice versa.

Visual approaches are believed to complement and counterbalance the discursive approaches to children's media practices that have dominated the field so far. Research with children can benefit from a variety of visual methods that have been employed in ethnographic media research, including: the video-tour, with participants showing a researcher around their home (Pink & Mackley, 2012); the video re-enactment, whereby participants are invited to re-enact their daily routines while explaining them in detail (Pink & Mackley, 2014); and following and filming participants while engaged in their daily activities. Other methods have already been successfully experimented with in research projects focusing on young children's engagement with touchscreens. For example, Marsh et al. (2015) integrated a combination of visual methods in order to understand the socially situated affordances of tablets and apps for pre-schoolers. First, a play and creativity tour was undertaken, with a map drawn of the house, accompanied by children's and parent's narratives around places for and practices of play and creativity (and tablet use). Second, some children were invited to wear a Go Pro chest camera, in order to have an embodied view of children's play with apps and involve children in the data-collection process. Finally, parents were invited to video-record and photograph their children while using apps.

The engagement of parents as co-researchers in non-discursive methods is an established strategy, especially within education research focused on the nature of play and learning, with technologies in the home adopting an "ecocultural framework" (Marsh, Hannon, Lewis, & Ritchie, 2017; Plowman & Stevenson, 2012). The research project conducted by Lydia Plowman and Olivia Stevenson (2012) engaged parents as co-researchers through mobile phone diaries: on an agreed Saturday, parents were asked to respond to text prompts sent by the researchers with a picture of their child along with a short text message explaining what they were doing and where they were. In a study by Marsh et al. (2017), parents were given a digital still camera and digital camcorder for the duration of the project and asked to record videos and images of children's digital literacy practices whenever they wished. While the engagement of parents in data collection is not unproblematic—both family practices and parents' expectations of their role in the research shape what is recorded—it provides researchers with access to situations

and practices that would otherwise be inaccessible. Beyond document-
ing children's everyday practices, pictures and videos taken by the child
and/or parents as co-researchers can also be fruitfully employed as initial
prompts for interviews (Noppari et al., 2017).

Conclusion

In this chapter we have outlined a methodological approach to the
study of the Internet of Toys that sits at the intersection of two different epistemological traditions (the phenomenological and the non-
representational). We achieved this goal in two ways: theoretically, by
re-directing the focus of media research onto the practices through
which digital materialities are actualised and enacted; and on the methodological level, through the combination of the walkthrough method
with discourse-based and observational methods.

A materialist phenomenology, we believe, would be advantageous to
studies of children and media and could provide a way to reconcile a
child-centred perspective with the need to consider the unprecedented
agency gained by Internet-connected things.

Child-centred approaches have currently been accused of neglect-
ing the role of non-human agents in children's relational encounters
with the world (Spyrou, 2017). From a materialist-phenomenological
approach, however, such an accusation, and the idea that child-
centred research may be detrimental to a full understanding of the role
of technologies in children's lives, would not make sense if we understand digital materialities as being actualised in specific social contexts,
or communicative figurations (Couldry & Hepp, 2017) constituted by
actors, systems of meanings, and ensembles of media and technologies.

The research toolkit we have attempted to elaborate on in this chapter shows, instead, how it is possible to design a child-centred research
methodology that also employs methods, such as the walkthrough,
which partially de-centre the child in order to gain new insights related
to non-human agency and the autonomy of Internet-connected things.
As researchers mainly interested in children and media, though, we
argue for the heuristic and ethical value of a child-centred epistemology.

Note

1. Remote control and user programmable toys do use the virtual interface (apps) more often.

References

Aarsand, P. (2016). Children's media practices: Challenges and dilemmas for the qualitative researcher. *Journal of Children and Media, 10*(1), 90–97.

Barassi, V. (2017). BabyVeillance? Expecting parents, online surveillance and the cultural specificity of pregnancy apps. *Social Media + Society, 3*(2), 1–10. https://doi.org/10.1177/2056305117707188.

Cameron, H. (2005). Asking the tough questions: A guide to ethical practices in interviewing young children. *Early Child Development and Care, 175*(6), 597–610.

Chaudron, S., et al. (2018). Rules of engagement: Family rules on young children's access to and use of technologies. In S. Danby, M. Fleer, C. Davidson, & M. Hatzigianni (Eds.), *Digital childhoods: International perspectives on early childhood education and development* (pp. 131–145). Singapore: Springer.

Christensen, P., & Prout, A. (2002). Working with ethical symmetry in social research with children. *Childhood, 9*(4), 477–497.

Costa, E. (2018). Affordances-in-practice: An ethnographic critique of social media logic and context collapse. *New Media & Society*, online first.

Couldry, N. (2004). Theorising media as practice. *Social Semiotics, 14*(2), 115–132.

Couldry, N. (2012). *Media, society, world: Social theory and digital media practice.* Cambridge: Polity.

Couldry, N., & Hepp, A. (2017). *The mediated construction of reality.* Cambridge: Polity.

Davis, J. L., & Chouinard, J. B. (2016). Theorizing affordances: From request to refuse. *Bulletin of Science, Technology & Society, 36*(4), 241–248.

Du Gay, P., Hall, S., Janes, L., Madsen, A. K., Mackay, H., & Negus, K. (2013). *Doing cultural studies: The story of the Sony Walkman.* Second Edition (1st ed., 1997). London: Sage.

Evans, S. K., Pearce, K. E., Vitak, J., & Treem, J. W. (2017). Explicating affordances: A conceptual framework for understanding affordances in communication research. *Journal of Computer-Mediated Communication, 22*(1), 35–52.

Gibson, J. J. (1979). *The ecological approach to visual perception*. Boston: Houghton Mifflin.

Green, L., Stevenson, K., Holloway, D., et al. (2017). Like mother, like daughter? Unboxing an Etsy childhood. In M. Dezuanni (Ed.), *At home with digital media*. Brisbane: QUT Digital Media Research Centre.

Haddon, L., & Holloway D. (2018). Parental evaluations of young children's touchscreen technologies. In G. Mascheroni (Ed.), *Nordicom 2018 yearbook on digital parenting*. Gothenburg: Nordic Information Centre for Media and Cmmunication Research (Nordicom).

Hine, C. (2015). *Ethnography for the internet: Embedded, embodied and everyday*. London: Bloomsbury.

Holloway, D., & Green, L. (2016). The internet of toys. *Communication Research and Practice, 2*(4), 506–519.

Holloway, D., & Stevenson, K. (2017). Parent as field collaborator when interviewing the pre-verbal and early verbal child. *DigiLitEY Blog*. Retrieved from https://digilitey.wordpress.com/2017/01/24/parent-as-field-collaborator-when-interviewing-the-pre-verbal-and-early-verbal-child/.

Hutchby, I. (2001). Technologies, texts and affordances. *Sociology, 35*(2), 441–456.

Hutchby, I. (2014). Communicative affordances and participation frameworks in mediated interaction. *Journal of Pragmatics, 72*, 86–89.

Koller, D., & San Juan, V. (2015). Play-based interview methods for exploring young children's perspectives on inclusion. *International Journal of Qualitative Studies in Education, 28*(5), 610–631.

Lievrouw, L. A., & Livingstone, S. (2006). Introduction to the first edition (2002): The social shaping and consequences of ICTs. In L. A. Lievrouw & S. Livingstone (Eds.), *Handbook of new media* (pp. 15–32). London: Sage.

Light, B., Burgess, J., & Duguay, S. (2018). The walkthrough method: An approach to the study of apps. *New Media & Society, 20*(3), 881–900.

Manches, A., Duncan, P., Plowman, L., & Sabeti, S. (2015). Three questions about the internet of things and children. *TechTrends, 59*(1), 76–83.

Marsh, J. (2017). The internet of toys: A posthuman and multimodal analysis of connected play. *Teachers College Record, 119*(15), 1–32.

Marsh, J., Hannon, P., Lewis, M., & Ritchie, L. (2017). Young children's initiation into family literacy practices in the digital age. *Journal of Early Childhood Research, 15*(1), 47–60.

Marsh, J., Plowman, L., Yamada-Rice, D., Bishop, J.C., … Winter, P. (2015). *Exploring play and creativity in pre-schoolers' use of apps: Final project report*. Retrieved from www.techandplay.org.

Mascheroni, G., & Holloway, D. (Eds.). (2017). *The internet of toys: A report on media and social discourses around young children and IoToys.* DigiLitEY. Retrieved April 26, 2018 from http://digilitey.eu/wp-content/uploads/2017/01/IoToys-June-2017-reduced.pdf.

Noppari, E., Uusitalo, N., & Kupiainen, R. (2017). Talk to me! Possibilities of constructing children's voices in the domestic research context. *Childhood, 24*(1), 68–83.

Norman, D. A. (1988). *The psychology of everyday things.* New York: Basic Books.

Pink, S., & Mackley, K. L. (2012). Video and a sense of the invisible: Approaching domestic energy consumption through the sensory home. *Sociological Research Online, 17*(1), 3. Retrieved from http://www.socresonline.org.uk/17/1/3.html.

Pink, S., & Mackley, K. L. (2014). Re-enactment methodologies for everyday life research: Art therapy insights for video ethnography. *Visual Studies, 29*(2), 146–154.

Pink, S., Ardèvol, E., & Lanzeni, D. (Eds.). (2016a). *Digital materialities: Design and anthropology.* London: Bloomsbury.

Pink, S., Horst, H., Postill, J., Hjorth, L., Lewis, T., & Tacchi, J. (2016b). *Digital ethnography: Principles and practice.* London: Sage.

Plowman, L., & Stevenson, O. (2012). Using mobile phone diaries to explore children's everyday lives. *Childhood: A Global Journal of Child Research, 19*(4), 539–553.

Spyrou, S. (2017). Time to decenter childhood? *Childhood, 24*(4), 433–437.

Storm-Mathisen, A. (2016). Grasping children's media practices—theoretical and methodological challenges. *Journal of Children and Media, 10*(1), 81–89.

van Dijck, J. (2014). Datafication, dataism and dataveillance: Big data between scientific paradigm and ideology. *Surveillance and Society, 12*(2), 197–208.

Zuboff, S. (2015). Big other: Surveillance capitalism and the prospects of an information civilization. *Journal of Information Technology, 30*(1), 75–89.

Part IV

The Political Economy of IoToys

14

The Internet of Toys: Playing Games with Children's Data?

Ingrida Milkaite and Eva Lievens

Introduction

Children are increasingly the subject of data collection practices, leading to what has been labelled the "datafication" and "dataveillance" of children (Lupton & Williamson, 2017). A growing point of contention is the way in which the Internet of Things (IoT), and in particular the Internet of Toys, affects children. New devices and apps provide many positive opportunities for children, such as entertainment, enjoyment and reassurance, educational benefits, flexible learning environments, selfhood and identity practices, means to exercise control of one's online identity, engagement in self-development, positive contributions to

I. Milkaite · E. Lievens (✉)
Law and Technology, Faculty of Law & Criminology,
Ghent University, Ghent, Belgium
e-mail: E.Lievens@UGent.be

I. Milkaite
e-mail: Ingrida.Milkaite@UGent.be

© The Author(s) 2019
G. Mascheroni and D. Holloway (eds.), *The Internet of Toys*,
Studies in Childhood and Youth, https://doi.org/10.1007/978-3-030-10898-4_14

285

children's close relationships and well-being, and more possibilities for professional success in the future (Holloway & Green, 2016; Lupton & Williamson, 2017; Mascheroni & Holloway, 2017). At the same time, the Internet of Toys phenomenon may also pose serious risks to children's rights to privacy and data protection. These include corporate and government surveillance, data privacy and security issues, geolocation tracking, remote control of technologies and security failures (Chaudron et al., 2017; Holloway & Green, 2016). The construction of highly detailed personal profiles of children from a very young age onwards could lead to problematic and potentially discriminatory practices, such as excluding children with certain profiles from some types of education or refusing to grant specific health insurance policies (Rouvroy, 2016). In addition, the use of artificial intelligence technology which processes children's personal information (e.g. likes and dislikes), such as that integrated into the "Hello Barbie" doll, may lead to never-seen-before emotional bonds between children and objects (Jolin, 2017; Vincent, 2015).

Stories about hackers gaining access to digital baby monitors, speaking to infants directly through these devices and such Internet-connected dolls as "My Friend Cayla" and "Hello Barbie" being easily hacked have gained much media attention in recent years (Halzack, 2015). It is a fact that media discourse often concentrates on a fairly narrow representation of legal aspects of connected toys and tends to highlight infamous instances of security breaches, such as the hacking of connected dolls (Huggler, 2017; Newcomb, 2017). Questions related to the data that they collect, store and (or) transmit, and the impact this has on children's right to privacy, are much less elaborated upon (Mascheroni & Holloway, 2017). Hence, this chapter aims to map and analyse the rights and duties of the various actors involved in the Internet of Toys "chain" on the basis of current and future legislation in the US and the EU. They include children and parents, as well as the manufacturers of the devices, software, apps or platforms where data are stored.

Children's (Privacy and Data Protection) Rights Frameworks

In general, children are entitled to the protection of their private life on the basis of general human rights documents. First, this right is recognised by article 12 of the UDHR (Universal Declaration of Human Rights, 1948) and article 17 of the ICCPR (International Covenant on Civil and Political Rights, 1966). The child's right to privacy is laid down in the United Nations (UN) Convention on the Rights of the Child (UNCRC). Article 16 of the UNCRC provides for the protection of children's right to privacy, family, home, correspondence, honour and reputation. Children are also attributed, among others, the rights to participation, emancipation and to be heard in all matters affecting them (article 12 UNCRC), the rights to education and development (articles 6 and 28 UNCRC), the rights to freedom of expression and association (articles 13 and 15 UNCRC), the right to protection against economic exploitation (article 32 UNCRC) and other rights. It has been very clearly established, for instance by the UN Committee on the Rights of the Child, that these fundamental rights are as applicable in the "online" world as in the "offline" one (UN Committee on the Rights of the Child, 2014), which includes connected digital toys and IoT devices.

In terms of protection in Europe, the right to privacy is envisaged by key instruments adopted by the Council of Europe (CoE) and the European Union (EU). In the framework of the CoE, the right to privacy, including children's right to privacy, is enshrined in article 8 of the European Convention for the Protection of Human Rights and Fundamental Freedoms (ECHR, 1950) and Convention 108+ (Modernised Convention for the Protection of Individuals with Regard to the Automatic Processing of Individual Data, 2018). At the EU level, articles 7 and 8 of the EU Charter of Fundamental Rights (CFREU, 2000) provide, respectively, for protection of the right to respect for private and family life *and* the protection of personal data (European

Union, 2012). Children's rights in particular are also protected by article 24 of the CFREU, which acknowledges their right to such protection and care as is necessary for their well-being and their right to be heard, and it emphasises that in all actions that concern them, whether taken by public authorities or private institutions, the child's best interests must be a primary consideration (European Union, 2012).

US and EU Legal Frameworks for the Child's Rights to Privacy and Data Protection

Both in the United States (US) and the EU, specific legislation has been adopted to address concerns related to the processing of (children's) personal data in today's information society.

The Children's Online Privacy Protection Act and the Internet of Toys

The Children's Online Privacy Protection Act (COPPA) is a US federal law that was adopted in 1998 and became applicable in 2000. It imposes requirements on operators of websites or online services directed to children under 13 years of age, and it is also applicable to operators of other online services that know that they are collecting personal information online from a child under 13 years of age (Federal Trade Commission, 2013a). The main aim of the act is to give parents control over what personal data are collected from their young children online. It is vital to conduct an analysis of COPPA in this chapter, since it played a crucial role in EU data protection reform, as it served as inspiration for parts of the General Data Protection Regulation (GDPR).

Under COPPA, a "child" is an individual under the age of 13. An "operator" is any person who operates a website or an online service and collects or maintains personal information from or about the users of or visitors to such website or online services, or on whose behalf such information is collected or maintained. Under COPPA rules, personal information is individually identifiable information about an individual collected online, including first and last name, home or other physical address, including street name and name of a city or town, email address, telephone number, social security number, screen or username, a persistent identifier that can be used to recognise a user over time and across different websites or online services, a photograph, video or audio file, where such a file contains a child's image or voice, geolocation information sufficient to identify a street name and the name of a city or town and other information that could be combined with other pieces of information in order to identify a person (United States Congress, 1998; Federal Trade Commission, 2015). The Federal Trade Commission (FTC) also specified a very broad meaning of the term "online services", which includes *any* service available over the Internet, or that connects to the Internet (FTC, 2015). As such, this broad interpretation appears to cover toys that are connected to the Internet and associated services.

The main legislative rationale behind COPPA is that the personal data of children under 13 years of age must not be processed by an operator unless parental consent is obtained. COPPA obliges website or online service providers to provide notice that they are collecting children's personal information (through a clear and comprehensive online privacy policy), and to collect verifiable parental consent. Avoiding obtaining such consent is one (or the) reason why many online services (e.g. Facebook and Google) set 13 years as the minimum age for participation (United States Congress, 1998; Holloway & Green, 2016; Montgomery & Chester, 2017). COPPA states that the term "verifiable parental consent" means any reasonable effort, taking into consideration available technology, to ensure that a parent of a child receives notice of the operator's personal information collection, use and disclosure practices, and authorises them, before that information is collected from that child. The FTC has approved a number of different verification methods which differ depending on whether the operator is planning to use children's personal information for internal purposes only or whether it plans to disclose that information to third parties or allow children to make it publicly available. In the latter case, an operator must ensure that the person providing consent is the child's parent. Such verification methods include providing a consent form to be signed by the parent, and returned via US mail, fax or electronic scan (the "print-and-send" method); requiring the parent to use a credit card, debit card or other online payment system; having the parent call a toll-free telephone number staffed by trained personnel, or have the parent connect to trained personnel via video-conference; or verifying a parent's identity by checking a form of government-issued identification against databases of such information (FTC, 2015).

In 2013 the FTC approved the use of knowledge-based authentication methods, as long as "the specific process uses dynamic, multiple-choice questions with enough options to ensure that the chances of a child guessing the correct answers is low and the questions used are of sufficient difficulty that it would be difficult for a child in the household to figure out the answers" (FTC, 2013b). Previously, the FTC had also approved the Social Security number verification method (Tabor, 2013). In November 2015, the FTC approved another method allowing entities to use facial recognition technology to obtain the parental consent required under COPPA.

When the information collected from children is only used for internal purposes (thus, it will not be disclosed to third parties or made publicly available), the operator can use any of the methods mentioned above or the "email plus" method of parental consent. "Email plus" allows the operator to request (in a direct notice sent to the parent's online contact address) that the parent indicates consent in a return message (FTC, 2015), and afterwards take an additional step towards confirmation after receiving the parent's message.

The parental consent requirement is applicable not only to online websites or services that direct their services to children or target them but also to those who have *actual knowledge* that their services are in fact used by children (Montgomery, Chester, & Milosevic, 2017). The FTC has explained that a number of factors may help to determine whether a website or online service is directed at children, such as the subject matter of the site or service, its visual content, the use of animated characters or child-oriented activities and incentives, music, age of models, presence of child celebrities, language or other characteristics, advertising directed at children and audience composition, as well as the intended audience of the site or service and actual knowledge that personal information is collected directly from another website or service which is directed at children (FTC, 2015). Parents must have access to their child's personal information to review and (or) have the information deleted, and they must also have the opportunity to prevent further use or online collection of a child's personal information. Operators are obliged to maintain the confidentiality, security and integrity of information they collect from children, and they must also retain such personal information for only as long as is necessary to fulfil the purpose for which it was collected (FTC, 2015).

In terms of Internet-connected toys and devices, there is little doubt that COPPA is applicable. Toys and associated services target (especially young) children directly, they are connected to the Internet and often, if not always, collect and process children's personal information. Hence, it has been claimed that COPPA requires operators, including Internet of Toys actors, to inform children and parents about the exact information that is being collected and processed, how it is used and obtain real informed consent before enabling a device (Turner, 2016). In 2016, privacy advocates from the Future of Privacy Forum and Family Online Safety Institute argued that the COPPA rules should be enforced in relation to Internet-connected toys due to possibly unfair information collection practices (Future of Privacy Forum & Family Online Safety Institute, 2016). Their position was confirmed by the FTC six months later. In 2017 the FTC explicitly stated that COPPA applies to IoT devices, including Internet-connected toys (Gray, 2017). A month later, the US Federal Bureau of Investigation (FBI) released a consumer notice stating that such toys could raise privacy and contact concerns for children and listed COPPA as one of the applicable legislative measures protecting consumers against possible privacy and other risks (FBI, 2017).

One of the most recent examples of a legal case against an Internet-connected toy operator in the US is the FTC case against VTech Electronics Limited (FTC, 2018a). The US subsidiary of the electronic toy manufacturer VTech agreed to settle charges brought against it by the FTC stating that the company violated COPPA "by collecting personal information from children [and their parents] without providing direct notice and obtaining their parent's consent, and failing to take reasonable steps to secure the data it collected" and pay $650,000 as part of the settlement agreement (FTC, 2018b). Previously, the same company, which also manufactures digital baby monitors and educational toys, was hacked and the personal data of more than 5 million user accounts and the profiles of child customers were compromised, with the stolen data including children's names, birth dates, mailing and email addresses (Lupton & Williamson, 2017).

Furthermore, legal uncertainty still surrounds other IoT devices, which are often not directly intended for children but as such do collect their data. Amazon Echo, Alexa, Apple's Siri and HomePod 'smart home assistants' are the most recent examples of such devices, which stay on stand-by mode in order to assist their owners with various enquiries they may have (such as answering questions and playing music). Crucially, they are widely used by children, as well as parents, and analyse all the information they are supplied with and store voice recordings (Harris, 2016), irrespective of whether the voice belongs to an adult or a child. More importantly, they are increasingly targeting children. Examples of these practices are advertisements for, among others, a newly released Google Home device which entails a young boy talking to it, while his sister uses it to get help with her schoolwork; the virtual assistant Siri is advertised by not only showing a young girl interacting with it but also features the Cookie Monster from Sesame Street (Harris, 2016). It has therefore been claimed that by showing pre-teenage children using voice-activated artificial intelligence devices and featuring celebrities appealing to them, Amazon, Google and Apple are aiming their services at children (Harris, 2016), and hence fall within the scope of COPPA.

The Internet of Toys and the General Data Protection Regulation

In the EU, the GDPR lays down rules relating to the protection of natural persons with regard to the processing of personal data (article 1). It provides for a wide material and territorial scope and strict sanctions and emphasises the rights of data subjects and concepts such as privacy by design. Key principles relate to the fact that personal data must be processed lawfully, fairly and in a transparent manner (article 5). The lawfulness requirement entails that there must be a legitimate ground on the basis of which data are processed. Possible grounds are (freely given, specific, informed and unambiguous) consent, necessity for the performance of a contract, legal obligation, vital interests of the data subject, tasks in the public interest or the legitimate interests of the controller (article 6). In addition, data must be collected for specified, explicit and legitimate purposes, be adequate, relevant and limited to what is necessary in relation to the purposes for which they are processed, accurate and, where necessary, kept up to date, stored for no longer than is necessary for the purposes for which the personal data are processed, and processed in a manner that ensures appropriate security of personal data (article 5).

Insofar as providers of Internet of Toys related products and services process personal data, the GDPR will be applicable. As a variety of actors may be involved (e.g. device manufacturers, software developers, cloud service providers, third parties) it will be essential to establish which of these actors act as data controllers and which should be classified as data processors. A data controller is a natural or legal person which determines the purposes and means of the processing of personal data (article 4(7)), while a data processor is a natural or legal person which processes personal data on behalf of the controller (article 4(8)). It is the controller who carries the main responsibility and who will need to implement appropriate technical and organisational measures to ensure and be able to demonstrate that processing is performed in accordance with the GDPR (article 24).

Unlike the 1995 Data Protection Directive (DPD), which it replaces, the GDPR includes a number of provisions that explicitly aim to protect a child data subject's right to data protection. First and foremost, recital 38 GDPR provides that children merit specific protection with regard to their personal data, as they may be less aware of the risks, consequences, safeguards and rights in relation to the processing of personal data, in particular in relation to marketing or creating personality or user profiles.

In addition to this general acknowledgment of the specific need for protection, article 8 provides for particular conditions applicable to a child's consent in relation to information society services being directly offered to him or her. Information society services are services normally provided (1) for remuneration, (2) at a distance, (3) by electronic means, and (4) at the individual request of a recipient. Article 8 states that when consent is the ground for data processing, and information society services are offered directly to a child, data processing shall be lawful when the data subject is at least 16 years old. In situations where the child is less than 16 years old, consent must be given by the holder of parental responsibility in order for data processing to be legal under the GDPR. According to paragraph 2, controllers must make reasonable efforts to verify that consent is given or authorised by the holder of parental responsibility over the child. This provision mirrors the obligations under COPPA, although the age limit differs. That said, EU Member States do have the opportunity to derogate and choose a lower age than 16, provided it is not below 13 years. It means that the 28 Member States must decide whether to lower the age threshold to 15, 14 or 13. These particular decisions concerning the age of consent for children's data processing under the GDPR are not the focus of this chapter, but it is nevertheless important to mention that research into (ongoing) national legislative processes demonstrates that a fragmented landscape is gradually emerging across the EU (Milkaite & Lievens, 2018), which may have significant practical implications for data controllers.

In its Guidelines on Consent under GDPR, the Article 29 Working Party (A29WP; a body that consisted of the 28 EU Data Protection Authorities and has since been replaced by the European Data Protection Board) has specified that to obtain parental consent "a proportionate approach may be to focus on obtaining a limited amount of information, such as contact details of a parent or guardian" (A29WP, 2018b). Indeed, what is reasonable when both acquiring consent and verifying the parental relationship between a child and the holder of parental responsibility will depend on the risks inherent in the processing and the available technology (A29WP, 2018b). According to A29WP, email verification may be sufficient in low-risk cases, but in high-risk cases it might be appropriate to obtain more proof in order for the controller to be able to verify and retain parental consent information (for instance, a parent could be asked to make a small payment via a bank transaction or trusted third party verification services could be used).

Article 8 raises many important questions regarding its practical implementation and the subsequent impact on children's rights, also in the context of the Internet of Toys. At the moment, it is still unclear how service providers will implement the requirement to verify the age of their users, and whether consent is actually given by parents. Although the GDPR does not contain an explicit requirement that the age of data subjects needs to be verified, this seems to be inevitable, as relying on the consent of an underage child will entail the processing of his or her personal data being unlawful (A29WP, 2018b; Borgesius & Lievens, 2019). In addition, it has been argued that parents may in fact not be best suited to protect their children online and should not be relied upon, as many are unaware or unable to mediate their children's online activities (Livingstone & Haddon, 2009). Parents do not "always know best" and often lack digital literacy skills themselves. According to recent research, many parents feel their children know the Internet better and might not always be able to give freely given, specific, informed and unambiguous consent, since often they are not familiar with the services their child wants to join, do not have the time or patience to read privacy policies and, even if they do, the legal texts are complex, raising questions as to what extent consent is actually informed (van der Hof, 2017). This issue is closely linked with the GDPR requirement to provide information in a concise, transparent, intelligible and easily accessible form, using clear and plain language (recital 58, article 12). According to the A29WP, this means that "the vocabulary, tone and style of the language used is appropriate to and resonates with children so that the child addressee of the information recognises that the message or information is being directed at them" (A29WP, 2018c). These obligations are crucial for Internet of Toys service providers.

Moreover, it is clear that practices such as marketing and the profiling of children are covered by the specific protection requirement in recital 38, which is particularly relevant in relation to the Internet of Toys as such devices may collect children's personal data and use them for these purposes. Under the GDPR, when children are the subject of profiling (recital 71, article 22) or marketing, specific protection should be afforded to them (Information Commissioner's Office, 2017; Verdoodt & Lievens, 2017). In fact, it has already been argued that children should not be subjected to intrusive profiling or behavioural advertising practices at all (Verdoodt & Lievens, 2017).

Data controllers should in certain instances conduct data protection impact assessments (DPIA) under recital 75 and article 35 (van der Hof & Lievens, 2018). These provisions may also be relevant for Internet of Toys actors. According to the A29WP, IoT devices, and hence Internet of Toys technologies and applications, may be covered by the data protection impact assessment requirement (A29WP, 2017b). The innovative use of new technologies, including IoT devices, is one of the criteria provided by A29WP which helps to determine whether data processing is likely to result in high-risk processing. IoT devices are listed as a specific example, since "certain Internet of Things applications could have a significant impact on individuals' daily lives and privacy and therefore require a DPIA" (A29WP, 2017b). In relation to the Internet of Toys, this criterion can be combined with another one, that of vulnerable data subjects, which mentions children as a prime example. The A29WP has clarified that processing operations which meet at least two criteria will require a DPIA (A29WP, 2017b). Hence, Internet of Toys providers will need to undertake a DPIA.

In addition, Internet of Toys companies should respect the privacy by design and privacy by default requirements (article 25; van der Hof & Lievens, 2018). In fact, in its recent consultation on Children and GDPR Guidance, the UK Information Commissioner's Office already recommends that companies protect children's personal data from the outset and design their systems and processes with this in mind (Information Commissioner's Office, 2017).

The Internet of Toys and Future ePrivacy Regulation

A second relevant EU legislative instrument, the so-called ePrivacy Directive (Directive 2002/58/EC), contains rules for the processing of personal data in the electronic communication sector, the free movement of such data and of electronic communication equipment and services. This Directive will be replaced by the ePrivacy Regulation in the coming years. A proposal for the new Regulation was introduced by the European Commission in January 2017.

The ePrivacy Regulation will particularise and complement the GDPR in the field of the provision and use of electronic communications services and is thus a *lex specialis* vis-à-vis the GDPR. The proposed ePrivacy Regulation applies to the "processing of electronic communications data carried out in connection with the provision and the use of electronic communications services and to information related to the terminal equipment of end-users" (European Commission, 2017). The ePrivacy framework is very closely linked to the GDPR as electronic communications data may, in many cases, include personal data as defined in the GDPR, and hence, will affect similar digital and online activities, which are also used by children.

The key points of the Commission proposal include the extension of the scope of the ePrivacy Regulation to "Over the Top" (OTT) communication services such as WhatsApp, Facebook Messenger, Skype, Gmail, iMessage and Viber, and its applicability to IoT devices (recital 12). The regulation also strengthens the protection for metadata (e.g. the time of a call and its geolocation), as this type of data may also reveal very sensitive and personal information (recital 2), which is equally true with regard to children. The October 2017 European Parliament (EP) Draft Legislative Resolution includes an extension of the principle of confidentiality of communications to data related to or processed by terminal equipment, the prohibition of so-called "cookie-walls", the introduction of granular consent and the introduction and promotion of end-to-end encryption. All of these developments are particularly important for the IoT and Internet of Toys market players.

While the GDPR explicitly recognises children as a vulnerable group of individuals who deserve specific protection when it comes to the processing of their personal data, especially in the context of profiling and marketing, the proposed ePrivacy Regulation does not mention children at all. This has been criticised by scholars (Verdoodt & Lievens, 2017), as well as consumer protection organisations. The European Consumer Organisation (2017), for instance, has argued that it is necessary to introduce specific provisions in the proposed Regulation to safeguard the privacy of children.

One of the EU Parliamentary Committees, the Committee on the Internal Market and Consumer Protection, proposed that the ePrivacy

Regulation should also explicitly pay special attention to the protection of children's privacy, and that specific safeguards are necessary, notably for the purposes of marketing and the creation of personality or user profiles of children (EP Committee on the Internal Market and Consumer Protection, 2017). With regard to terminal equipment intended particularly for children's use, they proposed an obligation to "prevent access to the equipment's storage and processing capabilities for the purpose of profiling of its users or tracking their behaviour with commercial intent". These proposed amendments would have had a significant effect on current, especially commercial, practices in relation to children, also in the context of the Internet of Toys. However, in the end, these amendments were not included in the EP Draft Legislative Resolution.

In terms of data processing practices in relation to Internet of Toys devices, enhanced protection for children could be integrated into the ePrivacy Regulation, in addition to default limits on processing children's data for the purposes of marketing, and especially in relation to profiling for behavioural advertising purposes (A29WP, 2018a; Information Commissioner's Office, 2017). Notably, terminal equipment used by children (including connected toys), as well as services offered to them, should by default offer privacy protective measures and settings, thus reinforcing article 25 GDPR in general, and taking into account the best interests of the child in particular (A29WP, 2017a; European Data Protection Supervisor, 2017). In cases where a child is an end user, and consent is needed, it can be assumed that article 8 GDPR will be applicable in relation to information society services as recital 3 of the proposed ePrivacy Regulation refers back to the GDPR in relation to consent.

Finally, in terms of the processing of metadata, the child's right to privacy and development should be taken into account in cases where Internet of Toys devices are used. Traffic data or metadata "may make it possible to create a both faithful and exhaustive map of a large portion of a person's conduct strictly forming part of his private life, or even a complete and accurate picture of his private identity" (van Hoboken & Zuiderveen Borgesius, 2015). It has already been shown that the processing of metadata can be just as intrusive as processing the content of communications—intimate details about a person's lifestyle and beliefs, political associations, medical issues, sexual orientation or habits of religious worship can be discovered through mobile phone traffic data (European Data Protection Supervisor, 2017; Lievens & Verdoodt, 2018; Manning, 2016). Especially for children who are developing and exploring their identity, such processing could be considered contrary to their best interests. This also entails that, in the context of the Internet of Toys, it should be very carefully considered to what extent it is necessary to process this type of data, and that consent to process it should not be relied upon where children are concerned, as it will be very hard to understand the exact consequences thereof.

Recommendations

Recommendations for Internet of Toys Actors

In the context of the Internet of Toys, the distinction between the different actors involved and mapping their exact responsibilities in relation to children's rights to privacy and data protection is not evident. These actors include toy designers, device manufacturers, software providers, app and platform creators, cloud service providers, artificial intelligence developers and speech recognition service providers. Insofar as they process the personal data of children, actors must not only comply with their legal obligations but should also go the extra mile in respect of children's data protection. First of all, this entails better communication and information practices. According to Gray (2017), full privacy policies on toy boxes should be replaced by very clear cues disclosing the steps parents will have to take before they can turn on a connected toy. Creative and intuitive audio and visual notifications to inform both children and parents of data collection and processing practices should also be adopted by developers. It is crucial that parents and children actually understand that a toy may record children, store their voice recordings and use the child's conversations to advance the algorithms that are used. Secondly, strong data security practices must be established for every Internet-connected toy before they are released.

This could be done by implementing strong encryption standards, ensuring technical standards preventing the toy from communicating with unauthorised devices and re-evaluating the need (from a data minimisation perspective) to store voice recordings or send them to the cloud (Gray, 2017; McReynolds et al., 2017).

Both COPPA and the GDPR promote industry self-regulation through codes of conduct and best practices. Internet of Toys actors should adopt a high standard of children's rights protection through such codes and abide by them.

Recommendations for Policymakers and Regulators

The Internet of Toys phenomenon is still relatively new, but spreading rapidly. This means that both Internet of Toy actors and consumers—children and parents—will need guidance. Policymakers should provide guidance to industry, promote best practice examples, foster codes of conduct and introduce certification seals that are easy to understand for data subjects (Holloway & Green, 2016). Moreover, special consumer education programmes should be widely adopted and shared, possibly with the help of non-governmental organisations and Data Protection Authorities (DPAs), to raise awareness and enhance the digital literacy skills of both children and parents. As educators are particularly important in terms of digital literacy, sufficient resources must be attributed to educational actors in this area (Livingstone & O'Neill, 2014).

Furthermore, aside from approving codes of conduct and providing clarification on the interpretation of certain vague concepts, the DPAs and the European Data Protection Board are key actors in the actual enforcement of the obligations of Internet of Toys actors vis-à-vis children and their parents. They will play a crucial role in ensuring that the specific protection that children merit is also put into practice.

Finally, it is evident that connected toys are not the only Internet-connected devices that children are using today. Toys receive more and more scrutiny, yet other IoT devices that impact on children's lives and rights, such as smart home assistants, should also be the subject of regulatory compliance checks (McReynolds et al., 2017).

Conclusion

As technology is such an integral part of children's day-to-day reality, and data are being collected about them throughout their lives from birth onwards, children do not only merit specific protection, they also merit a consistent and coherent data protection framework. This is true in relation to the IoT environment in general, and the Internet of Toys context in particular.

Children's rights to privacy and data protection are protected by conventions and legislative acts—on the international, regional and national levels. Yet, their implementation and enforcement are challenging. In the EU, the new data protection framework presents an opportunity for the consistent application of important principles and tools that may realise children's rights in practice, both in the context of the GDPR and the future ePrivacy Regulation. The principles of privacy by design and privacy by default, for instance, could play a very important role in relation to processing the personal data of children, leading to a "de-responsibilisation" of children and parents, for whom data processing processes are opaque and hard to understand. In the same vein, carrying out DPIAs before personal data of children are processed in the Internet of Toys context, including an assessment of the risks to children's rights, should become standard practice.

Finally, consistency in implementation and enforcement will be crucial. Children merit DPAs that are child rights-minded, and that not only look at the processing of personal data of children through a narrow data protection lens, but also take into account the potential impact of the implementation of the data protection framework on the full range of children's rights (Lievens et al., 2018).

References

Article 29 Working Party. (2017a). Opinion 01/2017 on the Proposed Regulation for the ePrivacy Regulation (2002/58/EC) WP 247.

Article 29 Working Party. (2017b). Guidelines on Data Protection Impact Assessment (DPIA) WP 248 REV 01.

Article 29 Working Party. (2018a). Guidelines on Automated Individual Decision-Making and Profiling for the Purposes of Regulation 2016/679 WP 251 REV 01.

Article 29 Working Party. (2018b). Guidelines on Consent under Regulation 2016/679 WP 259 REV 01.

Article 29 Working Party. (2018c). Guidelines on Transparency under Regulation 2016/679 WP 260 REV 01.

Borgesius, F. Z., & Lievens, E. (2019). Commentary Article 8 GDPR, Conditions applicable to child's consent in relation to information society services. In M. Cole & F. Boehm (Eds.), *Commentary on the general data protection regulation*. Cheltenham: Edward Elgar (forthcoming).

Chaudron, S., Di Gioia, R., Gemo, M., Holloway, D., Marsh, J., Mascheroni, G., & Yamada-Rice, D. (2017). *Kaleidoscope on the internet of toys—Safety, security, privacy and societal insights* (No. EUR 28397 EN). Luxembourg: European Union.

Council of Europe, European Convention for the Protection of Human Rights and Fundamental Freedoms, 4 November 1950, ETS 5.

Council of Europe, Modernised Convention for the Protection of Individuals with Regard to the Automatic Processing of Individual Data, 10 October 2018, CETS 223.

European Commission. (2017). *Proposed regulation on privacy and electronic communications.*

European Consumer Organisation. (2017). *Proposal for a Regulation on Privacy and Electronic Communications (e-Privacy).* BEUC Position Paper, BEUC-X-2017–059—09/06/2017.

European Data Protection Supervisor. (2017). *Opinion 6/2017 on the Proposal for a Regulation on Privacy and Electronic Communications (ePrivacy Regulation).*

European Parliament Committee on the Internal Market and Consumer Protection. (2017, October 23). Opinion on the proposal for a regulation of the European Parliament and of the Council concerning the respect for private life and the protection of personal data in electronic communications and repealing Directive 2002/58/EC (Regulation on Privacy and Electronic Communications).

European Union. (2012). Charter of Fundamental Rights of the European Union, 26 October 2012, /C 326/02.

Federal Bureau of Investigation. (2017, July 17). *Consumer notice: Internet-connected toys could present privacy and contact concerns for children.* https://www.ic3.gov/media/2017/170717.aspx.

Federal Trade Commission. (2013a). *Children's online privacy protection rule ('COPPA').* 26 February 2018. https://www.ftc.gov/enforcement/rules/rulemaking-regulatory-reform-proceedings/childrens-online-privacy-protection-rule.

Federal Trade Commission. (2013b). *FTC grants approval for new COPPA verifiable parental consent method.* 26 February 2018. https://www.ftc.gov/news-events/press-releases/2013/12/ftc-grants-approval-new-coppa-verifiable-parental-consent-method.

Federal Trade Commission. (2015). *Complying with COPPA: Frequently asked questions.* 26 February 2018. https://www.ftc.gov/tips-advice/business-center/guidance/complying-coppa-frequently-asked-questions.

Federal Trade Commission. (2018a, February 26). *VTech Electronics Limited.* https://www.ftc.gov/enforcement/cases-proceedings/162-3032/vtech-electronics-limited.

Federal Trade Commission. (2018b, February 15). *Electronic toy maker VTech settles FTC allegations that it violated children's privacy law and the FTC act.* https://www.ftc.gov/news-events/press-releases/2018/01/electronic-toy-maker-vtech-settles-ftc-allegations-it-violated.

Future of Privacy Forum, & Family Online Safety Institute. (2016). *Kids & the connected home: Privacy in the age of connected dolls, talking dinosaurs, and battling robots.* https://www.fosi.org/policy-research/kids-connected-home-privacy-age-connected-dolls-talking-dinosaurs-and-battling-robots/.

Gray, S. (2017). *Federal trade commission: COPPA applies to connected toys.* February 26, 2018. https://fpf.org/2017/06/26/federal-trade-commission-coppa-applies-connected-toys/.

Halzack, S. (2015, March 11). Privacy advocates try to keep 'creepy,' 'eavesdropping' Hello Barbie from hitting shelves. *Washington Post.*

Harris, M. (2016, May 26). Virtual assistants such as Amazon's Echo break US child privacy law, experts say. *The Guardian.*

Holloway, D., & Green, L. (2016). The internet of toys. *Communication Research and Practice, 2*(4), 506–519. https://doi.org/10.1080/22041451.2016.1266124.

Huggler, J. (2017). *Germany bans internet-connected dolls over fears hackers could target children.* http://www.telegraph.co.uk/news/2017/02/17/germany-bans-internet-connected-dolls-fears-hackers-could-target/.

Information Commissioner's Office. (2017). *Consultation: Children and the GDPR guidance.* https://ico.org.uk/media/about-the-ico/consultations/2172913/children-and-the-gdpr-consultation-guidance-20171221.pdf.

Jolin, D. (2017). *Would you want a robot to be your child's best friend?* https://
www.theguardian.com/technology/2017/sep/10/should-robot-be-your-
childs-best-friend?CMP=twt_a-technology_b-gdntech.

Lievens, E., Livingstone, S., McLaughlin, S., O'Neill, B., & Verdoodt,
V. (2018). Children's rights and digital technologies. In U. Kilkelly &
T. Liefaard (Eds.), *International human rights of children*. https://doi.
org/10.1007/978-981-10-3182-3_16-1

Lievens, E., & Verdoodt, V. (2018). Looking for needles in a haystack: Key
issues affecting children's rights in the general data protection regulation.
Computer Law & Security Review, 34(2), 269–278.

Livingstone, S., & Haddon, L. (2009). *EU kids online: Final report*. LSE.
London: EU Kids Online (EC Safer Internet Plus Programme Deliverable
D6.5).

Livingstone, S., & O'Neill, B. (2014). Children's rights online: Challenges,
dilemmas and emerging directions. In S. van der Hof, B. van den Berg, &
B. Schermer (Eds.), *Minding minors wandering the web: Regulating online
child safety* (pp. 19–38). The Hague and The Netherlands: Springer with T.
M. C. Asser Press.

Lupton, D., & Williamson, B. (2017). The datafied child: The dataveillance
of children and implications for their rights. *New Media & Society, 19*(5),
780–794.

Manning, C. (2016). *Challenges posed by big data to European data protection
law*. http://dx.doi.org/10.2139/ssrn.2728624.

Mascheroni, G., & Holloway, D. (2017). *The internet of toys: A report on media
and social discourses around young children and IoToys*. DigiLitEY.

McReynolds, E., Hubbard, S., Lau, T., Saraf, A., Cakmak, M., & Roesner, F.
(2017). *Toys that listen: A study of parents, children, and internet-connected
toys*. ACM Press. https://doi.org/10.1145/3025453.3025735.

Milkaite, I., & Lievens, E. (2018, May). *GDPR is here: Mapping the GDPR age
of consent across the EU*. Better Internet for Kids. https://www.betterinter-
netforkids.eu/web/portal/practice/awareness/detail?articleId=3017751.

Montgomery, K., & Chester, J. (2017). Data protection for youth in the
digital age: Developing a rights-based global framework. *European Data
Protection Law Review, 1*(4), 277–291.

Montgomery, K. C., Chester, J., & Milosevic, T. (2017). Ensuring young people's digital privacy as a fundamental right. In *International handbook of
media literacy education*. London: Routledge.

Newcomb, A. (2017). *That chatty smart toy your kid loves is now part of an FBI alert.* February 18, 2018. https://www.nbcnews.com/tech/security/fbi-warns-parents-privacy-risks-internet-connected-toys-n784126.

Rouvroy, A. (2016). *'Of data and men': Fundamental rights and freedoms in a world of big data.* Council of Europe, T-PD-BUR(2015)09REV.

Tabor, A. J. (2013). *Imperium, LLC proposed verifiable parental consent method application.* https://www.ftc.gov/sites/default/files/attachments/press-releases/ftc-grants-approval-new-coppa-verifiable-parental-con-sent-method/131223imperiumcoppa-app.pdf.

Turner, K. (2016, June 6). Analysis: The internet of things has a child privacy problem. *Washington Post.*

UN Committee on the Rights of the Child. (2014). *Report of the 2014 day of general discussion "Digital media and children's rights".*

UN General Assembly, Convention on the Rights of the Child, November 20, 1989,1577 UNTS 3.

UN General Assembly, International Covenant on Civil and Political Rights, December 16, 1966, 999 UNTS 171.

UN General Assembly, Universal Declaration of Human Rights, December 10, 1948, 217 A(III).

United States Congress. (1998). Children Online Privacy Protection Act, 15 U.S.C. §§ 6501–6506.

van der Hof, S. (2017). I agree … Or do I?—A rights-based analysis of the law on children's consent in the digital world. *Wisconsin International Law Journal, 34*(2), 101–136.

van der Hof, S., & Lievens, E. (2018). The importance of privacy by design and data protection impact assessments in strengthening protection of children's personal data under the GDPR. *Communications Law, 23*(1), 33–43.

van Hoboken, J., & Zuiderveen Borgesius, F. J. (2015). Scoping electronic communication privacy rules: Data, services and values. *JIPITEC, 6,* 198.

Verdoodt, V., & Lievens, E. (2017). Targeting children with personalised advertising: How to reconcile the best interests of children and advertisers. In G. Vermeulen & E. Lievens (Eds.), *Data protection and privacy under pressure: Transatlantic tensions, EU surveillance, and big data.* Antwerp: Maklu.

Vincent, J. (2015). *This 'smart' Barbie is raising concerns over children's privacy.* https://www.theverge.com/2015/3/16/8223251/hello-barbie-speech-recognition-privacy.

15

RETRACTED CHAPTER: Covert Advertising on IoToys

Esther Martínez Pastor and Patricia Núñez

The authors are retracting the chapter Esther Martínez Pastor and Patricia Núñez, 'Covert Advertising on IoToys', due to factual discrepancies. Both authors agree to this retraction.

© The Author(s) 2019
G. Mascheroni and D. Holloway (eds.), *The Internet of Toys*,
Studies in Childhood and Youth, https://doi.org/10.1007/978-3-030-10898-4_15

RETRACTED CHAPTER

16

The Industry of Smart Toys: Cultural Implications from the Political Economy

Vilmantė Liubinienė and Ana Jorge

Introduction

The globalisation of electronic communications has spurred the development of Internet-connected children's toys using voice and/or image recognition; "app-enabled toys … toys-to-life, which connect action figures to video games … puzzle and building games … and children's tech wearables such as smart watches and fitness trackers" (Holloway & Green, 2016, p. 507). On the one hand, smart toys can offer children a plethora of opportunities, especially for entertainment, discovery, conversation, challenging play-time and educational activities (Sefton-Green, Marsh, Erstad, & Flewitt, 2016). They can also help them to

V. Liubinienė (✉)
Faculty of Social Sciences, Arts and Humanities, Kaunas University of
Technology, Kaunas, Lithuania
e-mail: vilmante.liubiniene@ktu.lt

A. Jorge
Universidade Católica Portuguesa, Lisbon, Portugal
e-mail: anajorge@fch.lisboa.ucp.pt

© The Author(s) 2019
G. Mascheroni and D. Holloway (eds.), *The Internet of Toys*,
Studies in Childhood and Youth, https://doi.org/10.1007/978-3-030-10898-4_16

"develop cognitive, social, and behavioral abilities" (Cagiltay, Kara, & Aydin, 2014, p. 703). On the other hand, academic (Chaudron et al., 2017; Holloway & Green, 2016) and public discourse (Mascheroni & Holloway, 2017) have emphasised the risks associated with smart toys, such as privacy invasion and data security.

Despite the considerable cultural symbolic power of brands in children's lives, consumption patterns of global technologies, including smart toys, differ around the world. In addition to "unequal living conditions and disparities, illiteracy and inadequate education, [and] other social realities" (Kotilainen & Suoninen, 2013, p. 141), "inequality of media access [exists] among the young in different areas, i.e. between the North and the South and between urban and rural areas in the Southern countries" (ibid., p. 157). As Livingstone and Third (2017, p. 664) state, "although the Internet is an increasingly global network, the digital environments accessible to children are heavily shaped by differences in language, geography, culture and power—as defined by the state, commerce or, most locally, family and community".

The aim of this chapter is to discuss the implications of this "global communications industry 'dominated by commercial interests' (as cited in Holloway & Green, 2016, p. 507) for linguistic identities and the cultural possibilities" (Holloway & Green, 2016, p. 507). We analyse the provision and promotion of smart toys and their different affordances to children and families. The theoretical framework combines the perspectives of globalisation and localisation, the political economy of children's media and leisure and cultural and creative industries literature. The research is based on a comparative project on the Internet of Toys (IoToys), and the COST Action DigiLitEY performing content analysis of media and advertising discourses on this technology and product websites involving 11 European countries (Austria, Finland, Germany, Italy, Lithuania, Malta, Portugal, Romania, Serbia, Slovenia and Spain) and Australia. As well as secondary data on children, technology and digital literacy, we include case studies from Lithuania and Portugal, two small countries in Southern and Eastern Europe.

Global Production Versus Local Consumption Patterns of Smart Toys

In addition to economic, financial and political flows, globalisation involves the movement of technology, media images and cultural ideologies (Barker & Jane, 2016; Lash & Lury, 2007). As a result, a variety of commodities have become easily available across the globe, and information about newly developed items can be easily accessed via media promotional campaigns, as well as online searches. Producers rely on media to project meanings to consumers. Toys are one such case in which packaging, advertising and marketing suggest modes of use, and the product itself "is, at the very least, a referent in the production of meaning" (Mato, 2009, p. 77). One example is the Barbie doll, considered to favour one specific representation of the female body and ethnicity; another classic example is Disney, which has "a reputation of being conservative, patriotic, and 'All American'" (Wasko in Birkinbine, Gómez, & Wasko, 2017, p. 11) and has been criticised "for problematic presentations of women and minorities, Americanization of folk and fairy tales, as well as for the company's excessive commercialization and merchandising" (ibid., p. 23).

However, the production of meanings is not deterministic as "meaning is constructed in conjunction with the context" (Mato, 2009, p. 77). Thus, although globalisation entails greater involvement in networks that extend far beyond our immediate physical locations, and increased levels of networking, meeting and mixing are distinctive features of contemporary culture, the values and cultural meanings attached to place remain significant (Barker & Jane, 2016, p. 188). Localisation can be understood as an extreme "domestication" strategy that erases all elements of foreignness in products (Toto, 2014, p. 200). Localisation can be performed for continents, regions and countries where people speak different languages and have different cultures. This strategy plays a great role in the ability to sell products and obtain a return on investment in them (Nair & Dambal, 2011). O'Hagan and Mangiron (2013, p. 87) argue that "localization has gained recognition in a relatively short period of time as an essential industrial process required by businesses for the efficient globalization of products in electronic form".

According to Jiménez-Crespo, localisation practices have evolved with the emergence of electronic products and content, first software and later wider spheres, such as websites, that need to be adjusted for the local language and other region-specific conventions. "Localization has expanded from its origins in software products for personal computing in the 1980s to a wider array of digitally mediated communications, such as software (Esselink, 2001), web (Yunker, 2003, as cited in Jiménez-Crespo, 2013, p. 28), videogames (Chandler & O'Malley, 2011, Mangiron & O'Hagan, 2006, as cited in Jiménez-Crespo, 2013, p. 28; O'Hagan & Mangiron, 2013), smartphone apps, small device localization (Börjel, 2007, Musale, 2001, as cited in Jiménez-Crespo, 2013, p. 28), and web search engine marketing" (Jiménez-Crespo, 2013, p. 28). While these localisation types still exist today, emerging types, genres and categories are redefining the goals and needs of localisation. One new category is the Internet of Things, the linking of digital and physical entities through information and communication technologies, including the subcategory of smart toys. Especially through mobile devices and applications, the market already offers new services. For instance, people can control objects through remote access and use smartphone apps to monitor physical aspects, such as sleep, exercise and health. The localisation of Internet-connected children's toys opens up new markets and expands business possibilities, targeting not only children as the youngest group of users but also their parents, who are persuaded to buy smart toys for educational and entertainment purposes (Nixon & Hateley, 2013). This new type of localisation involves blending and redefining existing types of localisation. However, the localisation of a business greatly depends on the size of the market in which it localises, and consequently, small markets remain on the periphery of this strategy.

Testing the popularity and availability of smart toys via media promotional campaigns was the goal of an international team of researchers within COST Action DigiLitEY. In the Christmas season of 2016, the IoToys project investigated the discursive environment of smart toys by analysing the contents of their representations in media commentaries and commercial advertisements (Mascheroni & Holloway, 2017). A purposive online search using keywords related to the themes and names of products was conducted in 11 European countries and Australia. This research was based on the assumption that the Christmas season might represent the most intense moment of promotion and public visibility for these commodities targeting children.

We found that media coverage of the smart toys topic was scarce in Lithuania, Malta, Serbia and Slovenia, but more extensive in Germany, Portugal and Italy. We hypothesised that this could be related to economic factors, such as the size of the economy and, by extension, local markets and the price of smart toys in relation to the country's purchasing power. As shown in Table 16.1, the correlation between the intensity of media coverage of IoToys and countries' gross domestic product (GDP) was high, except for the case of Spain. Some smaller countries and markets, such as Slovenia and Malta, saw less coverage despite being relatively wealthy from the perspective of the per capita GDP. Smart toys cost approximately €100, so not all families could afford them, even as Christmas presents. The data collected in Lithuania showed that the most frequent question discussed among mummy bloggers was the price of toys.

However, economics is not the most fundamental issue. Perhaps more important is whether these toys and the apps that support them are available in children and parents' native languages. We, therefore, considered the size of linguistic communities to understand the possibilities for software adaptation beyond the size of countries and their economies. As seen in Table 16.1, the Spanish (437 million), Portuguese (219 million), German (76.8 million) and Italian (63.4 million) linguistic communities are not comparable to Lithuanian (2.9 million) and Slovenian (2.5 million) ones. The Spanish and Portuguese linguistic communities far exceed their population due to their colonial past. The size of linguistic communities helps to explain why the localisation of global products is not profitable for all markets.

Moreover, the size of linguistic markets should be seen in connection with the knowledge and skills associated with foreign languages, which open up opportunities to enter the global community and pursue common goals in education and employment. As a proxy for the orientation towards using foreign languages, we include the English First (EF) English Proficiency Index (the average level of English-language skills among adults taking an EF test) in Table 16.1. This shows that the Finnish population had a high level of proficiency in English as a

Table 16.1 Media commentary on IoToys by country, economic and linguistic indicators

Country	Number of items found in news media and commentary in IoToys	GDP ranking	GDP per capita and purchasing power parity ranking	Official language(s)	Linguistic community (number of native speakers, in millions)	EF English proficiency index ranking
Germany	58	4	19	German	76.8	11
Italy	28	8	37	Italian	63.4	28
Australia	15	13	10	English (de facto)	335	N/A
Spain	4	14	36	Spanish	437	23
Austria	19	29	16	German	76.8	10
Finland	18	44	29	Finnish, Swedish	5.4, 9.2	5
Portugal	31	47	46	Portuguese	219	13
Romania	12	51	61	Romanian	24	16
Slovenia	5	84	41	Slovene	2.5	6
Lithuania	5	86	44	Lithuanian	2.9	25
Serbia	6	92	90	Serbian	8.7	17 (2016)
Malta	4	132	33	Maltese, English	0.5, 335	N/A

Source *Number of items found in news media*: 2016, IoToys Project (Mascheroni & Holloway, 2017). *GDP ranking, GDP per capita and purchasing power parity*: October 2016, International Monetary Fund. *Linguistic community*: Ethnologue: 2016, English, Spanish, Portuguese, German, Italian and Swedish, 2015, Finnish; Statistical Office of the Republic of Slovenia: 2006, Slovene and Serbian. *EF English proficiency index* (average level of English language skills among the adults who took the EF test): 2015, except Serbia, 2016, https://www.ef.com/

foreign language (ranking no. 5). Although our sample did not include other Nordic countries, we believe that the Finnish case is representative of Northern Europe, a region with high English proficiency. From the linguistic perspective, therefore, the periphery is relative in this case. The same can be said of Slovenia (English Proficiency Index ranking 6) but, in contrast, Lithuania ranks only 25 in the same index. English proficiency as an indicator of global orientation might explain the relatively few items on smart toys appearing in the news media and commentary in Lithuania prior to Christmas 2016 and why smart toys are not as popular or widespread there as in Germany, Italy and elsewhere. Lithuania puts great emphasis on preserving the local language, and acquisition of the native language and the development of linguistic identity remain the primary goals during children's education and primary socialisation. However, it should also be mentioned that the situation regarding English language proficiency in Lithuania is changing.

Examining the available languages used in the software for the major smart toys in the market in 2016, we found that the most frequently selected languages for uploading toy apps were English, German, Italian, French, Spanish and, in some cases, Finnish and Portuguese. The software was not localised or adapted to the users of relatively small local communities, so toys' inability to respond to children and parents' commands or understand children's native languages could jeopardise their appeal. An analysis of websites of the smart toys found online in the IoToys project, presented in Table 16.2, was intended to identify the language used in the official materials on smart toys in the 12 countries participating in the IoToys project. The results revealed common tendencies: most toys had website versions in German, Spanish, Italian and French, some in Finnish and Portuguese, and none or very few in Romanian, Slovenian, Lithuanian and Serbian. Analysing the available languages of product websites by different manufacturers (start-ups, national toy and leisure companies and global brands, such as Disney or Lego), we found that, as expected, global producers mostly targeted the biggest and most valuable markets, whereas local brands targeted mostly national—in some cases, regional—markets. This was especially true in the cases of the Italian brands Clementoni and Lisciani and the Spanish brand Famosa, given Italy's and Spain's low English proficiency, as seen

Table 16.2 Language of smart toys' websites by type of producer

Type of producer	Smart toy	Language									
		English	Spanish	Portuguese	German	Italian	Romanian	Serbian	Finnish	Lithuanian	Slovene
Global brands	Hatchimals (Spinmaster)	•	•		•	•					
	Zoomer Interactive Puppy	•	•		•	•			•		
	My Friend Cayla	•	•		•						
	i-Que	•			•						
	Smart interactive toy (Fisher Price)	•									
	Lego dimensions	•	•		•	•					
	Sphero SPRK	•	•		•	•			•		
	Skylanders	•	•		•	•	•		•		
	Furby (Hasbro)	•	•	•	•	•	•				•
	Kidi Fluffies, Vtech	•	•		•	•	•				
	Amiibo Pokemon (Nintendo)	•	•		•	•					
	Codeapillar (Fisher Price)	•		•	•	•	•		•	•	•
National toy companies	Mio Amico Robot (Lisciani group)	•		•		•					
	Nenuco Happy School (Famosa)	•	•			•					
	Little Live Pets	•		•							
	Doc Robottino (Clementoni)	•	•	•	•	•			•		
	Evolution Robot (Clementoni)	•	•	•	•	•			•		
	Springfree Trampoline	•	•		•		•				

(continued)

Table 16.2 (continued)

Type of producer	Smart toy	Language									
		English	Spanish	Portuguese	German	Italian	Romanian	Serbian	Finnish	Lithuanian	Slovene
Start-up companies developing only smart toys	VaiKai	•									
	Magik play	•									
	MagikBee	•									
	Mon-mon	•									
	Woogie	•									
	Cozmo	•			•						
	Trefolino Teksta Kitty, Zoomer Zuppy, T-rex, Puppy	•									
	Smart Monkey (Science4you)	•		•							
	Dash and Dot	•			•						
	Anki Overdrive	•			•						
	BB8 Droid	•	•		•	•					
	OSMO Game System for iPad	•	•		•	•					
	Mardles	•									
	My Puppy Pal	•	•								
	Robosapiens X (WowWee)	•									

The websites were searched in January 2018 and only analysed for the languages spoken in the 11 countries in the IoToys project in Table 16.1. An interesting and unexpected finding was that start-ups privileged the English language, and some did not even include national languages on their websites. This indicates that start-ups had to position themselves in technological, international markets dominated by English or did not have the resources to localise content.

Technology in Children's Culture

Throughout the twentieth century, "children's popular culture was 'sold separately' to the child and the parent", as Seiter demonstrates, and the media and entertainment industries were key to involving children in the consumer society (as cited in Nixon & Hateley, 2013, p. 28). As economies have become more globalised, there has been "an increasing commodification of childhood and commercialisation of children's culture" (Woodyer in Bragg & Kehily, 2013, p. 91) achieved by (a wider range of) media directly addressing children (Buckingham, 2011). Stig Hjavard (2004, p. 48) argues that running in parallel with globalisation and commercialisation is mediatization, "a process through which core elements of a social or cultural activity … assume media form". Crucially, Hjavard (2004) claims, this has happened in the toy industry through computers and the Internet. Taking Lego as a case study, Hjavard argues that technologies have become more integrated into toys at the same time that they have become increasingly invested with symbolic content and narratives. Ultimately, play itself has been mediatised, "invested with consumer values", pushing "the toys—and the children—even further into a consumer culture" (ibid., p. 60). In the media discourses on smart toys during the 2016 Christmas season, we found echoes of a campaign by a consumers association from Norway concerned about privacy violations, data safety and data-mining by toy producers. These techniques may allow companies to gain more power over young consumers (Buckingham, 2011) by, for instance, using data on children's forms of use of toys to inform their continued development and suggest other products and services.

To further explore this line of argument, we adopted a case study approach, searching for information on policies and smart toy producers in Portugal and Lithuania on official websites, in news media and academic work.

Technology for children has been sold to parents not only by markets but also by governments through "the ideologies of playing to learn, and the need for lifelong learning from birth to ensure future success" to parents (Nixon & Hateley, 2013, p. 31). In the post-industrial era, states have promoted digital technologies, notably in education, to facilitate economic development. These initiatives have included the distribution of hardware and laptops to children, an idea that has spread around the world. In Portugal, the distribution of laptops to schoolchildren was one of the flagship programmes under the "Technological Plan" of the government in power from 2005 to 2011. In September 2008, then-Prime Minister José Sócrates announced the distribution of half a million laptops (for free or at reduced prices for the most disadvantaged families), declaring that "'we want the computer to be part of the school supplies in every school' (*Jornal de Notícias*, 29 July 2009) [and that] 'this new generation will be better prepared and will be able to contribute more towards the modernisation and development of Portugal'" (Pereira, Pereira, & Melro, 2015, p. 33). Another goal was to use children to promote Internet use by digitally excluded families, but there were also economic motives: the computer Magalhães (named after the explorer Magellan) was produced in and exported from Portugal. The programme became involved in an economic scandal and was suspended, due to a financial crisis in the country, after 2011.

In Lithuania, a group of stakeholders and business people announced an initiative to donate a microcomputer to each child in December 2016 as an alternative to another idea announced by Parliament members: to donate a national costume to each child (Vietoje tautinio kostiumopo mikrokompiuterį, 2016). Municipalities throughout Lithuania took up and further developed this idea with the support of stakeholders, such as BITĖ Lietuva, one of the country's leading mobile operators. The principles of crowdfunding and sponsorship were used to implement the idea, so it gained support from many other companies and individuals.[1] These programmes were in line with the principles of the 2000 Lisbon Strategy, re-released by the European Council in 2005, and the 2010 Digital Agenda for Europe from the European

Commission. The principles of these documents are based on the modernisation of the information systems of European Union (EU) member-states and the integration of European citizens iton the Information and Knowledge Society, by fostering job creation based on information and communication technologies. Digital technologies are at the centre of these strategies for innovation and economic growth.

In addition to the distribution of hardware and the promotion of Internet access, international institutions such as the United Nations Educational, Scientific and Cultural Organisation (UNESCO) and the European Commission (EC) have promoted digital literacy as a priority for citizens (Frau-Meigs, Velez, & Michel, 2017). The EC has made digital education a priority to implement by the end of 2020 and, after the Gothenburg Summit, in November 2017, it accordingly adopted new initiatives to improve the key competences and digital skills of European residents. Among the three initiatives proposed by the EC (2018a) on 17 January 2018, the second relates exclusively to digital education. The Digital Education Action has three key objectives: to make better use of digital technologies for teaching and learning, developing the digital skills of children needed for living and working in an age of rapid digital change and improving education through better data analysis and foresight. Specific initiatives include supporting schools with high-speed broadband access and a public awareness campaign on online safety, media literacy and cyber hygiene. To further promote coding, the EC works with the EU Code Week ambassadors, eTwinning network, Digital Skills and Jobs Coalition, Digital Champions and other interested bodies and organisations. The EC's goal is to involve at least half of schools in EU Code Week by 2020. Education in digital skills has been informed by a discourse that combines the civic and economic dimensions of promoting the enlightened use of digital media by children and young people as the least-reached population groups. "Learnability, problem-solving, critical thinking, and entrepreneurship" are skills needed for the generation that will form the digital workforce of tomorrow (EC, 2018b).

According to a Digital Skills in Europe Factsheet issued by the Tallinn Digital Summit (2017), the Lithuanian (52%) and Portuguese

(48%) populations have basic digital skills lower than the EU28 average (56%). This points to the need for deeper analysis of young children's engagement with digital technologies to strengthen children's and young people's critical thinking and media literacy. When comparing these two countries, it is important to take into account different factors that shed light on the current situation and which might help to outline global and European trends in digital education and to compare local contexts and initiatives. Lithuania ranks 13th and Portugal 15th in the Digital Economy and Society Index (DESI) 2017. Lithuania has better performance than the EU average in all dimensions—connectivity, Internet use, integration of digital technology and digital public services—except for human capital, where it has made limited progress. Lithuania continues to perform well in connectivity but is growing more slowly than the EU average, while it has improved significantly in the integration of digital technologies and in digital public services. In comparison, Portugal has improved its scores in all DESI dimensions, except for digital public services. It has made the greatest progress in fixed and mobile broadband take-up (connectivity) and the corporate use of digital technologies. Given the historical lag in the education system, Portugal's greatest challenge lies in raising the overall digital skills levels of its general population.

Moreover, in the face of increasing market concentration, conglomeration, transnationalisation and financialisation in the cultural and media markets, the EC and other transnational entities, such as UNESCO, have intervened to counter the effects of reduced cultural diversity (Hesmondhalgh, 2012). The provision of access and content paying attention to linguistic and cultural diversity is crucial so that language does not create an additional source of disadvantage. Support for smaller, local players can contribute to more than cultural and linguistic diversity. For instance, notably, in the late 1990s, the UK government presented its creative industries programme as a strategy to overcome the transformation of the industrial economy (Hesmondhalgh, 2012). In this new paradigm, the creative industries include software and computer services, so they are expected, of course, economically, to create value and export high-value services and products.

We can locate start-ups producing smart toys within this wider frame of countries' investment in the digital economy. Smart toy producer Vai-kai provides an apt illustration of the intersection of the global influence of digital technologies with the local tradition of craftmaking, supported by the creative industries model. "Traditional craftsmanship with the standards of the twenty-first century", "digital heart beating in a wooden body", "a combination of talented handcraft with super precise technology", we can read on the brand's website (Vai-Kai, n.d.), are the characteristic features of Vai-kai, whose name in Lithuanian means "children". The original idea for the toy belongs to the company's founders: Justyna Zubrycka and Matas Petrikas. The website describes the chief executive officer, Petrikas: born in a family of craftsmen, he played with ceramics and woodwork from early childhood and later produced music and interactive media in both his native Lithuania and Berlin, a city well known for its creative orientation. In 2008, he joined SoundCloud as one of its first software engineers, where he later managed the launch of the biggest music-creator platform. Today, Petrikas wants to give his daughters and other children access to a more human-connected world (Vai-Kai, n.d). Other start-up companies also make such biographical connections. For instance, LeapFrog (n.d.), the creator of My Puppy Pal, "was founded in 1995 by a father who revolutionised technology-based learning solutions to help his child learn how to read".

The workshop producing the smart wooden toys Vai-Kai lies in Kreuzberg, Berlin, but the creators and founders label the origin of the toy as "handmade in Europe" (Vai-Kai, n.d.). Narrating the story of the toy's creation, they tie the expert skills of "woodmakers in Poland" with "the highest quality ecological and child-friendly colours by the Swiss company Zuelch™". Thus, the Lithuanian tradition of wooden crafts may be spread globally with new inspiration and the addition of technology. As seen in the analysis of the websites' languages in Table 16.2, connections to local cultures in design are made through cultural heritage rather than language, as Vai-Kai's website is only available in English.

Smart Monkey was created by the start-up Science4You (n.d.), "a 100% Portuguese company dedicated to developing, producing and

selling educational and scientific toys as well as activities for children",
primarily those younger than age 16 years. Miguel Pina Martins created the start-up as a project at Lisbon University in 2007 and officially launched it in 2008. It received venture funding and support
from the Small and Medium Enterprises (SMEs) and Innovation
programme and was promoted, by the media and the government,
as an example of successful entrepreneurship during the financial
crisis in Portugal. The company distributes more than 350 products
online and through its own shops and technology and toys shops.
Science4You released Smart Monkey for the 2015 Christmas season
and it has developed a technological line of products, including smart
watches, drones, tablets, an action camera, robots and a smart ball,
offering education through products and consumption. The company has benefitted from EU programmes, receiving €481,000 from
a programme to support SMEs (2016–2018) "to buy a new production line" which, among other objectives, "represent[s] the status
of national culture, science and technology through its products"
(Science4You, n.d.). It also received €615,000 from a programme
to support internationalisation (2016–2018) to "diversify high add-
ed-value products" in international markets (Science4You, n.d.). The
success of this strategy was publicised in 2017, when Science4You
announced its products would be sold in 1800 shops of Target,
a United States retailer (Pimentel, 2017).

This support from national and European public funding is a key
component of Science4You's market orientation, which is linked to
job creation, specialisation and internationalisation. The impact on the
national economy and the reinforcement of popular culture can also
be seen in the case of the British start-up Mardles (n.d.): "All Mardles
products have been designed and developed right here in the UK—a
British success story!" In other cases, private companies are even associated with public services: Spanish toy brand Famosa (n.d.) developed the Nenuco Happy School "with the pedagogic consultancy of
the Technological Institute of Children's Products and Leisure". These
examples demonstrate how nation-states share an interest with both
start-ups and established toy producers in pushing technology into children's spaces of play.

Conclusion

The trends in the production and promotion of smart toys still largely depend on the logics of the global market, putting small linguistic communities and poorer countries in a disadvantaged position to access these new technologies. Here, the political economy framework has permitted discussing imbalances in relations of power (Wasko, 2005), but it can also serve as a basis for debates on solutions and alternatives, especially if we consider the framework of children's digital rights (Livingstone & Bulger, 2014; Livingstone & Third, 2017). Commercial interests primarily rely on successful marketing and promotional campaigns to sell smart toys, but local cultural and linguistic implications should also be taken into account. If smart toys offer opportunities for children's development and well-being, some children may miss out on those opportunities as they do not have access to toys in their market or native language. From the perspective of children's rights, particularly digital rights, there is an urgent need to provide "educational technology, online information and creative resources (…) in an equitable way (taking into account relevant languages)" (Livingstone & Bulger, 2014, p. 320).

Investment in the creative economy as a way to create a new economy is the leitmotif for the technological start-ups we find among smart toy producers. Aspects of local heritage seem to be a starting point, but not local language, as some start-ups only present themselves in English. Among both start-ups and national toy producers, the symbolic investment in local culture serves as the basis for economic and marketing strategies, in some cases supported by governments and European bodies.

Analysing the media and advertising discourses on smart toys in IoToys and the content of the toys' websites, as well as other economic and linguistic factors and the case studies of Portugal and Lithuania, we have discussed a particular kind of subject that smart toys contribute to creating among young children. MyFriendCayla, Codeapillar and Smart Monkey, among others, are part of a wider model of economic development around technologies in which digital literacy is invested in as a tool for the new workers of tomorrow, and foreign language proficiency—which, in most cases, means proficiency in English as a foreign language—is a highly important skill (*vide* the EC model of digital education that combines digital and foreign language skills). The model of smart toys, albeit for private consumption, mostly in the family leisure context, also sees leisure as a way of learning, which can (and should) happen throughout life. Therefore, contextualised research on children's digital literacy—among family, school and peers—which some chapters in this volume address, becomes all the more necessary.

Acknowledgements The authors acknowledge the support of COST DigiLitEY for a short-term scientific mission to produce this chapter.

Note

1. The aim of this initiative is to supply 265.62m children with microcomputers. So far, funds have been collected for 1,790,484 microcomputers, 67.41% of the total goal. The results of this initiative and the full list of supporters are available on the website Kompiuteriukai vaikams (2018).

References

Barker, C., & Jane, E. A. (2016). *Cultural studies*. London: Sage.

Birkinbine, B. J., Gómez, R., & Wasko, J. (2017). *Global media giants*. London and New York: Routledge.

Bragg, S., & Kehily, M. J. (2013). *Children and young people's cultural worlds*. London: Policy Press.

Buckingham, D. (2011). *The material child: Growing up in consumer culture*. Cambridge: Polity.

Cagiltay, K., Kara, N., & Aydin, C. (2014). Smart toy based learning. In J. M. Spector, M. D. Merrill, J. Elen, & M. J. Bishop (Eds.), *Handbook of research on educational communications and technology* (pp. 703–711). New York: Springer.

Chaudron, S., Di Gioia, R., Gemo, M., Holloway, D., Marsh, J., Mascheroni, G., … Yamada-Rice, D. (2017). *Kaleidoscope on the internet of toys—Safety, security, privacy and societal insights.* Luxembourg: Publications Office of the European Union. https://doi.org/10.2788/05383 and http://publications.jrc.ec.europa.eu/repository/bitstream/JRC105061/jrc105061_final_online.pdf.

Digital Economy and Society Index (DESI). (2017). Retrieved January 18, 2018, from https://ec.europa.eu/digital-single-market/en/news/digital-economy-and-society-index-desi-2017.

Esselink, B. (2001). *A practical guide to localization.* Amsterdam and Philadelphia: John Benjamins.

European Commission. (2018a, January 17). *Press release: New measures to boost key competences and digital skills, as well as the European dimension of education.* Retrieved January 18, 2018, from http://europa.eu/rapid/press-release_IP-18-102_en.htm.

European Commission. (2018b, January 17). *Fact sheet education and training initiatives.* Retrieved January 18, 2018, from http://europa.eu/rapid/press-release_MEMO-18-103_en.htm.

Famosa. (n.d.). *Nenuco hAPPy School.* Retrieved January 19, 2018, from http://www.nenucofamosa.es/pt/brinquedos/nenuco-happy-school/.

Frau-Meigs, D., Velez, I., & Michel, J. F. (2017). *Public policies in media and information literacy in Europe: Cross-country comparisons.* Abingdon, Oxon: Routledge.

Hesmondhalgh, D. (2012). *The cultural industries* (3rd ed.). London: Sage.

Hjavard, S. (2004). From bricks to bytes: The mediatization of a global toy industry. In P. Golding & I. Bondebjerg (Eds.), *European culture and the media* (pp. 43–63). New York: Routledge.

Holloway, D., & Green, L. (2016). The internet of toys. *Communication Research and Practice, 2*(4), 506–519.

Jiménez-Crespo, M. A. (2013). *Translation and web localisation.* New York and London: Routledge.

Kompiuteriukai vaikams/(Mini-computers for children). (2018). Retrieved January 17, 2018, from http://www.kompiuteriukai.lt/parama/rezultatai/.

Kotilainen, S., & Suoninen, A. (2013). Cultures of media and information literacies among the young: South-North viewpoints. In U. Carlsson & S. H. Culver (Eds.), *Media and information literacy and intercultural dialogue* (pp. 141–162). Gothenburg: Nordicom.

Lash, S., & Lury, C. (2007). *Global cultural industry: The mediation of things.* London: Wiley.

LeapFrog. (n.d.). Retrieved January 18, 2018, from http://www.leapfrog.com/en-us/home.

Livingstone, S., & Bulger, M. (2014). A global research agenda for children's rights in the digital age. *Journal of Children and Media, 8*(4), 317–335.

Livingstone, S., & Third, A. (2017). Children and young people's rights in the digital age: An emerging agenda. *New Media & Society, 19*(5), 657–670.

Mardles. (n.d.). Retrieved January 17, 2018, from https://mardleslife.com.

Mascheroni, G., & Holloway, D. (2017). *The internet of toys: A report on media and social discourses around young children and IoToys.* DigiLitEY. Retrieved December 4, 2017, from http://digilitey.eu/wp-content/uploads/2017/01/IoToys-June-2017-reduced.pdf.

Mato, D. (2009). All industries are cultural: A critique of the idea of 'cultural industries' and new possibilities for research. *Cultural Studies, 23*(1), 70–87.

Nair, S., & Dambal, G. (2011). *Technical writing to localization: An emerging career path.* Retrieved January 10, 2018, from http://indus.stc-india.org/2011/02/technical-writing-to-localization-an-emerging-career-path/.

Nixon, H., & Hateley, E. (2013). Books, toys, and tablets: Playing and learning in the age of digital media. In K. Hall, T. Cremin, B. Comber, & L. Moll (Eds.), *International handbook of research on children's literacy, learning and culture* (pp. 28–41). Malden, MA: Wiley.

O'Hagan, M., & Mangiron, C. (2013). *Game localization: Translating for the global digital entertainment industry.* Amsterdam: John Benjamins.

Pereira, S., Pereira, L., & Melro, A. (2015). The Portuguese programme one laptop per child: Political, educational and social impact. In S. Pereira (Ed.), *Digital literacy, technology and social inclusion: Making sense of one-to-one computer programmes around the world* (pp. 21–100). Vila Nova de Famalicão: Humus.

Pimentel, A. (2017). *Brinquedos da Science4you à venda em 1800 lojas Target nos EUA* [Science4you toys for sale in 1800 Target stores in the USA]. Retrieved January 19, 2018, from http://observador.pt/2017/09/28/brinquedos-da-science4you-a-venda-em-1800-lojas-target-nos-eua/.

Science4You. (n.d.). Retrieved January 19, 2018, from https://brinquedos.science4you.pt.

Sefton-Green, J., Marsh, J., Erstad, O., & Flewitt, R. (2016). Establishing a research agenda for the digital literacy practices of young children: A white paper for COST action IS1410. Retrieved December 10, 2017, from http://digilitey.eu.

Tallinn Digital Summit: Digital Skills in Europe. (2017). Retrieved January 18, 2018, from https://ec.europa.eu/commission/sites/beta-political/files/digital-skills-factsheet-tallinn_en.pdf.

Toto, P. A. (2014, January). Review of Jiménez-Crespo, Miguel A. (2013). *Translation and Web Localisation.* New York and London: Routledge. *The Journal of Specialised Translation* (21).

Vai-kai. (n.d.). Retrieved February 12, 2018, from https://vaikai.com/.

Vietoje tautinio kostiumo – po mikrokompiuterį/(Micro-computer instead of national costume). (2016). Retrieved February 10, 2018, from http://www.vz.lt/sektoriai/informacines-technologijos-telekomunikacijos/2016/12/19/vietoje-tautinio-kostiumo–po-mikrokompiuteri.

Wasko, J. (2005). Studying the political economy of media and information. *Comunicação e Sociedade, 7,* 25–48.

17

Concluding the Internet of Toys

Giovanna Mascheroni and Donell Holloway

Introduction

We introduced this volume with the proposition that IoToys should be conceived of as media, if we want to understand how digital materialities—that is, the entanglement of things, practices and data— unfold in the context of, and reshape, everyday childhoods. This means

---

In accordance with the Italian academic convention, we specify that while the general structure and the conceptual framework of the chapter were designed by the two authors jointly, Giovanna Mascheroni specifically wrote the section *Dataveillance and the Future of Citizenship*, while Donell Holloway wrote the section *Surveillance Capitalism*.

G. Mascheroni (✉)
Department of Communication, Catholic University of the Sacred Heart, Milan, Italy
e-mail: giovanna.mascheroni@unicatt.it

D. Holloway
School of Arts and Humanities, Edith Cowan University, Mt Lawley, WA, Australia
e-mail: donell.holloway@ecu.edu.au

taking into account the interdependencies between (a) the toys' materiality and the materiality of the communication infrastructures to which they are connected; (b) the varied (communicative, play, data) practices that such technological artefacts enable and encourage (and the practices they discourage as well); and (c) the societal processes that constitute both the outcome and pre-condition of artefacts and practices, namely datafication and surveillance capitalism. Each chapter has added to our understanding of IoToys as media constituted at the intersection of material objects, practices and broader institutional arrangements. More specifically, the first part set out key notions—robotification, connected play, post-digitality, the uncanny—that help us to theorise the new playthings and associated play practices; the second part explored how the Internet of Toys is being domesticated in both homes and playgrounds; the following chapters introduced the reader to research and design methodologies; while the fourth and final part delved into the political economy of IoToys, exploring issues such as privacy, hidden advertising, the commodification of childhood and children's rights.

Along the same lines, in this conclusion we revisit the concepts of datafication and surveillance capitalism in order to emphasise critical questions and map out possible trajectories that future research in the field could address and pursue.

Surveillance Capitalism

Made popular by Shoshana Zuboff in 2015, the term surveillance capitalism refers to the economic conditions, practices and systems responsible for the monetisation of data obtained through digital surveillance. Growing corporate power in the online world has led to this new economic circumstance whereby online information (data) is transformed into valuable commodities, and where the production of these commodities (data) is reliant on mass surveillance via the Internet (Zuboff, 2015). Zuboff argues that surveillance capitalism depends on "a global architecture of computer mediation [...] which produces a distributed and mostly uncontested new expression of power that I [she] christen[s]: 'Big Other'" (p. 75). The "Big Others", such as Google and Facebook, now amass and control unprecedented quantities of user data which they turn "into products and services that have fuelled stunning commercial growth" (Moore, 2016, p. ii). Children's growing online presence also sees them positioned as data sources within a surveillance economy. Under surveillance capitalism, therefore, children are positioned both as objects of economic activity (digital labourers) and subjects of market relations (digital consumers) (Andrejevic, 2014; Zuboff, 2015). As such, this is the first time that the activities of children have been of any significant economic value in the global north since children retreated from the paid labour force in the late nineteenth and early twentieth centuries.

Children's previous engagement in the market economy (as both producers and consumers) occurred during Industrial Revolution times, when child labour was common. Initially, this child labour was seen as an economic opportunity rather than an ethical problem, especially for poorer families who often moved from the countryside to the growing industrial cities so that they could make a better living. However, the Romantic Movement, that took up the theme of children's original innocence and need for protection, and Liberal Protestants, (particularly in North America) who believed that children had innocent souls that needed to be turned towards God, swayed public opinion. Subsequently, a succession of child labour reforms in the late nineteenth and twentieth centuries, as well as the introduction of compulsory education beginning in the late nineteenth century, saw children begin to retreat from the workforce into more unproductive domestic spaces and schools. At the start of the twentieth century, nevertheless, children became a discrete consumer group with the appearance of separate children's departments in larger department stores and advertisements directly aimed at them (Ellis, 2011). Previously, children tended to consume whatever "their parents made or prepared for them" (Leach, 2011, p. 85). Media also played a leading role in shaping children's consumer culture. Illustrated stories and comic strips introduced characters whose images appeared in dolls, games and toys from the 1890s. Media-integrated marketing further intensified with the sale of movie merchandise before the release of Disney's Snow White and the Seven Dwarfs in 1937 (Ellis, 2011). The advent of widespread television further intensified a children's consumer culture. A similar children's consumer culture continues today, although it is also firmly embedded in the online world, thus making children (via the surveillance economy) producers of economic activity—as well as consumers.

Therefore, this is the first time since children retreated from the paid labour force in the late nineteenth and early twentieth centuries that their production activities are of any significant economic value. Under our surveillance economy, data collection, analysis and on-selling by corporate bodies now includes data from minors—from babies, children and young people (Harris, 2017; Lupton & Williamson, 2017; Mascheroni & Holloway, in press; Montgomery, 2015). Children's cognisance of these data collection practices is limited, with many children too young to consent to understand the possible consequences of todays' data collecting practices; and, as partial citizens, they lack the political and/or legal agency to counter or oppose these moves (Third & Collin, 2016). Concerns about children's data privacy and security have long been raised, particularly in relation to children's websites and apps (Grimes, 2008; Montgomery, 2002; Steeves, 2006). The arrival of the Internet of Toys (IoTs) and children's wearables (as well as digital devices not actually produced for, but used by, children like smart home assistants) intensifies opportunities for the collection, analysis and use of children's data; compromising further the data security and privacy of children (Baraniuk, 2016; Harris, 2017; Holloway & Green, 2016). Moreover, children's accumulated data will quickly be outstripping the data gathered on their parents, with the implications of lifelong data collection and accumulation being a concern (Harris, 2017; Holloway, in press).

Hence, throughout this book, concerns have been raised about the commercial and organisational appropriation of children's online data and how this appropriation and accumulation compromises the privacy and data security of children today, and into their future, as well as their individual and cultural identities. These concerns include undercover advertising to children as a result of data collection, analytics and targeted marketing; the loss of children's cultural or linguistic identities due to corporate globalisation of the industry; the need to support and advocate children's digital rights to provision, protection and participation; and vulnerabilities within the design and data flow architecture of connected toys that permit the open flow of large amounts of children's data.

Zuboff suggests that within our surveillance economy, the power of the "Big Others" who use algorithmic personalisation approaches to an individual's data, such as Facebook, Google and Apple, goes mostly unchallenged and operates without any meaningful procedures for individual consent (2015). In the case of children, it is often parents and guardians, as legally responsible for them, who are left without any substantial or meaningful process of consent on behalf of their children. The use of ambiguously worded "terms and conditions" and the opt-in opt-out choices given to parents on behalf of their children leave parents with limited choices regarding their children's data security and privacy. For instance, when making decisions around the "terms and services" and "privacy policies" associated with connected toys, parents who choose not to agree to the terms and conditions essentially opt-out and exclude their child from playing with the full affordances the connected toy provides. So, while opting-out is a choice parents can make, by doing so they also severely limit the digital play affordances provided by the connected toy they have just bought for their child. The burden of protecting children's data, therefore, has been left solely to parents and not to designers, merchandisers or online service providers—and to some degree by policymakers and government authorities who also deem parent consent an adequate safeguard for the safety of children's data and privacy.

> [T]his [also] reflects a neo-liberal regulatory regime that places the burden of protecting children on parents. Data protection legislation purports to give parents control by requiring web sites that target children to solicit parental consent before collecting, using and disclosing personal information from children, by convention those who are less than 13 years of age. (Steeves, 2012, p. 356)

Consequently, parents enter into long-term contractual agreements that transfer legal responsibility for the collection, analysis and distribution of children's data away from toy companies and their service providers. This essentially gives these commercial entities the power to continue and conceivably expand upon data-collecting and sharing practices (Holloway & Green, 2016; van Dijck, 2014). Connected toys (and other IoTs) also mark a major change in how we think about consumption, purchase and ownership in a surveillance capitalism economy. This is because most smart toys are "hybrid" products—where the physical object (the toy) is owned by the customer, yet the presence of embedded and connected software means that the toy and its owner are subject to ongoing contractual terms and conditions with toy companies and their service providers.

Children's data collection is now entangled with the new "logic of accumulation" (Zuboff, 2015) of surveillance capitalism. Connected toys and wearables are equipped with a growing number of sensors such as audio, visual, haptic, location, movement, temperature and moisture sensors (think of smart nappies, for example). These numerous sensors increase the number of transmission points and subsequent data points available for collection, thus taking data collection possibilities to a whole new level. Unsurprisingly, data security failures have already occurred. These include the hacking of VTech's Learning Lodge (Nov, 2015) and Mattel's Wi-Fi Hello Barbie (Nov, 2015). There have also been privacy and regulatory responses, such as the bans made by the Federal Network Agency in Germany regarding iQue Robot and the My Friend Cayla doll (Walker, 2017), as well as children's smart watches (Singleton, 2017; Wakefield, 2017).

Concerns have also been raised about the long-term accumulation of children's learning data (Montgomery, 2015) available through educational connected toys and children's health data obtained via wearables for babies and children (Mascheroni & Holloway, in press), and the use of these data into the future. Owlet, a company producing connected baby socks that tracks babies' heart rates and oxygen levels via pulse oximeters, stores and owns the babies' sensitive health data (Turner, 2017). Various hospitals and health insurers are already procuring consumers' personal information from data brokers in order to identify patients who are high-risk in terms of insurance or care (Jennings, 2014; Osbourne, 2018). In addition, health providers' own databanks are particularly vulnerable to hacking and their contents put on sale on the dark Web. For instance, in Australia this year, almost a quarter of all data breaches have involved healthcare data sources (Minion, 2018).

As children's bodies, activities and social experiences are being tracked and datafied, even newer technologies are being designed to capture and respond to children's everyday experiences in an ever more seamless manner. So, while the possible benefits and risks of connected toys and things for children are still by and large unpredictable, the future implications of data collection, analysis, sharing and on-selling need thoughtful consideration, regulation and the possibility of consequential enforcement. Concerning also is the manner in which surveillance practices are becoming normalised and socially accepted by children and their parents, as well as the way in which surveillance capitalism shapes and influences children's civic, political and social rights into the future (see below).

Dataveillance and the Future of Citizenship

Whereas privacy risks are the most powerful effect of dataveillance in the short term, its long-term social consequences can only be speculated about at this stage, but they are likely to alter the conditions under which individuals and collectivities enact themselves as citizens through acts of claiming rights (Isin & Ruppert, 2015).

The transformations that involve citizenship are grounded in the very ways in which the notion of privacy, and the boundaries between the private and the public, is being shifted and reconfigured through the almost ubiquitous datafication and quantification of online and offline activities, interactions and even emotions. Data about whom we are and what we do become valuable because, on this basis and through algorithmic calculations, we are assigned to "measurable types" (Cheney-Lippold, 2017), i.e. averaged datafied templates of "women" vs "men", "children" vs "adults" and "seniors", "citizens", "foreigners" etc. The algorithms that analyse, interpret and compare such data are "formally indifferent" (Zuboff, 2015, p. 76) to the embodied individuals they affect. On this basis, Cheney-Lippold argues that predictive analytics does not lead to personalisation, where individuals are communicated to as distinctive persons. Rather, algorithms classify individuals in dynamic and mutable user profiles based on "the intersections of categorical meaning that allow our data, but not necessarily us, to be 'gendered', 'raced' and 'classed'" (Cheney-Lippold, 2017, p. 87). Notwithstanding, or precisely because of such indifference to the individual user, algorithm-based predictive analyses govern and regulate people's access to resources and opportunities, such as health, education, employment and credit. "Predictive privacy harms" (Crawford & Schultz, 2014) affect different populations in disparate ways. A growing body of literature documents how algorithmic interpretations are already shaping the material conditions and future opportunities of those who are profiled in a way that contributes to further marginalising and disempowering the most vulnerable categories, such as the poor, immigrants and people with disabilities (Eubanks, 2018; Gangadharan, 2017; Madden, 2017; Marwick & boyd, 2018).

When it comes to children, serious concerns have been raised regarding their "digital dossiers", which may be, and often are, initiated by parents through sharenting practices—such as the sharing of ultrasound images (Leaver, 2015), health and biometric data on the unborn (Barassi, 2017) and babies (Leaver, 2017), and other representations of children (Blum-Ross & Livingstone, 2017). Once they grow up, as we have seen, children become data sources in their own right, through their use of touchscreens, apps, IoToys and IoT devices. The preoccupation is that such digital dossiers "could follow young people into adulthood, affecting their access to education, employment, healthcare, and financial services" (Montgomery, 2015, p. 268). Dataveillance, then, affects citizenship to the extent that it potentially undermines the civic, political and social rights of citizens. The consequences, we argue, are more serious for children, who are positioned as partial citizens or citizens-in-the-making and have few opportunities to be engaged in institutionally legitimised acts of claiming and having their voices heard. Rather, children are more likely to be targeted as in need of both protection and socialisation in order to successfully become a "good (digital) citizen" (Third & Collin, 2016).

Dataveillance is also likely to impact on citizenship in subtler but equally enduring ways. That is, by feeding the imaginaries and practices of the "good citizen". Children grow up in a datafied environment where they are socialised into a surveillance culture (Lyon, 2017) well before they directly engage in such practices. Lyon theorises a shift from surveillance as a "technologically enhanced mode of social discipline or control" typical of modernity, to surveillance as a culture that "is now internalized and forms part of everyday reflections on how things are and of the repertoire of everyday practices" (Lyon, 2017, p. 825). Surveillance culture is being normalised in both the form of surveillance practices and surveillance imaginaries, which emerge from people's everyday involvement with surveillance and from media and public discourses. Surveillances imaginaries and practices are co-constituted, since the former provide shared schemata of action, interpretation and evaluation, whereas the latter contribute to reproducing such imaginaries. The normalisation of surveillance means that surveillance practices have become socially accepted and even desirable, as the examples of self-tracking and "intimate surveillance" show. Self-tracking (Lupton, 2016) is constructed as a virtuous practice by which individuals monitor their health, sports performance and work productivity and are encouraged to improve their achievements accordingly, on the basis of the data collected by apps and wearables and analysed by algorithms. Similarly, intimate surveillance—i.e. the well-intentioned technologically mediated monitoring of children's data and behaviour—is also discursively constructed as a "necessary culture of care" (Leaver, 2017, p. 2). Through its social legitimation and its incorporation within parental imaginaries, intimate surveillance is thus becoming a normalised parenting practice.

According to Lupton and Williamson (2017), due to their exposure to surveillance practices initiated by others, and as a consequence of their own engagement in surveillance practices from a very young age—through the use of touchscreens and apps, IoToys and, later, school and educational platforms like ClassDojo—children become "calculable persons" who are simultaneously calculated and calculating (Lupton & Williamson, 2017, p. 8). They learn to quantify mundane aspects of their lives and compare their performances against peers' measures. We cannot but ask: are children condemned to growing up as "passive data subjects" (Isin & Ruppert, 2015, p. 4)?

There is no evidence to assume that, as a consequence of datafication, citizenship will be reduced to a passive subject position that is defined solely by algorithmic identifications. Rather, critical data studies converge in understanding digital citizenship as both the product of automated calculations and users' acts of citizenship (Hintz, Dencik, & Wahl-Jorgensen, 2017; Isin & Ruppert, 2015). Digital citizens are positioned as both "objects of data (about whom data is produced)" and "subjects of data (those whose engagement drives how data is produced)" (Ruppert, Isin, & Bigo, 2017, p. 3). These scholars look at the material contexts in which datafication is experienced and enacted, based on the assumption that everyday life opens up opportunities for contesting acts of citizenship. Surveillance practices and imaginaries are always socially situated, enacted, negotiated, resisted and made sense of in the context of everyday life. In so doing, individuals reproduce, but also, potentially, transform, surveillance culture through acts of citizenship, as claim-makers of rights that they already have or are yet to exist.

It is on the basis of such a notion of citizenship as performative, processual and contingent that we can think of children as citizens (Hartley, 2010; Third & Collin, 2016). The ambiguous position of children as simultaneously non-citizens and citizens-in-the-making is precisely what grants them the opportunity to reinvent citizenship. As Hartley writes:

> Children are thus at one and the same time the least important component of institutionalised citizenship, since they remain non-citizens, and its most important "subjects", since they necessarily and continuously constitute the practice of citizenship formation. (2010, p. 3)

Drawing on de Certeau (1984) and his notion of strategies and tactics, Third and Collin conclude that the incorporation of the digital, and of dataveillance, in everyday activities operates strategically, by pervading imaginaries and practices. "However, it is precisely in the totalising reach of its strategic impulses that the (digital) everyday is exposed to the potentiality of tactical disruption" (2016). That is, children are capable of tactical acts that reinvent digital citizenship by claiming rights that are not yet institutionally recognised, by contesting adult-based definitions of rights and by disrupting participatory habits and conventions.

How can we extend these theoretical achievements in studies of surveillance capitalism and digital citizenship to the topic of our book, which is the Internet of Toys? Contributors to this book have expressed unease about the appropriation of children's online data under a surveillance economy. This surveillance economy is founded on socially constructed corporate practices involving a "deeply intentional and highly consequential new logic of accumulation [...] that vie for hegemony in today's networked spaces" (Zubboff, 2015, pp. 76–78). Implicated within this new logic of accumulation are data-consent contracts, which often contain non-negotiable terms and conditions that are unilaterally drafted by the companies who control the data (Rhoen, 2016). Thus, while it may seem that parents agree to the collection and accumulation of their children's data in return for the digital affordances of the connected toys they buy for their children, we need to ask: To what degree is this assumed reciprocity the product of legitimate consent? In addition, and in light of children's partial citizenship and lack of political or legal agency in the present, we should also consider children's rights to reclaim, wipe or disconnect from their previously collected data portfolios as adults in the future.

The contributions in this volume have also demonstrated how children encounter the digital materialities of IoToys in diverse ways, at the intersection of datafication and play. Datafication can be conceived of as a strategy, since the precondition of IoToys is that users agree to their (play and personal) data being collected through sensors, stored in online clouds, and analysed. However, children's play with IoToys is fundamentally tactical, and involves the physical materiality along with the digital materiality of such playthings in ways that are not, and cannot be, fully determined by the producers. Connected play, as a socially situated practice, is potentially subversive of algorithmic identifications, because both children and their parents may generate nonlinear, discontinuous and at times contradictory digital traces. When contextualised in the contexts and relations of everyday lives, therefore, datafication positions users as both datafied citizens and data citizen subjects, subjects of obedience and power (Isin & Ruppert, 2015).

References

Andrejevic, M. (2014). Surveillance in the big data era. In *Emerging pervasive information and communication technologies* (PICT) (pp. 55–69). New York: Springer.

Baraniuk, C. (2016, December 6). Call for privacy probes over Cayla doll and i-Que toys. *BBC News*. Retrieved from http://www.bbc.com/news/technology-38222472.

Barassi, V. (2017). BabyVeillance? Expecting parents, online surveillance and the cultural specificity of pregnancy apps. *Social Media + Society, 3*(2), 1–10. https://doi.org/10.1177/2056305117707188.

Blum-Ross, A., & Livingstone, S. (2017). "Sharenting", parent blogging and the boundaries of the digital self. *Popular Communication, 15*(2), 110–125.

Cheney-Lippold, J. (2017). *We are data: Algorithms and the making of our digital selves*. New York: New York University Press.

Crawford, K., & Schultz, J. (2014). Big data and due process: Toward a framework to redress predictive privacy harms. *Boston College Law Review, 55*(1), 93–128.

De Certeau, M. (1984). *The practice of everyday life*. Berkeley: University of California Press.

Ellis, L. (2011). *Towards a contemporary sociology of children and consumption*. Durham: Durham University.

Eubanks, V. (2018). *Automating inequality: How high-tech tools profile, police and punish the poor*. New York: St. Martin's Press.

Gangadharan, S. P. (2017). The downside of digital inclusion: Expectations and experiences of privacy and surveillance among marginal internet users. *New Media & Society, 19*(4), 597–615.

Grimes, S. M. (2008). Kids' ad play: Regulating children's advergames in the converging media context. *International Journal of Communication, Law and Policy, 8*, 161–369.

Harris, M. (2017, December 27). 72 M data points collected on children in spite of COPPA. *App Developer Magazine*. Retrieved from https://appdeveloper magazine.com/5769/2017/12/27/72m-data-points-collected-on-children-in-spite-of-coppa/.

Hartley, J. (2010). Silly citizenship. *Critical Discourse Studies, 7*(4), 233–248.

Hintz, A., Dencik, L., & Wahl-Jorgensen, K. (2017). Digital citizenship and surveillance society: Introduction. *International Journal of Communication, 2017*(11), 731–739.

Holloway, D. (in press). Surveillance capitalism and children's data: The Internet of Toys and Things (IoTTs) for children. *Media International Australia.*

Holloway, D., & Green, L. (2016). The internet of toys. *Communication Research and Practice, 2*(4), 506–519.

Isin, E., & Ruppert, E. (2015). *Being digital citizens.* London: Rowman & Littlefield.

Jennings, K. (2014, July 10). How your doctor and insurer will know your secrets—Even if you never tell them. *Business Insider Australia.* Retrieved from https://www.businessinsider.com.au/hospitals-and-health-insurers-using-data-brokers-2014-7?r=US&IR=T.

Leach, W. R. (2011). *Land of desire: Merchants, power, and the rise of a new American culture.* New York: Vintage.

Leaver, T. (2015). Born digital? Presence, privacy, and intimate surveillance. In J. Hartley & W. Qu (Eds.), *Re-orientation: Translingual transcultural transmedia studies in narrative, language, identity, and knowledge* (pp. 149–160). Shanghai: Fudan University Press.

Leaver, T. (2017). Intimate surveillance: Normalizing parental monitoring and mediation of infants online. *Social Media + Society, 3*(2), 1–10. https://doi.org/10.1177/2056305117707192.

Lupton, D. (2016). *The quantified self.* Cambridge: Polity Press.

Lupton, D., & Williamson, B. (2017). The datafied child: The dataveillance of children and implications for their rights. *New Media & Society, 19*(5), 780–794.

Lyon, D. (2017). Digital citizenship and surveillance| surveillance culture: Engagement, exposure, and ethics in digital modernity. *International Journal of Communication, 11,* 19.

Madden, M. (2017). *Privacy, security, and digital inequality: How technology experiences and resources vary by socioeconomic status, race, and ethnicity.* New York: Data & Society. Retrieved from https://datasociety.net/pubs/prv/DataAndSociety_PrivacySecurityandDigitalInequality.pdf. Accessed 23 March 2018.

Marwick, A. E., & boyd, d. (2018). Understanding privacy at the margins. *International Journal of Communication, 12,* 1157–1165.

Mascheroni, G., & Holloway, D. (in press). The quantified child: Discourses and practices of dataveillance in different life stages. In O. Erstad, R. Flewitt, B. Kümmerling-Meibauer, & I. S. Pires Pereira (Eds.), *Routledge handbook of digital literacies in early childhood.* London: Routledge.

Minion, L. (2018, April 11). Healthcare suffers almost a quarter of data breaches, as reports skyrocket under mandatory notification scheme. *Healthcare IT*. Retrieved from http://www.healthcareit.com.au/article/healthcare-suffers-almost-quarter-data-breaches-reports-skyrocket-under-mandatory.

Montgomery, K. (2002). Digital kids: The new on-line children's consumer culture. In C. Von Feilitzen & U. Carlsson (Eds.), *Children, young people and media globalization* (pp. 189–208). Göteborg: Nordicom, The UNESCO International Clearinghouse on Children, Youth and Media.

Montgomery, K. (2015). Children's media culture in a big data world. *Journal of Children and Media, 9*(2), 266–271.

Moore, M. (2016). *Tech giants and civic power*. King's College London, Centre for the Study of Media, Communication and Power.

Osborne, C. (2018, May 1). Healthcare was a top target for ransomware families in 2017. *ZDNet*. Retrieved from https://www.zdnet.com/article/ransomware-operators-select-the-healthcare-industry-as-a-top-target/.

Rhoen, M. (2016). Beyond consent: Improving data protection through consumer protection law. *Internet Policy Review, 5*(1).

Ruppert, E., Isin, E., & Bigo, D. (2017). Data politics. *Big Data & Society, 4*(2). https://doi.org/10.1177/2053951717717749.

Singleton, M. (2017). Germany bans smartwatches for kids and asks parents to destroy them. *The Verge*. Retrieved from https://www.theverge.com/circuitbreaker/2017/11/19/16671428/germany-bans-smartwatches-kids-parents-destruction.

Steeves, V. (2006). It's not child's play: The online invasion of children's privacy. *University of Ottawa Law and Technology Journal, 3*(1), 169–188.

Steeves, V. (2012). Hide and seek: Surveillance of young people on the internet. In K. Haggerty & D. Lyon (Eds.), *The Routledge handbook of surveillance studies* (pp. 342–360). London: Routledge.

Third, A., & Collin, P. (2016). Rethinking (children's and young people's) citizenship through dialogues on digital practice. In A. McCosker, S. Vivienne, & A. Johns (Eds.), *Negotiating digital citizenship: Control, contest and culture* (pp. 41–59). London: Rowman & Littlefield.

Turner, R. (2017, September 12). Owlet Smart Sock prompts warning for parents, fears over babies' sensitive health data. *ABC News*. Retrieved from http://www.abc.net.au/news/2017-09-12/owlet-smart-sock-prompts-warning-for-parents-privacy-concerns/8893104.

van Dijck, J. (2014). Datafication, dataism and dataveillance: Big data between scientific paradigm and ideology. *Surveillance & Society, 12*(2), 197–208.

Wakefield, J. (2017, November 17). Germany bans children's smartwatches. *BBC News*. Retrieved from http://www.bbc.com/news/technology-42030109.

Walker, H. (2017, February 18). Terrified German parents urged to destroy doll 'that can spy on children'. *Daily Express*. Retrieved from http://www.express.co.uk/news/world/768924/My-Friend-Cayla-German-parents-childs-doll-destroy-hacking-internet-smart-technology.

Zuboff, S. (2015). Big other: Surveillance capitalism and the prospects of an information civilization. *Journal of Information Technology, 30*(1), 75–89.

Index

The manufacturer's authorised representative in the EU is Springer
Nature Customer Service Centre GmbH, Europaplatz 3, 69115 Heidelberg,
Germany. If you have any concerns regarding our products, please
contact ProductSafety@springernature.com

Printed and bound by CPI Group (UK) Ltd, Croydon, CR0 4YY

29/04/2026

02099450-0009